Th

MW01483932

THE HARD ROAD

BRENDAN HENEGHAN

Copyright © 2023 Brendan Heneghan

Cover art by Cody Sexton of Anxiety Driven Graphics
Editing by author Remo Macartney
Additional formatting design by editor Paige Johnson

www.Outcast-Press.com

All rights reserved.

(e-book): ASIN: B0CRVXX9RP
(print): ISBN: 978-1-960882-08-0

This is a work of fiction. All characters, names, incidents, and dialogue, except for incidental references to public figures, historical events, and businesses are either products of the author's imagination or used in a fictitious manner not intended to refer to any living persons or disparage any company.

ACKNOWLEDGMENTS

Thank you everyone,
for everything.

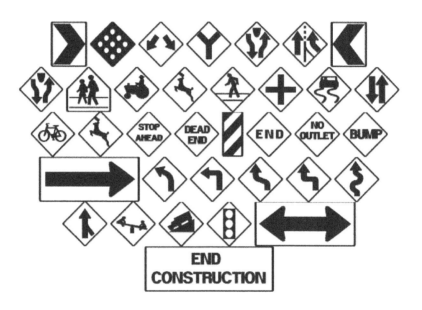

____"Midway upon this journey of our life, I found myself within a forest dark, for the straightforward pathway had been lost."

--Dante Alighieri

Part One:

The West

Prelude to a Journey

I was born in a state of war. I can confirm that. At age 12, a gang of cops arrested me for stealing my own bike outside a Wendy's. A motorist on Harlem Avenue fell under the impression that I was stealing the bike I let my two friends borrow an hour earlier. Unable to believe the pleas from a 12-year-old in a wifebeater, she called the executioners, and they placed me under arrest. It wasn't until they allowed a phone call that my father could explain my innocence.

Four years later, in high school, Johnny Law tried pulling another fast one on me... A drinking ticket for not drinking. I suppose those assholes love their power enough to fine or imprison anybody. My father was furious.

"What message are you sending these kids, giving him the same punishment as everybody else? He didn't drink. This ticket provides a record of him blowing zeroes. What you're telling these kids is that doing the right thing doesn't matter. You'll still punish them regardless of their decision. Guilt by association in this matter is not justice."

We went home, phoned an attorney, and won the case in a six-month court battle. The attorney didn't charge us a penny either—I cut his grass for years as the CEO of a one-man lawn service. It takes a village and, damn, it felt nice to beat the power.

I'm sure you get the picture. I don't care much for authority. Neither does my generation. Why should we respect authority if authority doesn't give us a reason to respect it? If the power structure in this fine land radically reforms and gives us something to *believe* in, fair enough, I'm all ears. But such a feat may never be achieved in my lifetime.

For years, I was a clean-cut conservative: Mr. Fifties. It wasn't until I moved to Baton Rouge from Chicago to study at Louisiana State University in August of 2017 that I underwent a stark metamorphosis. In what ways, you may be wondering? In a sentence, my outlook on life...society, class, and a tornado of other subjects. Nietzsche taught me infinity.

Homer taught me heroism. Camus taught me how to handle chaos. And, Christ, crazy old Hunter Thompson taught me how to live free. I have too much to say, and too much to do, but I suppose for now you have enough context about my character and what I believe...

A vast array of events brought me where I wound up on July 10, 2020—a stoned primate soaring through the Rocky Mountains at 100 miles per hour. Pine trees and jagged cliffs along the highway pointed to Heaven. Joe Torres sat right beside me at the wheel. Tony Cerrone slumped over in the back seat, sucking dabs like a hashish-smoking sultan. My intoxicated mind was locked in a state of intense paranoia. The trees looked as if they were reaching for the car to drag us into the woods. A slow, painful death, far away from anybody I'd ever known or loved. I did everything in my power to hold onto my sanity. I ate too many mushrooms in Denver while picking up Tony.

My friends met in kindergarten. I never ended up in homeroom with either of them until the third grade, but The Great Recession of '07 hit my folks hard. We could either leave the only city we'd ever known or transfer to the local Chicago public school. Mom and Dad sat with my siblings and me, and transferring schools was the unanimous decision. For three years, I barely spoke to the guys, but the sparks of our friendship reignited in high school.

Joe's a humble guy. He won't hurt a soul as long as nobody messes with him or his. If a Mexican Tom Petty exists, he is it—a lean, all-American kid brainwashed by an obsession with the blues, rock, and rap—like me. Tom O'Shea says he looks like Dave Franco in *Superbad*. On the other hand, Tony is a gambling, fighting, old-school Italian with a grand heart and the humor of a clown who smokes what I estimate to be 10 joints a day. Tony Cerrone, Joe Torres, and I, Pat Morrison... Together, I'll take this moment to claim our status as the Triumvirate of the Road.

In the car, I was petrified from the mushrooms, yearning for memories long buried in the dust. The road that day piqued my enthusiasm for life, and the time had come to push further than ever before.

I'm not joking about the mushrooms. I couldn't fall asleep. I couldn't feign sobriety while the drug ravaged my head. A bad psychedelic trip is a waiting game, and if I were fortunate enough, the psychosis would take an upward turn. The drugs, a damn pandemic, a hopeless election looming— 2020 proved a dastardly year, and I found everything about society utterly repulsive.

Nietzsche says modern man is defined by decadence, and who am I to disagree? Our slumber is fed by endless waves of microplastics, preservative-laced fast food, bullshit TV shows we have the gall to brand as "reality," and bourgeoisie bosses with moneybags in their eyes. They steal our vitality and dreams while we chase a facade known as the dollar. Tame, bipedal zoo animals stumble through slabs of gray concrete atop the earth in metropolitan jungles, *serving* tirelessly.

Is this America's national motto? "Serve, serve, serve! Serve people who don't give a shit about you until you're nothing more than a broken soul with nothing left to give but unfulfilled desires!"

We are, after all, at the mercy of a service economy.

I'm wrapped in what irks me. The vacation was a pilgrimage, and the escape was absolutely necessary. Ahead of us, the road twisted, curved, and jutted into mountains. A metaphor? Our world is ruled by uncertainty, and the road is one with the unknown. Where would it take us? What perils lay in wait? We were not in control. Nobody's ever in control. If this pandemic's taught me anything, it's that our passions, lives, and everything we've ever loved, cherished, or worked for can be instantly snuffed out—like a candle in a dark house.

"Immortal" by Kid Cudi opened on the radio, a damn fine song. It mellowed the mind games, but not enough. My terror remained, wading beneath the surface. Driving with two childhood friends served as the only redeeming thing in such an intolerable psychedelic nightmare. *Toughen up, you dipshit*, I thought. *Your psychedelic trip is the genesis of a long ride, and you better get used to it.* Thanks to funds from our summer jobs, we amassed a lovely collection of drugs and alcohol, with no intention of slowing pace. Our biggest concern was not getting arrested. There's a fantastic freedom, having nothing to lose. Not a penny between us saved for retirement. Our checking accounts rarely touched triple digits. Youth was our punishment, and whatever waited ahead would come from an insatiable hunger to live. Perhaps a third eye could be our lantern in the dark.

In the vast, confusing universe of drugs, intensity is what I crave. Downers like heroin, Xanax, or codeine are of zero interest because there's no thrill to be found in a morgue. The 2010s saw opioid overdoses double, and the carnage has spilled into this decade. Drug abuse spiraled out of control as pandemic lockdowns ushered people indoors, depressed by the spring rain, with nothing to do. The hopelessness and general monotony of a modern dystopia exacerbated this problem into a morbid frenzy. Back in Chicago, a bleak picture was painted.

To this day, someone driving on Harlem near the blue line across from Taco Burrito King might find needles in the street or junk fiends panhandling to fuel their addiction. Folks sticking needles in their arms is not a welcoming sight. Needles *are* the gutter. Heroin constitutes a death wish, and it is neither possible nor right to paint the entirety of drugs in the same picture. Trip safely and expand your mind is what I say. It's part of what brought me to the road.

Life sucked the entire year. I grew sick and tired of faceless "experts" telling us how to "stay safe" by hunkering down in our homes, hoping and praying for a safety that didn't exist. Our westward push meant liberation. We'd rise above the lockdowns, above the politicians, above the mundane cycle of 9-to-5s, sentencing us all to a premature death. Our interest in taking psychedelic drugs and roaming the West reached a peak during the pandemic summer.

Joe and I studied shamanism—religious rites and beliefs of North America's Indigenous peoples, especially tribes in the

Southwest. We both read several works by Carlos Castaneda, who wrote a series of books documenting his experimentation with psychedelics under the tutelage of Yaqui tribe elder Don Juan in Mexico. The idea of tripping balls in the desert to expand our minds in the land of the Navajo (Diné), Anasazi, and Zuni attracted us. What would we learn? Paraphrasing Huxley, what doors of perception would we open?

The juncture in life for a 22-year-old overflows with unrealistic expectations. The pressure is on. Get a job, make money, find an apartment, buy a car. Partake in the cold, unfulfilling streams of materialism and stress, or else it's obvious there's something seriously wrong with you. Dreams are for children! the system conditions us to believe.

Between Joe, Tony, and myself, we sought answers. Our quest for freedom, knowledge, experience, self-discovery, and pure adventure teemed with notions of escape. This was no ordinary vacation. When society collapses before your eyes, curiosity is an inevitable consequence. Especially when old rich people fought tooth and nail to rob us of our youth. I sigh, weep, and punch holes in walls for our generation—a generation without a destination. Never have we known a world where people didn't live chained to the wall by their own fear; a life free of fearing the police, free of economic angst, free of partisan propaganda and imposed division, driving us all into whirlwinds of nonsensical polarization.

Despite the horror, I was unfathomably alive, as if I'd die at any moment. Eating mushrooms is akin to poisoning yourself, but they aren't toxic. I've never heard of a psilocybin overdose. It's the microdose of poison that elicits hallucinations and head games. Hell broke loose when we stopped in Eagle at a Kum and Go. It was Friday evening, and the place was busy. Joe suggested I step out of the car for fresh air. Not a chance in Hell.

"Are you nuts?" I asked him. "These people are onto me. I can tell."

"You're still fucked up, huh?" he replied.

"Yeah, I ain't goin' anywhere."

"I'll fill the car," Tony volunteered in his thick Chicago accent.

"Cool, I'm getting some snacks inside. Either of you want something?"

"Water please," I groaned.

"What about you, Tony?"

"I'm straight. Since we're at a Kum and Go, I'll just sit here and jack off."

After chuckling at Tony's raunchy joke, Joe disappeared into the convenience store, and madness danced like a band of skeletons in my head. I was certain all those innocent families with children, reinforced by armies of elderly folks in campers, would report me to the highway Gestapo if I stepped one foot outside of the 2017 Jeep Patriot. A couple of long minutes passed before Joe returned with water bottles and a bag of sausage links.

I chugged the water and in seconds we were back in the saddle. Tony retreated like a prairie dog into his makeshift den in the back seat. And relief swept over me on the interstate, away from stroller-pushing fascists and retirees who still think the police are here to protect and serve. I found a brief peace, but it didn't last... *Jesus, carry me through these mountains!* The sooner we reached Grand Junction, the better.

To the West, a blood-red sun set sluggishly, two hours away from fading behind the mountains, and the deep blue sky transitioned into shades of purple, pink, and orange over a rocky, tree-filled wilderness ruled by animals. And the Bureau of Land Management. For another hour, the powerful drugs tore at my psyche until the come down slowly closed in.

Strangely enough, it coincided with our descent from the Rockies, and the environment rapidly changed. Green forests, dark mountains, and rivers transformed into brown, dusty hills. "Waiting for the Sun" by The Doors echoed from the radio. Joe sang along.

"Great song," I said.

"Hey, Joe—" Tony began before I cut him off.

"You gonna shoot somebody?"

They appreciated my Hendrix joke.

"How much time 'til we reach Grand Junction?" Tony asked, this time uninterrupted.

"An hour probably."

"That Denver weed will get us feelin' good!"

"Fuck yeah, Morrison. Finally coming out of your shell, eh?"

"Yes. Thank God."

"I've never done this before."

"Done what, Joe?"

"Driven this far, aside from family vacations. We're on our own out here. I love it." A hypnotic grin covered his face.

"Neither have I, man. I've flown to all sorts of cities but never driven across the country like this," Tony said.

"Well, y'all, the only long-distance trip I've ever been on with friends was to Argentina last summer. But I ain't complaining."

"I wish I was there, man. You and Flynn came back with some insane stories!"

"We got plenty of time to go there... Fuck!"

"You alright, Morrison?" Tony chuckled.

"Yeah, I'm fine, thanks. Thought something was crawlin' on me."

"Those damn mushrooms, I told ya, man! You should've waited 'til we're in the desert to eat some!"

"I know, you ain't gotta be a dick."

"Besides, we basically have the whole bag left, and there's a hell of a ton more traveling to do."

"True, Joe," Tony conceded, "but what would this trip be without some ball-busting, eh?"

"Shit, you're not wrong, man."

"Facts though, Morrison... There's a million more trips we can take."

"I'll tell you this, Tony. I prefer road trips to flying because, when you drive across this land, you actually see the country. You witness and experience how other people in different regions live. You're not cooped up in some TSA line like a farm animal, getting fondled and told what to do. It builds character."

"I gotta say, boys," Tony interjected, "there's something awesome about not knowing where you'll eat or sleep next that keeps you on your toes."

"With modernity, the comfort zone is the status quo, and I don't think people are supposed to live like this, with big ole houses, offices, and suffocating levels of comfort." I sighed, still bothered by the wars in my head.

"What are you saying? Should we go back to living in caves?" Tony asked.

"Hell no. What I'm trying to say is we need balance. There's no balance here in the States—or anywhere for that matter. By balance, I am intentionally making it sound as general as possible. Economically, environmentally, politically... Everything. I just think our country needs a return to its agrarian roots, where people grow and hunt their own food in close-knit communities. Think of how the tribes out here once lived or how folks did on the frontier. But today, we have great medicine and technological advances to the point where we could live such a life. There would be challenges, but infant mortality wouldn't be high like it was and people could still live for a long time. Free, sustainable, independent but cooperative lives. Every person an individual!"

"Sounds like a utopia," he replied.

"I understand how it sounds. But it's not impossible. What has happened can be reversed. Whenever somebody accuses my views of being utopian, here's my question for them... Are the people we elect not trying for some type of utopia? A utopia *they're* in charge of?"

"True. Beats the mess we have today where everything's so controlled and fake," Joe chimed in.

"You're damn right, man."

We zoomed on the highway. Full-throttle, blood burning like fire through our veins. Freedom rang through the air, and there was nothing to worry about but the moment. Faster and faster, the sun sank. An omen?

Probably not, but my superstitious mind couldn't help itself. Rolling down that deserted mountain highway with pure intentions, life was beautiful. Our journey was inspired by a common dream of escape. And although freedom tasted sweet, I suffered the terrible reality that we'd find trouble on our journey.

A Quiet Desert Night

We pulled into the hotel at 8 o'clock, just as the last rays of sunlight vanished over the mountains. A Shell gas station and a La Quinta Inn sandwiched our hotel. Adjacent to I-70, it gave off *No Country for Old Men* vibes. Before the trip, I lectured the boys about the dangers of Anton Chigurh. If we stumbled across that pyromaniac in the desert, we'd hightail away at the speed of light! In the absence of the psychopathic killer, we dragged our luggage inside the lobby, and all Hell broke loose. Again.

The fucking place was on fire! Here I was, seconds away from screaming it. Somebody had to do something, or the place would be finished, and we'd be shit out of luck for lodging. My skin scorched as embers fell on my arms and legs. I eyeballed the fire extinguisher behind the desk... *Wait a second... Joe and Tony don't notice this Hellish blaze. Neither does the receptionist. Phew!*

My mind played tricks on me, thank God. I jumped the gun assuming my sobriety. Talking with the receptionist would be Hell. She was small, thin, roughly our age, and looked Latina, but I remained on edge because there was an elephant trunk where her nose should've been, and her hair looked like a bunch of snakes. *Don't make a damn fool of yourself, don't make a fool of yourself. Secure the keys and be on your way.*

She exhibited strange behavior—slurring her words and unable to maintain eye contact. The poor girl was drugged out, higher than Mount fucking Everest. She struggled to keep her eyes open, but I could tell it wasn't from mere drowsiness. She was banged up on pills. Probably downers, I figured Xanax. Benzos are among the dumbest drugs a person can use. At times, it's difficult to distinguish whether someone's barred out on pills or belligerently drunk. When popping benzos, you feel alright. You're shitfaced, weed compliments it, and you think you're having a good time but, in reality, you're a walking Alzheimer's patient. Basic speech is impaired, balancing yourself becomes a challenge, and falling on your ass in front of a crowd usually isn't fun.

I've been there. During the Summer of 2019, I popped Xanax like candy and slugged codeine. I sniffed ketamine on special occasions. I once awoke in Baton Rouge at 4:30 on a Saturday morning, keeled over on the balcony floor after a night of too much whiskey and a handful of Xans. I'm lucky to be alive. But those days are long gone... Good riddance.

I hate witnessing anybody fall down the well, but it honestly took a load off, knowing the receptionist was more fucked up than me. Struggling through a workday and dealing with the public is *not* the ideal time to bear the title "highest in the room." We climbed the staircase to drop our bags off in the room. Tony graced us with his blunt-rolling skills. Before leaving Denver, we had stopped at a dispensary. Weed in Colorado is quality product. A better bang for your buck is always welcome during an era of inflation.

Within minutes, we were smoking outside on a bench in the designated smoking section. The land darkened, and the sun went entirely behind the mountains surrounding Grand Junction. Dusk rendered them invisible—a bummer because, if one can't get high within nature, it's at least nice to *see* it. When you're from the Midwest, mountains always have an intimidating but borderline spiritual impression. Humility is the closest emotion that comes to mind. Beggars can't be choosers, however, because other breathtaking sights lay within yards of us.

The handsome Shell gas station glowed across the parking lot as cars roared down I-70, and an Applebee's sign flashed across a vacant lot.

"It's a relief being over the Rockies," Joe said, exhaling a cloud of smoke.

"Say less, a breakthrough," Tony replied. "We're officially on the other side of the country."

"Until today, the furthest west I'd ever been was Omaha. Morrison, take this."

"I'm excited for Monument Valley," I said, sucking the blunt.

"Those pictures you showed me looked unreal," Joe replied.

"You won't see a place with more stars at night. There's something about that area of the desert. I can't explain, but it hits different. You'll see for yourself."

"It's wild being out here. I haven't been able to travel much lately," Joe said. "I feel freer than I ever have at any point in my life, and we've only been on the road for a day."

"It's a high. The road does that to you. When you got nothin' to do but drive to the next destination, surrounded by mountains and shit, without obligations... It's pure freedom. Breathtaking, even. Salt of the earth shit."

"Imagine if our generation said fuck it and millions of us resorted to life on the road."

"*Okay, Kerouac!*" I shouted. "I like where you're going though, Tony. I think we all should stick it to the old 9-to-5 bullshit and chase our dreams while we're young. Save money, abandon the repetition, and see what's out there. Life is miserable without a passion."

"You sound like Camus!" Joe laughed.

Maybe I did. Joe shared a love for the existentialists, from Satre to Camus to Nietzsche.

"I read *The Plague* last week!"

"Relevant," Joe said, referring to the "new normal"—a phrase the news beat to exhaustion over the pandemic.

"I've only read *The Stranger*," Tony replied, "but I'm tryna get my feet wet still. I was gonna stop at Barnes and Noble last Thursday before flying to Denver, but I was stoned and lookin' at memes all morning. Before I knew it, I had to get to O'Hare for my flight."

"I guess it's a good thing. Now you have a few solid recommendations."

"I know damn well I'm in good company with you guys when it comes to books!"

Tony wasn't as versed as Joe and me. He was particularly apolitical, but he shared our lust for knowledge. We loved learning but hated school. How's that for a paradox?

Soft, dry gusts of wind complimented the cooling temperature. We smoked like kings, discussing literature, expectations of the road ahead, memories of growing up together, and events of that annoying year. We found ourselves trapped amid a foul era. 2010s America is where we came of age. Polarization, civil unrest, social change, racial tensions, and the ongoing technological boom radically changed the country. Widespread college protests resurfaced from their dormant depths—further evidence of a world screaming, kicking, and contorting for change in spasms of rage.

Long gone were the fake, flag-waving, pseudo-patriotic days of the 2000s sparked in the aftermath of September 11, 2001. Parents raised their children to respect authority, taught us the police were heroes, and that brown strangers who follow a strange religion 6,000 miles across the Atlantic, two continents away, were hellbent on eradicating us for our alleged freedom. The previous 10 years shattered these illusions for many, myself included. For Generation Z, the 2000s were our '50s, and the 2010s shaped up as our '60s. 50-year flashbacks to the Love Era occurred until New Year's Day, 2020.

Unfortunately, at present, there's no unified counterculture. America's mobs remain distracted by culture wars and, save for the pandemic, the early 2020s are an extension of the 2010s. A wise man in olden times declared, "We must live together as brothers or perish together as fools[1], " and we've unapologetically chosen the latter option. But, out west, a massive wall of mountains and forests separated us from the exhausting polarization. We were high according to every definition of the word.

Joe leaned against the wall, his eyes bloodshot. Tony teased him. I would've joined in, but I knew damn well my eyes were glassy, so I let Joe take one for the team. Our routine of smoking and relentlessly roasting each other marched on, unwavering. We'll be 90-years-old doing the same thing if we play our cards right.

"Y'all trying to head in?" I asked.

---

[1] King, Martin Luther. *Why We Can't Wait.* Penguin Books.

"Sure," Tony said. "This blunt is cashed. But let me get this straight. We're going to Monument Valley tomorrow, Vegas the next day, and L.A. after?"

"Yeah, unless there's any objections. We'll figure out our next course of action once we hit the Pacific."

"Thank you, sir," I said as Joe held the door for us.

"No prob."

"I'm getting a fat night of sleep in preparation for tomorrow," I muttered.

"Facts," Tony replied as we entered the room. "Lotta traveling left."

"I gotta take a shit," Joe said, rising from his bed.

"Thanks for the update, prick." Tony scowled.

"You stoned?" I asked.

"I'm high, alright. Good thing we stopped at the dispo in Denver."

"I agree, solid deals there too. We won't be so lucky in Vegas or California."

"True, but it doesn't matter, we're on vacation, aren't we?"

"Facts. You said you've been to L.A. before?"

"Yessir! Venice Beach, the Sunset Strip, the Hollywood Hills, all that."

"Good shit. You'll be our guide when we're out there. I've never been to the West Coast."

"I figured, since Joe hasn't either. Given the circumstances we're in it won't be the same, but it'll be chill no matter what. We'll find open beaches and some good dispos."

"I dig the optimism, Tony. We'll need it."

"A good mentality is what it's all about, especially considering all the drugs we'll be doing. By the way, how are we doin' on drugs? I know we have weed and them shrooms. We got anything else?"

"Indeed, we do. We have a bag full of mushrooms, probably half a pound of weed, a sheet of acid, a fifth of Southern Comfort, and a fifth of Jack Daniel's. They're tucked away in Joe's red bag at the bottom of our luggage for discretion. I'll tell you, man, my trip today was something else. Humbling is the best word that comes to mind. A fucking nightmare, but I appreciate it. I survived and have a story to tell. I jotted down three pages of thoughts in my notebook I brought."

"I saw you writing in it back in Vail. A journal's a good idea. You'll look back and reflect 30, 40, even 50 years from now and think, *that's what I was like when I was young. That's what the world was like.* All the events we've seen growin' up will affect us, I just wonder how."

"You more or less read my mind. Documenting the times is becoming a passion of mine."

"Think you'll try to get published someday?"

I paused. "Yeah—but I have to wait 'til the time's right. Publishing companies need reasons to invest in writers. I'd have to prove myself. If I do, it's years down the line."

"Well, when you write a damn book, I'll be the first one to buy a copy." He laughed.

"Means a lot, my brother," I said as Joe emerged from the shitter.

"I'm calling it," he announced.

"Me too." I followed. "Long day ahead of us. The reservation will be an experience."

"Wait," Tony said. "You boys wanna drop acid when we make it to Monument Valley?"

"Yes," Joe replied.

"I thought it went without saying!"

"Good, I've tripped hiking in the Rockies but never the desert."

"We'll need lots of water and a couple blunts," I suggested.

"Oh, for sure."

A *South Park* marathon on Comedy Central lulled us to sleep, the episode where Stan notices he's getting older, and everything turns to shit. It's one of the few shows I'll make time to watch. I generally avoid watching TV because I have a theory that everything we're exposed to on television sets, from the news to the average commercial, slowly conditions us into weak, fearful robots incapable of recognizing what's worth fighting for—or fighting at all. Something about millions of people constantly gathering in front of a screen indoors for hours on end is deeply saddening.

Every day during the pandemic's opening months, I'd wake up, read some French or Russian anarchist, trudge to work, come home, write poems and essays, read again, smoke, and crash. The everyday routine bothered me, but I tried hard to spend my days engaging in productive activities. I crave love, adventure, and creation. To Hell with drudgery.

Hit The Road, Jack, It's 7 AM

Getting out of bed was easy, thanks to our grand but vague expectations. How easily one can wake up when anticipating adventure! We checked out of the hotel, and hurried to the car, content as children, ready to burn rubber deeper into the West. Grand Junction has a number of roundabouts, which are a rarity in Chicago and Louisiana, where I've lived. My dumb ass was hardly able to navigate them, but after aimlessly circling the same roundabouts, fast food chains, and gas stations, I broke free. From there, we had two options: Ride I-70 clean into Utah or take the lengthier route along the Colorado River. We unanimously agreed on the scenic route.

After a brief interstate cruise, Google Maps led us to a sketchy country road. It was paved at first, then potholed and bumpy, until reduced to a dusty, unpaved path, taking us to God-knows-where. *Did I miss a turn?* There's hardly any connection out there, and the directions served as the only sign of life. Mountains, sandy hills, and shrubs spanned for miles. About 30 minutes passed since exiting I-70, so I grew a little concerned. The temperature rose, and I did my best to maintain a straight face. *Stay calm*, I thought—*according to Google Maps, you're heading in the right direction*. We pushed deeper into the desert, and I wasn't sure where. With a car full of drugs, to boot.

Dust clouds left a trail in the rearview, rendering whatever was behind us invisible. After crossing over a hill, we noticed a few buildings. A town? Strange. We had no reason to think it was inhabited. We'd never seen a ghost town before. The deteriorating buildings gave off eerie vibrations and made me glad I wasn't on drugs. If we broke down, I would've shit my pants. I was sure the buildings had been there for a century at least. With no water or highways for dozens of miles, it made sense the place didn't last.

Suddenly, the blood in my veins turned to ice at the sight of a spray-painted message on a slab of concrete. **VANISHING POINT**, it read. To make matters worse, piles of needles marred the dirt, shining in the sunlight alongside footprints leading in and out of a couple decrepit buildings. A recently extinguished fire smoked in a doorway. We were not alone. *Time to go!* I jammed my foot on the gas—pedal to the metal. *Who lives here? Why? How do they survive?*

I imagined homicidal heroin addicts forming a community of sadistic inbreds in the desert, like a disorganized, less-glamorous Manson cult. Whoever they were, they probably butchered unsuspecting travelers like hogs, so they weren't taking us alive.

My heart stopped as I glanced back to the ghost town. Two hooded figures stood in the road. One of them wielding a long blade. Chills ran down my spine. I saw red and slammed on the brakes. "Joe, grab my .44 from the glove compartment!"

"What the fuck? Okay," he said, handing me the piece.

"She's loaded. Cover your ears, boys! I'ma scare these fuckers!" I fired a few rounds into the air and saw the two hoodlums retreat behind the **VANISHING POINT** sign.

"Jesus Christ, Morrison, are you crazy?" Tony shouted, his eyes wide.

"A bit. Those psychos back there'll think twice before scarin' some travelers next time."

"Good shit. I didn't know you had a .44, man. I'm surprised!" Tony cackled, shook up.

My ears still rang from the shots. "It was a gift from my dad. Got it when I turned 18. There's a box of ammo behind the passenger seat. I've heard a .44 Magnum can take down a buffalo."

"I saw you throw it in the glove compartment when we packed the car Wednesday night. I was like, 'Yup, we're taken care of.'"

"Hold up, boys. Am I the only person here who didn't know we were strapped?" Tony asked, befuddled.

"I guess so," Joe laughed.

"You bastards! That's a load off."

"My dad always said that young people coming up in a tough world should have the means to protect themselves. Y'all know him...a blue-collar Democrat, union man... He's valued the right to bear arms since he got his first gun from my grandpa way back in 1974. He got a 12-gauge for his twelfth birthday. How about it?"

"Dope. I wish parents were that cool nowadays."

"Yeah, Tony, my old man was beaten senseless all the time, and once was locked in an oven, but at least Dear Ole Grandad gave him a shotgun."

"Smartass! You get my point."

"Nah, there's truth in what you're saying. Parents back then were laxer in some areas but harsher in others. Helicopter parents rule the world today."

"What a story we have already... You never know what you'll see out here. I love it."

"Hell yeah, Joe. We have more than a week ahead of us. Shit will go down. It's inevitable."

"Do you own any other guns?" Tony asked me.

"I don't, personally. My dad's got his shotgun and half a dozen handguns but hasn't bought any new ones in years. My mom has no issues with gun ownership, but she's uneasy around 'em. I think she's still traumatized from when my grandpa shot their dog Tinker in their yard when she was a kid. He was an old dog...couldn't eat anything. If they didn't put him down, he would've starved to death."

"Fuckin' brutal! I see why she'd be uncomfortable."

"At the end of the day, y'all, guns are tools. Like any tool, they can be used for a variety of purposes, good or bad."

"Good point," Joe said, "in a world where guns exist, I'd rather be somebody with one than without."

"Damn right. Our encounter a few minutes ago proves it."

"Reminds me of 'Heartbreaker!'"

"Awesome song, Tony, let's turn it on," I suggested.

Listening to Mick Jagger's voice at top volume during a moment of high intensity is unrivaled. Somebody better be praying for whoever's on the wrong side of a gun. I'm not a violent man, but if the occasion calls for it, I will shoot. I've almost died before, and I'm not going out unless it's on God's terms.

We found the Colorado River 40 minutes later. Maps hadn't failed us. Auburn canyons wound along the river and, before we knew it, we'd entered Utah. We navigated rolling meadows, cattle ranches, and little country homes for a hundred miles before stopping in Monticello at a diner for lunch. **Trump 2020**, read the bumper sticker of a blue 2019 GMC Sierra in the parking lot. A woody scent stirred inside, likely due to the restaurant's log-cabin-styled interior.

We ordered our burger combos and claimed an empty table in the corner. Joe darted to the restroom to piss. He'd been bitching about having to go since crossing state lines. I was convinced he had a grandpa bladder. Meanwhile, Tony scrolled through his phone and, several feet away, two morbidly obese men in overalls engaged in a tense discussion about an impending socialist takeover of America.

"Can't you tell what this is? The 2020 election is the most important election of our lives. Can't you tell the socialist Left is taking over? Look at Joe Biden, he's in bed with the Chinese Communist Party, and the Democrats are gonna sell this country to China. That's what the news said the other day."

I'll be damned, something both sides of the aisle agree on, I thought. Every two to four years marks the "most important election of our lives," according to politicians and the gullible crowds who flock to their altars, unable to recognize doubletalk for what it is. These authoritarian, flag-worshiping knobheads wouldn't make it through a work of political theory if their IQs doubled. The man speaking was sweaty and had zits all over his neck. His friend donned a Make America Great Again hat and nodded without saying much. I couldn't resist the urge to join their conversation.

"Sir, excuse me, sir," I politely intervened.

"Hey. Can I help you?"

"I couldn't help overhearing your conversation. Do you really think Democrats are the sole problem in our country?"

"Well, yeah. The DNC wants to destroy this country."

"May I ask why you think that?"

Tony looked at me like I had lobsters crawling from my ears.

"It's all around you, man. They wanna open our borders, brainwash our kids, and demonize our police. Don't tell me you're voting for Sleepy Joe."

Every single person I've heard use the phrase "our police" has been White.

"No, sir. I'm a Christian, gun-loving American. But our problems run far deeper than the Democratic Party. I'd argue the GOP is just as bad, maybe worse."

"Well, they have all the RINOs who want to get rid of President Trump. They're no better than the Dems. Are you a liberal?"

Apparently, my admission of being a gun-loving American didn't appease him. "No. I'm not a fan of ideologies or parties for that matter. I'm curious, why do you think political allegiance has only two homes? There are more options than simply Republican/Democrat or conservative/liberal. You seem to agree with me that both parties are damn awful."

"You're wasting your vote if you go third party and, if you don't vote, you have no right to complain. You're a kid. You'll understand when you're a bit older."

"Maybe I will, maybe I won't. The truth is far more frightening than the superstitions your political party teaches you. Y'all have yourselves a nice meal." I clearly wasn't getting through to them.

"You too, young man."

I wasted my time and, worst of all, he hit me with the "when you're older" copout. It's an impossible endeavor, reasoning with idiots who think they've got everything under their thumb because they've blown out the candles 50 fucking times. Furthermore, who wants to trust their lives in the hands of rapacious demagogues? I once watched a Texas senator speak on TV to a crowd of like-minded people. He blamed communists and Democrats for the nation's problems. The crowd met each of his proclamations with rabid applause. Had the crowd not figured out the game? A rambling politician repeating bland, dishonest talking points to *whoop* them into arms against an invisible enemy, or worse, their fellow Americans? It made me sick. I sipped on a vanilla shake while dwelling on such.

"Interesting," Tony said, raising his eyebrows.

"I didn't expect to change any minds. I couldn't help myself. I like talkin' politics."

"You don't gotta tell me twice!"

Joe returned to the table as he spoke.

"Try your milkshake, Joe, they remind me of Nick's."

"Will do." He sipped his shake. "Damn, you're right!"

"Nick's is great," Tony replied. "But I prefer Brandy's."

"I'll say the gyros are better there. But the shakes at Nick's are king," I declared.

"I dig the skirt steak sandwiches at Nick's," Tony said as juice from the burger dripped from his chin onto the basket of fries.

"Bruh, I would eat those religiously! Every summer day back in 2009, I'd ride my bike there with DeShawn and Maurice. The old Greek guy would shout my order the second I'd step into the joint."

Marvelous memories. Upon entry to Nick's Drive-In, I'd hear the man yell, "Skirt steak on garlic bread and a vanilla shake!" Just like the old movies. We grew up as run-of-the-mill American kids and hailed from blue-collar families. At age 12, we'd terrorize the neighborhood, riding Mongooses, playing sports, wearing white T-shirts, gym shorts or blue jeans, and dirty old Air Force Ones. On rainy days, we invaded the movie theaters. Films like *Avatar*, *Zombieland*, and *Inglorious Basterds* dominated the box office. I guess we were the kind of kids you'd hear about in John Mellencamp songs.

To this day, I long for the past and, in the future, I'll long for the present too. The adage says, "The good ole days are best when you're aware you're living them," but I suppose our entire lives are "the good ole days" until we croak. We may as well leave a mark while we're here.

"You mentioned DeShawn and Maurice. How are they doing?" Tony asked me.

"They're alright. Maurice is in a tough spot. He got mixed up with the wrong people when he dropped out of school. You know how it goes. Last I heard, he's pulling himself together."

"True," he said. "A damn shame."

"But DeShawn's doin' well. He's in management at a dispo in Oak Park, movin' his way up. We smoked together in the yard a couple weeks ago and caught up. He says he may get an apartment soon, with hopes of going to DePaul when the pandemic's over. He raps in his spare time."

"Good for him," Joe said. "DeShawn's gotta be the nicest dude I've ever met. A hell of a straight shooter."

"I remember when we all boxed together in high school," Tony recalled.

"Him and I beat juniors as freshmen, the only two to pull it off. Every other freshman fighter who matched with an upperclassman got fucked up," I chimed in.

"I still got the picture of the three of us holding our medals after the fights."

"Send it to me when you get the chance. DeShawn would love to see it, I bet."

DeShawn, Maurice, and their siblings were the only Black kids in our neighborhood, Chicago being as segregated as it was—and *still* is. On numerous occasions, strangers called Chicago P.D. on us for the heinous crime of hooping at the local basketball courts. One neighbor of mine, a cop, even called them "animals," urging them to "move back to the West Side." He boasted about it at a Christmas party in front of my mother. Knowing damn well it was my friends he'd dehumanized, she gave that fascist neighbor of ours an earful.

Since the turn of the century, more than 250,000 Black people have fled Chicago for Southern cities like Dallas, Houston, and Atlanta. Meanwhile, Chicago is gentrifying. Our own neighborhood changed. Hordes of young professionals moved in from the suburbs, giddy and raising the property values, pricing us out. In many cities, particularly Chicago, poor Black neighborhoods don't gentrify, which intensifies racial segregation. Wealth is pouring into the Windy City at the expense of the Black, Hispanic, and White working classes. In fact, Chicago is so segregated that even

Caucasian ethnicities tend to steer clear of each other. The Irish claimed the far South and Northwest Sides, the Polish in Portage Park and Dunning, and Orthodox Jews in West Rogers Park.

A perfect storm is brewing. How can we understand each other if we all live in separate Americas? The working class will soon go extinct in the City of Chicago if trends continue, and dozens of other big cities are following the path. I read a solid article from *The Atlantic* when first stumbling across the phrase "the great American affordability crisis." Come to America and live a life you can't afford!

"What was your favorite spot to eat at in the neighborhood growin' up?" I asked Joe.

"This'll sound basic, but Wendy's near Harlem and Touhy. I can't figure out what was different about their food from other Wendy's locations, but it hit different. I ate there all the time as a kid. It was a block away!"

He had a point, we all ate there a million times while growing up.

"I was shocked when it closed last fall. First Walgreens on Touhy, then Wendy's. What's next? Our childhoods are being snuffed out!" I sighed, my voice ringing with as much disbelief as when I found out.

Joe was talking about a now-empty Wendy's. Lifeless buildings surrounded the dead restaurant. Same place I was arrested in front of. Fractured sidewalks, empty parking lots, and weeds pushing from cracks in the cement. Most of the neighborhood kids would go there to hang. Then we'd ride our bikes or play ball. But all pleasant experiences end, left behind in our memories.

While mourning the loss of a fast-food restaurant, it occurred to me how much the little things matter. Shortly after our trip down memory lane, we picked our baskets clean. The two obese country boys continued their right-wing circle jerk— prey in the partisan game. I digress. Full stomachs elevated our spirits. Right around the corner lay Monument Valley.

ALL ABOARD THE ACID BUS

The Navajo Nation drew closer, and the sun beamed higher and brighter. The car engine roared alongside Howlin' Wolf's screechy voice as we passed through the town of Bluff. The green valleys and ranches became red desert, crowned by buttes and mesas. Fallen pebbles kissed the feet of these formations, the stone faces carved by a thousand years of erosion. Somewhere around Mexican Hat, we found ourselves in Utah. The land looked postcard-perfect. The further west, the greater the thrill.

A native sun called our names, dragging our car deeper into the Painted Desert. For thousands of years, people called this barren place home. If we isolated a group of HR employees out there, chances are that buzzards would pick their bones clean in 48 hours.

"Mexican Hat... Funny name for a town." Tony chuckled.

"I bet some miners or homesteaders settled out here, saw my ancestors wearing sombreros, and didn't bother asking what they're called," Joe said.

"*This hee-yer town, we'll cawl Mexican Hat,*" Tony joked.

I laughed hysterically. "Y'all are probably right, that's the sad part!"

"Imagine being the first humans to discover this place."

"Well, shit, Joe, there's hardly anything out here now. I doubt it's changed much. The Navajo found this land a long time ago and made it home. Domesticated animals helped the people out here, but they didn't arrive until the 1600s. Sheep changed the game."

"This is untamed land, that's for sure," he replied.

"Thomas Jefferson acquired all this land in the Louisiana Purchase. People living back east thought they'd find mammoths and other extinct animals out here. Rumor has it that Jefferson sent Lewis and Clark west to confirm whether this was true."

"Wild times, man. I hear they wanna bring mammoths back."

"I've heard this before. Maybe it'll happen in our lifetimes."

"I can already see it. It's 2040, and I'm bringing my kids to the zoo to see a fucking mammoth."

"It's a possibility, Joe."

"How much more time do we got?"

"30 minutes or so."

We arrived at Monument Valley around 3 o'clock. You may have seen it in films like *Forrest Gump* and *Easy Rider*, cementing its status in American iconography. Name any Western movie set in a desert, chances are that they filmed it in Monument Valley.

We unpacked the car to set up the tent, embarrassing ourselves. Frontiersmen, we were not, but perhaps we broke a seal and paved the way for future adventures. As a child, I frequently played Cowboys and Indians with friends. I always wanted to be on the Native side, thanks to movies like *Dances with Wolves* or *Geronimo: An American Legend*. Unlike most of my peers, I considered the cowboys to be villains and their fierce opposition heroes. Few things are stranger than missing eras in which you've never existed. I glanced at the landscape and grabbed the bag of acid from my pocket.

We rolled two blunts before dropping the acid. LSD is an intense drug compared to other psychedelics. You might lose your mind, condemned to a life of madness after rapid abuse. Consider Charles Manson...

I tested the acid a week before on the Fourth of July, so I knew what I'd be getting us into. Thankfully, acid rarely leads to nausea, a common consequence of eating mushrooms on a full stomach. Discomfort increases the likelihood of a bad trip. I speak from experience. A month earlier, I curled up in the corner of my room, panicking with the lights off, convinced I'd been coming down with a terminal disease. Ghosts of the past returned to haunt me. I found salvation by listening to JFK's inspirational speech in Berlin on YouTube. I used it as a base to build from and, before long, the trip became an educational experience.

I felt calm and more connected to nature. All I wanted to do was climb a tree, as silly as that sounds. I chain-smoked joints, shirtless and barefoot, in my yard at two in the morning. I listened to Boston and stargazed with limited success, thanks to Chicago's light pollution. I was lucky that night. A bad trip can be a total dumpster fire, a fucking nightmare. Avoiding one requires a positive mindset and a healthy environment—tripping alongside trustworthy friends is important. A solo psychedelic ride is also fine, especially mixed with good music, a vital pillar among us psychonauts.

If used properly, psychedelics alter one's perceptions, eliciting mind expansion. You step into a world most wouldn't dare enter, accessing untapped parts of the brain. When you trip balls, you never see anything the way you did before. A few of my friends can testify. Before the trip, I had a history of using acid, and it's brought me to strange places. Aldous Huxley knew. He's ranked next to Timothy Leary and other pioneers. Tribes all over the Americas believed mushrooms and mescaline, among other plants with psychoactive components, were "teachers," manifesting entities—some masculine in their effects, others feminine, casting one who consumes them into alternate realities.

The psychedelic experience proves that there is more to the world around us than what we regularly see.

After a brief return to the highway, we arrived at a place called Valley of the Gods, where the acid hit us like Conor McGregor socking Jose Aldo at UFC 194. Tony lit the cannabis torch: the first of two. Doing drugs in the desert is risky, especially when it's 106 degrees. The threat of heat stroke looms over you since acid is known to raise body temperature. I envisioned national news about three acid-gobbling lunatics burning half the Navajo Nation to the ground as if the White Man hasn't put those people through enough. Running along the Utah-Arizona border, the Painted Desert is home to various tribes, a home we intended to respect.

"I'm fucked up," Joe said as we ventured from the Jeep.

"Me too," I replied. "Toss me a water."

"Look at 'em! Look, those things, what are they? They're everywhere!" Tony panicked.

"That's the last thing I need right now," Joe groaned.

"They want the weed, man! They're after the weed!"

"Fuck," I said. "Whatever they are, they gonna have to kill us for the stuff."

Tony saw things, and so did I. A band of stallions galloped between trickles of clouds, thundering through the air. The clouds expanded, constricted, expanded, and constricted while floating through the late afternoon, taking a devastating toll on our heads.

"Chill, y'all," I told them.

"Dude, I think I see Donald Trump's face over there. See that mesa?" Joe said, pointing toward the rusty sandstone in the distance.

"These hallucinations are intense. I'm losin' it."

"We're fine, Tone. Just breathe, we're gonna be fine."

"The plants," he said, "they're moving. I could use a cold pop right now."

"Joe's got water in the Cubs bag, bruh... Take this." He handed a bottle to Tony.

The bottle condensed from laying in the cooler but wouldn't stay chilled for long. The Utah sun beat down, trapping us in a damn Inferno. I turned around to gauge how far we'd walked from the car, and it was nowhere in sight. I doubted the possibility of theft. The Valley of the Gods is barren, empty—no other human beings for miles, as far as we knew. Communicating to the best of our abilities, our verdict compelled us to climb one of the nearby buttes. The white Jeep would be visible from higher ground, standing in stark contrast to the dirt surrounding it.

We engaged in a nerve-wracking climb, gripping each rock to avoid disaster. The butte was essentially a small mountain—rocky and full of crevices, and our drug-induced anxieties didn't improve the fragile situation. In the last push, I froze. I advised them to finish the climb; I'd wait. A dreadful feeling swarmed me as we parted ways.

I scanned the desert landscape, losing myself in bouts of curiosity. *What's the point of this trip? What are we doing out here?* We were men in revolt, escaping the pandemic, escaping bourgeois society—its demands, distractions, materialism, and nonsensical hierarchy, even if temporarily. Was it self-discovery? Defiance? Pursuit of freedom? To find God?

I can't answer these questions. Shit, perhaps we sought all those things, but sometimes I go too far. I dig too deep and end up coming face-to-face with something I don't understand. And I suppose I'll go to the grave with such questions left unanswered.

Minutes passed without a trace of my friends. I called their names, but only a gust of wind responded. If I listened closely to the wind, would it speak? And if it spoke, would I understand? Probably not. It too died down. Nothing left but piercing silence: eerie and deafening. I'd watched enough horror movies and my heart was seconds away from bursting through my chest. The heat preyed on me like the vultures I envisioned consuming my rancid corpse.

On the bright side, I suppose such a pretty, mysterious place wouldn't be the worst place to die. Bury me in the dry ground with thousands of coyote and rattlesnake carcasses, so I can rest forever, undisturbed in my country of birth. I can't help but sometimes wonder how many dead bodies lie beneath the ground I walk. *Quit plaguing yourself about death, you paranoid fuck. Acid and death do not mix!*

I exerted great energy to alter my thought process—to no avail. Horror movie trauma reignited the fear, locking me in unending trepidations. I had to make a break for it. Death was in the air. *Goddamn cave people emerged from their dwellings and kidnapped Joe and Tony. Cannibals! Maybe they're cannibals!* Some insane cult stole my childhood friends, dragging them to whatever rotten hole they crawled out of. *Jesus, save me from such horror!* Was I next? Would I even find the car if I tried searching for it?

I have to. There's no other choice. Go to the car, grab the gun, come back to this fucking hill, and figure out what the hell happened... Infinite absurdities shot through my brain like bullets. It's ridiculous how quickly the mind can slip into a frenzy under the hold of acid. I try to master the art of silence, which is an increasingly rare virtue these days.

Fuck it. We marched in a straight line from the trail. I'll find the damn car myself. I descended the big rock, clutching the water bottle for dear life.

"Find the car... Find the car... Don't think about mountain lions!" I glanced toward the butte, hoping Joe or Tony would reappear, but they didn't. I was weakened in a desert maze of heat, red rocks, and a sea of shrubs: all that remained of what was once an ocean.

Based on the sun gliding to the west, I pushed against it, heading east. The dirt path had to be nearby. With hardly any water left, the final tool at my disposal was a desire to live. As if the nightmare couldn't worsen, my phone died. Glass half full, it didn't matter—I doubted there was a trace of reception within 30 miles.

Fear infected me. I forgot about the heat until my mouth shriveled and dried. Without water, I'd be dead in an hour. Did I make the best decision?

No, definitely not... I should've wised up and climbed the last hurdle. I feigned good health as if everything were fine, but dehydration cursed me like never before. Either I'd fallen victim to a mirage, or the path was in sight, a football field's length away. This was no hallucination. There's a 50-50 chance I'd follow it to the car. Something inside told me I was being watched. By who? What? Why?

I didn't know. I was naked without a gun, blade, or anybody else. A compilation of strange, disembodied whispers shot through my ears. I burst into a full sprint.

I found the car 10 minutes later, unlocked it, and chugged a water bottle from the cooler before grabbing the .44. I slung a couple additional waters into my bag, locked the car, and jogged down the dusty road, pistol in hand. I was on a mission, eyes alert for trouble. Homer taught me the importance of heroism, a forgotten concept but an overused word in our time. I'd find my friends and rescue them from the clutches of a remote desert community of cannibals. A rescue, a daring rescue. No man left behind!

The clouds persisted in their shape-shifting as the sun peeked through. The Lord shined his light upon me!

"Saint Peter, I wish to meet you someday, but not today!" It was more than the drugs and setting that made everything fantastic. I was alive and it was good enough for me. I grabbed a handful of dirt and smeared lines beneath my eyes. *My war face.* After hiking for an unknown period, I found it—the butte we climbed, distinguished by a broken branch at the foot. How long had I been gone? 30 minutes? An hour? I climbed with caution since I didn't want to shoot myself.

Mustering some courage, I scaled the final crevice to the top. "Joe! Tony!" I shrieked, finding nothing but the whistling wind.

Seconds later, someone shouted, "Morrison! Where the fuck are you?"

I recognized Tony's voice, said, "I'm where we climbed up!"

He suggested I stay where I am.

Five minutes passed, and the other two gasped as they scaled the butte from the other side.

"There you are!" Joe exclaimed. "We were getting worried, man. What the fuck do you have the gun for? Have you had it with you this entire time? How'd you get so dirty?"

"No. I called out for y'all a few minutes and didn't hear nothing. So, fearing for y'all, I ran to the car and strapped myself. I smeared dirt on my face to blend in."

"You crazy motherfucker. Put the gun down, we're good. You really hiked all the way back to the car?"

"Damn right, I did. I was concerned! I feared the worst." I retired the gun to my bag.

"We couldn't call you because there isn't any service. We hiked in circles around this hill for an eternity!"

"Damn, I'm sorry, y'all... These drugs really got me fucked up. My phone's dead anyways."

"It's cool, we get it," Tony consoled me.

"On the lighter side of things, this view is unbelievable," I said.

"That sandstone formation to the west looks like a person. Maybe there's a giant trapped inside." Joe giggled.

"The tribes of this land actually told stories of giants. According to legend, they were a strong, advanced, and powerful group. Some say they were cannibals. Others say they were generally warlike. Minus the munchies."

"That's dope. Maybe giants did exist at some point. There's a whole lot of shit we haven't found yet. I doubt there were ever giants out here, but it doesn't hurt to keep an open mind," Tony said.

"True. I must say, as dope as Chicago's skyline is, I'd prefer to stare at these buttes and mesas every day of the week. I don't know when I'll pass from this life to the next, but when I do, bury me here or at least spread my ashes."

I've long desired a desert burial.

"Becoming one with the environment...literally! I dig it," Joe said.

From the peak, we could see the Jeep, and I came to grips with the fact I suffered dehydration and wandered astray. In my daze, I had traveled a couple miles. Low on water and still peaking on acid, light glowed at the end of the tunnel—the final stretch. The longtime friends by my side comforted me.

A gentle, ghostly breeze whistled through the ancient valley when the come-up reached its final peak. Tony lit the second blunt. The hypnotizing desert encircled us. Our mouths felt as dry as the cracked earth beneath us.

"What are y'all's plans after graduating?" I panted.

"I have no idea," Tony said. "But I don't wanna be tied down. I guess my dream is to travel or work remotely. That way I can go anywhere in the world, whenever I want! Workin' a livelihood I love while experiencing another culture would be perfect. That's what I can think of off the top of my head."

"You and me both, Tony. Chase that shit, man! Don't settle. At least in your twenties. What about you, Joe?"

"As long as I can live free and make life better for the people close to me, I'll be happy. I want to own some land somewhere someday and get away from the hive, so to speak."

I shrugged. "I feel both of you there."

"What about you? What are you trying to do? Write?"

"Yeah, it's dawning on me that I should be a writer. I probably fall somewhere between both of y'all, regarding how I want to live. Nietzsche's rants against mediocrity resonate with me. I don't want to be another brick in the wall. I want to go places: Rome, Cairo, Cape Town, Australia, Mykonos, Kilimanjaro... Maybe I'll write about it all someday, too. And when the time comes to ease up, I'll start a family and get a nice property in a small town near New Orleans. I imagine Spanish moss dripping from trees on a dirt road leading to a nice white house with a big ole porch where I can smoke and drink with my beloved. I'll raise any sons I may have to be good men, and my daughters to be smart and not take shit from anyone. My children will be warriors and scholars. I'll be the happiest man on earth if I can do those things."

"You really thought it all out. Hopefully, we have a world where our dreams are possible." Joe chuckled.

"What do you mean?" Tony asked.

"Look at the world around us, for fuck's sake! Our freedoms are being shit on because of this virus. Russia and China are getting more aggressive by the day. I don't have much hope in society, I guess. The shitstorm we're living through gives me enough doubt to believe that our futures are in jeopardy. If things weren't completely fucked pre-COVID, then they are now."

"You're right, Joe. I can't stand the worship of authority, control freaks. I despise it all and am deeply concerned for our futures. I try to be stoic about this shit, but it's easier said than done. All I ask for is freedom, even if it means freedom to live wild and flagrantly."

Tony raised his eyebrows. "I agree. It's not like our country was founded onna bloody war against a monarchy or anything."

"Exactly," said Joe. "But to be honest, as much as we've learned from our interests in philosophy and beat literature, we don't have any right to judge others for being asleep. We're just three 22-year-old drugheads who like to travel, drink, and read. This trip has been the only time I've willingly woken up before 10 AM. I'm a jackass."

"I feel that," I replied. "I've accepted that I'm a piece of shit in many ways, and it's a big reason why I ain't goin' into politics. Having my BA in political science, I'm constantly asked about running for office someday, and my response each time is a fat 'Hell no!' because when you learn enough about politics, you want nothin' to do with it."

"We always hear the same shit from older people to 'respect authority,' but I think it's a bunch of bullshit. What if authority doesn't give us a reason to respect it? Should the Germans have respected authority when Hitler rose to power? How about the Russians under Stalin, for that matter? Fuck no, and tons of people died fighting against those regimes. Obviously, our present scenario ain't as bad, but who's to say we're safe from totalitarianism? The government, the corporations... The elites and the system they uphold don't deserve a shred of a shit as respect. I don't like pointing fingers. But sometimes older generations look down on us for our dreams. I guess they've forgotten what it's like to be young and overwhelmed by expectations," Joe said after dragging the second blunt. Being a double major in poli sci and computer science, he's a jack of all trades.

Our respect for authority was as dead as the Great Barrier Reef. "I agree with both of ya," Tony said. "There's an underlying disease in the way people think and the generational disconnect is crippling us into something beyond recognition. 50 years ago, the old guard called us longhairs and draft dodgers, and now we're a buncha snowflakes."

"It's wild how the late '60s and early '70s rhyme with our own times. I think it's an opportunity to right the wrongs of history, but too few people will care enough to recognize the pattern. History is useless if we can't learn from it. I doubt our species ever will. Damn, I feel insane."

"Same here, Morrison, I'm definitely not in control of my own head right now. But you both are speaking facts, and the truth is worth telling, no matter how disturbing it may be," Joe said. "We're all fucked up and I'd love to stay here, looking at the desert, but my head's cooking like a damn tamale. We should get back to the campsite."

"Same... The acid, the heat...it's like a fuckin' oven out here. Let's head back." I hit the second blunt.

"Bet. We'll rip some dabs in the tent and knock back some cold ones."

"Sounds like a move, Tony," I said. "Let's get outta here before the police show up and put bullets in our backs."

Blistering heat nagged us without relenting. Our status as helpless foreigners to the arid environment taught us a pair of humbling lessons... Always go overboard while packing water, and never, under any circumstances, wander off alone. The humid summer heat east of the Rockies is what we'd been familiar with. While humid heat is repugnant, you're able to *feel* moisture abandoning your body. Dry heat inflicts sudden dehydration. I don't recall sweating during the hike. All three of us were blissfully unaware of our feeble state until it struck. A sharp pain stabbed my throat, my saliva nonexistent, and I had trouble swallowing as if a rusty nail lay lodged inside. The car remained some distance away, blocked by a series of hills.

"I'm out," I said, tossing an empty water bottle into my bag, along with the others.

"We'll share this one," Tony said in a cracked voice. "It's all we got left."

"*Let's give each other corona!*" I sarcastically exclaimed.

"Please give me some, I think I'm coming down with heatstroke. My head is killing me, and I can feel my body burning up," Joe said.

Tony obliged and passed him the water.

"We should reach the car soon. We ain't gettin' stuck out here," I declared, determined to sound confident—a weak attempt, I must admit. "We're gettin' closer." A bird screeched somewhere behind us.

"Vultures," Tony grimly muttered.

"Ain't no vultures," I scolded him. "Enough of that talk. We only have a little further to go." I surveyed the land around us. "It's hotter than the devil's armpit out here, but at least it's beautiful."

"Morrison, I appreciate nature a fuck ton, but let's focus on getting to the damn car," Joe muttered.

"Relax, it's about a quarter-mile away. We'll be fine. Just gotta count our blessings."

BURN CIVILIZATION, BURN

We tried to recover at the campsite. With an hour left until dark, we multitasked, chugging water while discreetly ripping dabs in the tent. Almost every vice imaginable is illegal on the reservation—tragically ironic since these harsh laws contribute to the area's high incarceration rate, but the winds of change are blowing as tribal leaders fight against these.

Dab wax funneled us deeper into our trances. We cheerfully threw around a football and knocked back beers, admiring the sun as it lowered over the horizon. Streaks of clouds flared across the heavens like golden flames.

Joe and Tony eventually retreated to the tent to get more stoned and, high as I was, I walked across the campground toward the desert. Sundown cooled the air, allowing the animals to come out to play in a nocturnal wasteland. Deer, coyotes, rattlesnakes, mountain lions, scorpions...

Fledgling sunlight faded over the landscape, reducing the mesas to silhouettes, and eerie noises from unknown creatures fired from every direction. I sensed the eyes studying us, but the drugs and alcohol numbed my anxiety. It was a quarter past 8 o'clock, and there I stood tripping, stoned, and five beers deep. Nearby, cliffs rose, and bushes and yellow Mojave yucca seduced me, complimented by distant tabletop mesas. My roots lie in the country, for better or worse. As royally fucked as the political climate is, amid so much bitterness, the desert remains constant, and will for ages to come.

The desolation provoked reflections. Since it was July, patriotism crossed my mind. *What defines a patriot? Does anybody ask themselves this question?* Patriotism has nothing to do with waving a flag or standing for an anthem. Patriots are rebels, outliers whose passion for liberty is so strong and pure that they'll protest government actions they deem oppressive. Scaring the shit out of society's corrupt fat cats by conscientiously objecting to their self-serving laws is the most patriotic thing anybody can do. After all, Stokely Carmichael once said, "Law is the agent of those in political power; it is the product of those powerful enough to define right and wrong."[2] Governments and laws, like all institutions, are constructs and may break down on a whim, tumbling into oblivion.

We committed multiple felonies in a single day. My confession sounds sinister at first glance, but who was hurt by our actions? Nobody but (almost) us. Philosopher Hannah Arendt observed our country's unique embrace of dangerous freedom which has allowed us to choose our paths, regardless of where they lead. It's not the government's duty to protect us from ourselves. Why is it okay for governments to drop bombs but not for people to drop acid? What in the wide world of fuck is wrong with us?

The experiment of dangerous freedom is fading as out-of-touch bureaucrats continuously dissolve freedom of choice. Politicians to this day are raising the smoking age to 21 in "progressive" cities. "Don't smoke but, by all means, fight in our wars," John McCain's ghost whispered in my ear. I wondered what's next. I don't *want* to see 18-year-olds smoking cigarettes or ripping vapes, however, they deserve the right to make their own decisions. Whether it's helicopter parents and special interests or censoring books to make them sound "nicer," a terrible trajectory is underway. Shielding our youth from life's ugliness won't make them into better people, but fearful shadows who are chained to a wall and unable to experience the light beyond the cave.

My contemplations rambled on like a Zeppelin song as the warm evening breeze kissed my skin. I finally was coming down. The trip mellowed out to a better high after hours of peak intensity. The sun had completely submerged below the horizon. My phone rang. It was Joe.

"What's up, man?" I asked.

---

[2] Ture, Kwame and Hamilton, Charles V. *Black Power: The Politics of Liberation*

"Dude, where are you?"

"Follow the sun."

"What?"

"Walk toward the sun, Joe. The last bit of light."

"Okay..."

"Wait... I think I hear you. You with Tony?"

"Yeah."

"Keep walking straight, I'm sittin' on a bench."

Pure darkness over the landscape. Seconds later, the other two joined me, marveling in the bliss of being cut off from civilization's poisons.

We didn't speak. Joe already changed into a T-shirt and pajama pants, while Tony and I still wore our cutoffs from hiking. Peace and quiet. I'm convinced our best friends are the ones with whom we can comfortably enjoy a stillness of time, the ones who understand, who recognize how we feel during any given moment, rendering words obsolete. I smiled and wondered if we'd found paradise—but it didn't last.

A barrage of bats circled us, so we beat it.

For the millionth time, we got zapped in the tent and drank for another two hours. Around midnight, the guys fell asleep, and I wasn't far behind them. I abandoned the tent to lie on the wooden table by the car, face the sky, and listen to music. *How long until I'll step foot here again?* I thought. *Who knows, I better seize as much of the night as possible.* The lunar glow was a sight to see, reinforced by stars against a jet-black sky. Nighttime in the desert speaks through the stars.

The acid had weakened, but the dabs kept me on cloud nine. In the stars, I saw the people I love.

Pale light calmed the mood but nevertheless, I couldn't see three feet in front of me. A vicious predator could've prowled in wait, ready to pounce, and I'd have no idea. Between the view and the whistling wind, shooting stars flared across the sky in a matter of minutes, causing me to brood over the poor bastards who've yet to see one. How do you tell somebody you're from a city without *really* telling them you're from a city? How can one begin to dream without looking at the stars?

I reminisced about the common comparisons between the wild and other planets. Nature is Earth in its purest form, hence a baffling irony... A large majority of people spend their lives in crowded metropolitan areas without ever testing themselves, me included. All we know are greed, control, fast-paced competitions, passionless one-night stands, and our own parochial interests. Every day is monotonous as we march onward to spiritual death and live for the weekend. We pass the other five days as zombies, forgetting our agrarian roots. As Nietzsche said, man is the tamest of animals. B.B. King's "The Thrill is Gone" rings in my head. The domestication of the human being is no less tragic than the taming of a lion. What's different is that a foreign species didn't kidnap and force us into captivity. We did it to *ourselves*.

Living free requires strength, which we needed on the road. All day, I was alive. Too alive. I experienced ecstasy, terror, humility, dread, fear, and happiness. My heart throbbed with adrenaline, thinking of creeps from the ghost town. An omen I didn't know what to make of. I was petrified, but at least I felt alive.

Current events funneled through my head about the society we were running from. A shitstorm of catastrophe during that odd year. The pandemic. George Floyd. Breonna Taylor. Police (State) violence, period. Tech addiction. Upcoming election blues. I am revolted by demagogues who lurk behind podiums of death, transforming normal individuals into moronic crowds, void of all critical thinking, clamoring like mad children for a savior before they scurry back into their recliners and television dens, where they complain. Complain about what?

About everything their candidate disapproves of. The masses never yearn to be free. Most of us fail to realize that truth is an ally disguised as the enemy. Across our country, cities suffered from unrest in fires stoked by a gross divide, but the flames and ashes burned far away from us. I sympathized with the riots and protests because civil disobedience is America's oldest tradition. Every now and then, this country goes berserk. Our parents and grandparents witnessed the strife of the '60s, and we're seeing it again in the present.

The times meant something to Joe, Tony, and me. Authority collapsed all around us, but we were numb to the breakdown. Besides, our generation was born in the wake of September 11. We spent the prime of our childhoods during the Great Recession. We lost our homes and our parents. Families with children panhandled on city streets from coast to coast. I don't remember my father ever working less than two jobs to feed my siblings and me. At times, he worked three. Time will tell how such turbulence will shape a generation.

Chicago destroyed itself in June of 2020. Our neighborhood along Northwestern Boulevard teemed with shuttered businesses and boarded windows. This was unprecedented. Mayor Lightfoot ordered curfews and lifted the bridges over the Chicago River connecting The Loop to the rest of the city. A few of us recall when some pranksters blasted *Purge* sirens from their cars. I often rode my bike on warm nights while cops patrolled every street corner. We never lived under overt authoritarianism before, and I'm forced to frequently ask myself what country I'm living in. Truth be told, millions of people live day-to-day, looking over their shoulders in this police state disguised as a glimmering republic. The illusion of freedom fades with each passing day.

But here we were, miles away, desert dogs roaming the West without a care. On the road, we dictated our universe and followed our instincts.

All the while, "The End" by The Doors played from my phone, and I understood why Jim Morrison chose the desert as an ideal place to take psychedelics. The land's ancient character is trance-inducing. Trippy lyrics rang in my ears about pain, serpents, incest, and patricide. The dark poetic nature of The Doors' lyrics inspired me to write a couple poems. Sporadic headlights of lone cars jutting down Highway 163 disappeared into the darkness. Another shooting star beamed across the sky, and I retired to the tent.

Viva Las Vegas

Instinctively, the Deep South, Appalachia, or declining Rust Belt cities come to mind with the mention of American poverty but rarely do the reservations. The Navajo Nation—the second largest of the great tribes—is no exception. Almost half the population live in poverty and lack running water. Most homes don't even have internet access.

We hit the road at first light. Breakfast consisted of bread and water we'd picked up at the Grand Junction Walmart. All around us, the reservation sprang to life. Rows of shacks and piles of garbage bordered the highway. Gas stations were frequented by panhandlers, fast food chains, and traces of a time forever gone haunted the land. Why don't we discuss the matter?

Red dirt in the shadows of corporate arches. Children played tag around overflowing dumpsters. We refueled the car when an old man with empty eyes asked if we had anything to spare. He hardly spoke. There was no backstory other than his hat, which indicated he was sent to Vietnam. He was not inclined to convince us why he needed money. We didn't have much cash, but we pooled together what we could. I grabbed a bottle of water from the trunk. He nodded and went across the street to a diner before turning around.

We made eye contact, and I wondered who this man's ancestors were, and how they lived before their land was scarred by greed and fossil fuel excavation. This man with empty eyes was far from alone. We hopped back into the car, wondering if these disparities before our eyes would ever be mended. This poverty was planned.

The blueprint probably sounded like this:

"You mean to say people already inhabit this continent? Throw those savages onto reservations so we can forget about them. This land ain't big enough for the two of us."

"There's still more to do, sir. What about the other problem? The elephant in the room?"

"Correct, we have a bone to pick with the millions of Black people whose ancestors arrived here involuntarily. Toss them into ghettos and invent something to keep them there. Jim Crow! Redlining! Drug wars!"

"The middle- and working-class White fools won't know what hit 'em. We'll spoon-feed those dumb honkeys some steaming bullshit with a side of propaganda called cable news to entrench each group against the other."

"Genius."

I apologize for the bleak humor, but coming of age under such turmoil takes a toll. Faction doesn't have to mean division. James Madison attempted to solve this dilemma in *The Federalist Papers*. Ignorance of our countrymen's plight poses as a mortal sin, tainting the fabric of Old Glory. Our experiences on the reservation, though limited, revealed to us an elusive injustice. North America knew freedom only when the Great Tribes were its sole inhabitants. Women too enjoyed far superior status in Indigenous communities compared to their Western counterparts, despite traditional gender roles. A passage from Benjamin Franklin is appropriate here:

"The Indian Men, when young, are Hunters and Warriors; when old, Counselors; for all their government is by the Counsel or Advice of the Sages; there is no Force, there are no Prisons, no Officers to compel Obedience, or inflict punishment. Hence, they generally study oratory; the best Speaker having the most Influence. The Indian Women till the Ground, dress the Food, nurse and bring up the Children, and preserve and hand down to Posterity the Memory of Public Transactions. The Employment of Men and Women is considered natural and honorable. Having few Artificial Wants, they have an abundance of Leisure for Improvement by Conversation. Our laborious manner of Life compared with theirs, they esteem slavish and base."[3]

---

[3] Franklin, Benjamin. *The Savages of North America.*

The first people of this fair land lived far superior lives before the arrival of Europeans. They didn't value excess, nor were their societies authoritarian. They lived sustainably and free of malevolent ideologies. Franklin's words are enough to force anybody to question whether what we've built on this continent is worth it. Three years earlier, when scaling the crest of a high mountain, I listened closely and heard the voices of the dead pleading for aid. I have a difficult time figuring out what I can do to mend the wrongs of history. Maybe there's nothing at all. Maybe there is. Hopefully, I recognize it when it spits on my shoes.

For four and a half hours, we rolled through a series of highways—U.S. Route 89, 160, AZ-98, and I-15. There's very little out there but red desert mountains and green shrubs scattered between Monument Valley and the Nevada state line. We sped past the edge of Zion National Park, through Hurricane and St. George, hauling ass into Nevada. At 1 o'clock, we stopped in Mesquite at a Sinclair for some gas, meeting the signature green dinosaur outside.

"Would you guys be down for some uppers when we get to Vegas?" Tony suggested, sitting behind the wheel.

"It's Vegas, why the hell not?" I answered.

"I dig," Joe replied, stepping out to grab the nozzle.

"Bet. There's a guy we can hit up when we get in. We used to play baseball together as kids before he moved out here. His name's Kenny but most people just call him Watts. He let me crash at his pad last time I was in town. He'll hook us up."

"Tony with the Vegas plug, you high-rollin' bastard!" I roared.

"Hell yeah!"

"Tonight'll be a hell of a time, I can sense it," I said, taking a drag of the one-hitter.

"Weed, shrooms, acid, coke... What's next?" Joe laughed as he filled the tank. "Morrison, you nuts? Smoking near a gas pump?"

"You know I'm nuts. There'd only be a problem if your dumb ass sprays gasoline into the car."

"Maybe I will, smartass."

"Shut up and fill the damn tank. We got a city to cause trouble in."

Tony grinned. "Tonight'll be a problem, I can tell."

"We're all set."

"Bet, let's burn some rubber."

While gliding past Joshua trees, we found an exceptional deal for the night. The pandemic restricted travel, so hotels and flights ran cheap. 20 bucks a piece to spend a night in the Strip. Fortune gave us its blessing since Sin City was apparently designed by a team of mad businessmen to deprive people of their money—an unsurprising characteristic of a town made by mobsters.

Soccer mom subdivisions and casino billboards are nestled along the Great Basin Highway leading into Las Vegas. Few Las Vegans are born there, and it's a booming place, brimming with transplants to the point of implosion. We took Exit 39 on Spring Mountain Road before hitting the Strip. Billboards advertised strip clubs, bars, and hotels, one of them showcasing a cowgirl in lingerie captioned, **Come west to get wild.**

Say less. We'd been pursuing "wild." We booked a reservation at The Stratosphere, Vegas' tallest building. It reminds me of Seattle's Space Needle. We cruised down Las Vegas Boulevard to our destination, met the valet, grabbed our bags, and entered the lobby to check in. The gold and scarlet carpet gave way to marble in the registration area. Unlike Grand Junction, we checked in with ease, secured the keys, and took the elevator to our room.

We were awestruck upon opening the door—two beds with silk sheets sat on a maroon carpet, and a bronze bust of a horse rested between them next to the lamp. Our room was on the 23rd floor and the entire Strip was in view. The Sahara, Treasure Island, The Paris Hotel, The Mirage, Caesars Palace, and a barrier of mountains in the distance.

"Won't you boys look at that?" Tony exclaimed. "We're living like kings tonight!"

"The view's dope as fuck," Joe said. "A proper Vegas welcome for sure. Morrison, you've stayed here before?"

"Yessir, back in 2017. Too bad the rooftop pool is closed. They got a big ole screen up there and a bar. And Lord have mercy, are the women fine. Absolute muses."

"Sounds like Heaven," Joe sighed.

"It's alright, we'll come back here after this covid bullshit's over. Y'all can see for yourselves."

"Sounds like a must," Tony said. "Who wants to hit the rig?"

"I'm good. I bet there'll be lots of people there and I'm still a bit spaced out from the smoke we had on the way in."

"I'm gonna wait 'til after we hit Planet 13," Joe said.

"Well, more for me," Tony chuckled.

"Go ahead, you goddamn fiend."

"I wear that title with pride, Morrison!"

"Hell, so do I. All three of us are damn fiends."

"I'll hit this, and we'll walk over."

"Yessir," Joe said. "Let's chug water before we go."

"Good idea," I concurred, tossing each of them bottles.

Planet 13 is the largest dispensary in the world. Stoners from all corners of the earth make their pilgrimage to the Mojave Desert's Sodom and Gomorrah. Unbothered by the 114-degree heat, we headed toward the stoner temple. Palm trees towered high, and their leaves glimmered in the sun. Enthusiasm replaced our road fatigue, complimented by the thrill of venturing through an unfamiliar city.

Outside Planet 13, a long line stretched around the red planet-like sphere in front of it. Nevertheless, the line moved quickly, and after about 10 minutes, we made it. Crowds of people packed the joint. The complex hosts a variety of stores in addition to the main floor, where you can buy different strains of flower. A true weed shopping mall. At the front of the line, employees checked IDs and handed out numbered tickets. The sheer variety of strains made this place a stoner's paradise. Glass cases protected the flower, edibles, and pre-rolls. Joe and I had to wait a half hour for our turn.

"Figure out what you're getting?" I asked him.

"Mad Russian Thunder Fuck."

"Damn, son, shit sounds intense."

"Right? Gonna cop an eighth; it's a sativa. I figure anything called Thunder Fuck has to be fire."

"I'd imagine. Tryna match later?"

"Yessir. What about you? Find something you want?"

"Yeah, Star Pie. I prefer sativas because I don't like to be a zombie. It's a hybrid."

"My Thunder Fuck should tilt the high towards the sativa anyways. Your Star Pie will balance it out."

"Bet."

Meanwhile, the girl behind the desk returned with the Star Pie, and I handed her my card.

"What's your number?" she asked Joe.

"708-121—"

"On your card, Joe."

"Oh God, that's embarrassing... 341,"

She grinned. "What would you like?"

"Mad Russian Thunderfuck."

"I think you mean Matanuska." She laughed.

He blushed and clenched his jaw. "Yeah, that's what I meant."

"Mad Russian. I'm dead," I chuckled.

"It's been a long day, I'm still spaced out from the ride in, and she's hot. It threw me off."

"Every woman in here is gorgeous," I said. "Vegas is shaping up to be my kinda town. The world suddenly turned blonde."

"It's a damn mystery what tonight will bring."

Meanwhile, Joe's crush reappeared, charging him $35 for the eighth. "And you?" she asked me.

"An eighth of Star Pie, please."

With our weed, we located Tony near the entrance. He stood, evaluating prices at a table selling pre-rolled blunts. "I was wondering where you guys were," he said. "You boys down to pitch in on some of these pre-rolls? Five for $75."

"Sure, what about you, Joe?"

"Let's do it. Pre-rolls at Venice Beach tomorrow will be a move. What's the strain?"

"Space Cake," answered the shop worker. She wore a T-shirt that read, **Went to Las Vegas, ended up on another planet.**

"51% THC!" Tony squealed like a child.

"Damn, ring us up," I commanded, energized. "We'll Venmo you, Tony."

"Bet."

Giddy, we wandered around to eventually settle behind a closed strip joint. We stood against a cinder block wall. Our recent purchases complimented our Denver weed and Durban Poison. Tony grabbed a cone from his pocket while Joe and I broke down our strains to match, giving him the broken bits. Up, up, and away!

"Damn, the dispo was outrageous. A weed shopping mall!" I exclaimed.

"Biggest dispo in the world, and we hit it!" Tony said.

"We've already put a dent in the bucket list, and it's our third day on the road," Joe said. "I can't wait for what lies ahead."

"Neither can I, brother. Speakin' of which, I'm not complaining—this weed is good as fuck, but I'll need an uplifting substance as night falls."

They immediately knew what I meant.

"Yeah, when are we copping from your guy, Tony?" Joe asked.

"We'll get the car at the hotel after we smoke and head his way. He lives in Paradise, and it ain't far from here."

"Bet," Joe and I answered simultaneously.

"I'm excited for baseball to start up again," I said, looking at the Cubs' schedule on my phone.

"Season starts in two weeks, right?"

"Yessir. We should be solid this year."

"Keep it rolling! We have a chance at being division champs," Joe said.

"I agree. The Brewers and the Cardinals ain't gonna do anything special. This ain't 2016, but I hope our boys keep playing well. I'm just relieved that baseball's comin' back."

"Yeah, I miss it," he replied.

"How do ya like Vegas, Joe?" Tony asked.

"I suppose it's different during regular times, but I can tell this place is wild. I'm excited for tonight."

Tony handed him the joint. "Last summer, I was drunk and trippin' on some mescaline at Harrah's. A lady in her forties kept hitting on me in front of her husband. That beer-bellied motherfucker kept telling me he was a cop and not afraid to kick my ass. I wasn't even doing anything. She wouldn't leave me alone! All I wanted to do was play some blackjack. Make no mistake, Torres, this place is unpredictable." His Chicago accent thickened.

"You sure you weren't doin' anything, Tony?" I teased.

"Of course not. Who do ya think I am? My folks raised me to be a good Catholic!"

"But you're agnostic!"

"Well, yeah, but it's the upbringing that counts."

"I know, I'm playin'. But you saw an off-duty cop on edge and lookin' for trouble, actin' all tough? *Shocker*."

"Sounds like the average barfly from our neighborhood," Joe said.

"Pass the joint, Joe, damn! I've been waitin' man! You're right though."

"Relax, Morrison. I got wrapped up in Tony's story. Trying to figure out what to expect in this town."

"No worries, just bustin' your balls."

"What time is it?"

"5:15."

"We should be getting back. I'll hit up my guy."

We hadn't interacted with many other people on the trip yet, aside from soul-crushed service sector employees. The pandemic conditioned folks to avoid each other. People strolling down the sidewalk would noticeably go around approaching strangers. It was unlike anything I'd ever seen. Throughout the day, random pedestrians would cross Sammy Davis Jr. Drive to avoid us.

How long will this be normal? Will it ever change? The enforcement of social distancing ties together with an entire apparatus of social media disillusion. *We are in the middle of the largest social experiment in human history, and we are the guinea pigs.* There's no use diving into all that. We had drugs to score, and a trip to the moon could help us forget the bullshit.

We briefly returned to the hotel. Tony motioned to the valet, who vanished for a minute before pulling in with the car.

Then we sped off to buy the drugs. The drive to Watts' place in Paradise lasted no longer than 10 minutes. Tony spoke with Watts on the phone to let him know we were on our way. Their conversation sounded cordial, but this failed to alleviate my anxiety. Perhaps we were hurling ourselves into a trap, a bust for low-level drug activity. An ominous weight pulled my heart down.

How well does Tony know this guy? Are they acquaintances or longtime friends? Will we die in Las Vegas, buried in a grave of fentanyl and sand? Streets grew desolate the further we drove from The Strip. The blood in my veins didn't flow, but boiled in place, because of the heat and fear. I was nauseous. Hardly anybody out on the pavement. Windows of homes were shut. We were locked in a post-apocalyptic wasteland. When we arrived, I didn't know how to feel. *Stay alert, carry yourself well. We'll be fine.*

We parked on a side street in a residential subdivision and walked a block to our destination. Rows of houses—stucco structures and Spanish roof tiles behind front lawns of gravel dotted the neighborhood. Tony pointed to his friend's house with a tall palm tree at the end of the street.

"Go to the side door," Tony said.

"Bet."

I got some hairy vibrations as we approached the house. I don't buy drugs from strangers, but I trusted Tony and suppressed my anxiety.

Watts waited outside the door. A dark beard lay in tangles on his cheeks. He stood a head above all of us, crossing his arms over his narrow chest.

"What's up, man, how the hell are ya? It's been a minute!" Tony greeted. "These are my boys Joe and Pat but, in Chicago, Pat goes by Morrison. We go way back."

"Watts, right?" I asked.

"That's my name. Pleasure. You grew up with Tony?" He spoke in a deep West Coast accent.

"Yeah, St. Bridget's in Chicago on the Northwest Side, a long time ago."

"You don't sound like it," he laughed.

"You're hearing Louisiana. I've called Baton Rouge home for a few years. I graduated from LSU in May."

"Explains a lot, congrats on the championship and graduation, man."

"Much appreciated. *Geaux Tiguhs!*"

Joe followed suit, introducing himself. Watts invited us inside, away from the heat. It appeared nobody else was home. The absence of sound was stronger than in the streets, and the ceiling fan cooled the blaze coursing our skin. Weight slowly lifted from our shoulders. A bong decorated the mahogany desk next to the bed in his room, alongside a Ziplock bag full of flower.

Watts reached under the bed and seized the drugs. "This is what I got." He held an impressive brick of cocaine.

"Yessir! Yessir!" Tony exclaimed. "Your room is drug Heaven."

"I've never seen such a big-ass brick of blow before," I said, ensorcelled by the sight.

"I got my connections. This is Vegas, isn't it?" He offered each of us a sample bump and took one himself, characteristic of a quality plug.

I sniffed my bump from the key, then Joe, then Tony. Strong stuff. Really strong stuff.

"Y'all are looking for an eight ball, correct?" Watts asked Tony.

"Yessir, how much?"

"$130. We go back and you've always been a real one Tony, so I'll hook you boys up. Besides, business has been hot lately. Lots of house parties this summer. This is quality stuff. Straight from south of the border."

"Bet. We appreciate you hooking us up, my brother."

We pooled $130 in cash, growing our drug arsenal into something impressive. Dancing on the edge is the surest way to feel alive. It was already a hard road we had chosen, and the pit grew deeper.

"Feel free to meet us at the Strip. We're gonna have ourselves a night," Tony offered Watts.

"I appreciate the offer, man, but I have business to take care of in the meantime. If I change my mind, I'll give you a call."

"Bet. I'm down to relive our adventures from last year!"

"Oh yeah, when you accidentally barfed in a lady's purse at the casino, mistaking it for a trash can after taking that peyote, huh?"

"You fucker!"

Joe and I stared at him with raised eyebrows.

"Say, 'hello,' to your people for me, Tony. Pleasure meeting y'all," Watts said as we left.

The setting sun cast a dark shadow over the horizon, and our excitement grew by the second.

"You got it."

Jim Morrison knew about the connection between drugs and gambling. Under the influence, you put a **for rent** sign in your brain, allowing the substances to move in with mind-altering baggage. We learned this on the reservation the day before, and would again come nighttime. We darted back through the pattern of dead streets and empty pavement with caution. Cocaine is an entirely different animal compared to our psychedelics. The prison time is harsh. Both Paradise and Vegas P.D. prowled the streets. We had to tow a line. The drive back ran much longer. It felt like an eternity, but we pulled into the hotel, ready to sprint into the night.

At 6:30, I unzipped the bag of mushrooms and stuffed three grams down my throat. Joe followed, then Tony calmly popped two tabs of acid under his tongue as he emptied blow onto the table by the window. I cracked open my bottle of Jack, and we killed it in under two hours, ripping dabs and coming up along the way. Sometime around 8:30, we left the hotel to satisfy our rumbling stomachs.

It was dark, and the lights of the Strip illuminated Las Vegas Valley. The psychedelics intensified our hallucinations. The Eiffel Tower and Lady Liberty replicas appeared wild, shifty, as if I could see everything's outline. We ventured past The Bellagio, Caesars Palace, The MGM, and The Luxor—a blue beam of light shot into the dark sky from atop the pyramid.

Las Vegas is an interesting town for psychedelic drugs. Large, flashing neon signs, glowing buildings, sculptures, and the vibrant atmosphere make it fun, but amid a trip, you could be described as insane. Anxieties rush through your head, clinging to the temporal lobe, wreaking havoc, creating scenarios of mere fiction outside the brain. Odd sensations take over and *anything* can come to mind. You plunge yourself into either Heaven or Hell and there's not a whole lot of control over which one you experience.

Good acid usually gravitates toward euphoria, but mushrooms are hit or miss. Tough cities like Vegas increase the fear of something bad happening. Sin City is an unpredictable urban jungle that has slain innumerable souls in its short existence. Grit is a vital quality in a land of wolves, and not everyone is fortunate enough to survive a modern Sodom and Gomorrah. The two biblical cities God destroyed come to mind for necessary reasons.

Las Vegas is a metaphor for America's future and perhaps, the world's. It sums up every element of cultural decay we've adopted in this country. Show business, materialism, people fucking just to fuck, and mindless entertainment while dollars flow into the checks of fat cats so they can continue growing the city like a cancer through the Mojave Desert.

I chucked the empty whiskey bottle from the car where it violently crashed against a **speed limit** sign. "10 points!" I yelled as the other two cussed me out. Hungry as we were, we cruised around the city for a half hour. Eyes out for pigs. A depraved monster sinking low enough to operate a vehicle under the influence can never be too careful. Cars sped past us outside the window. For once, we adhered to the speed limit. Aside from a few beers, my last experience in the Mojave Desert left me sober. Different vibrations on this Vegas summer night... It was almost 9 o'clock and we'd indulged in a milkshake of intoxicants.

We agreed to hit the drive-thru at In-N-Out Burger. Only Tony had eaten there before, so Joe and I anticipated a feast since we'd heard nothing but good reviews. We pulled back into the front of The Stratosphere, tipped the valet, and headed inside.

Dealing with the valet was one problem solved, but the clerk who checked our keys in the lobby horrified me. I glanced at Joe. He wasn't doing well, either. His teeth chattered. He wouldn't stop pointing his finger and moving it in circles. I read the clerk as a hardass. His demeanor exhibited misery and frustration. He refused to make eye contact, groaned, and huffed when Tony almost dropped his keycard—vibes you get from somebody who hates their job. I tried to sympathize, but the mushrooms made him look terrible. In front of us stood a sasquatch staring into our souls. This creature was fully aware of our intoxication and eager to turn us over to the authorities. We had to get away.

None of this happened. He checked our keys, and we found refuge in the room without trouble, happily feasting on burgers and fries. Our mouths watered excessively the whole time we ate. The beef, American cheese, tomatoes, and ketchup formed a glorious concoction. Our lean but toned bodies felt replenished. Joe scarfed his fries first, sticking to his tradition.

After concluding our meal, Tony emptied three thick lines from the bag, the white powder gently falling on the table. Joe tightened the lines with the edge of his debit card. Tony then passed around some beers—Millers, given we'd slammed enough hard liquor. The beds and walls shifted in a haze, and I felt dizzy. I didn't understand what was happening. The room began distorting, so I sat in the chair by the table to breathe and hydrate. Cottonmouth already. Tony turned on some music to elevate the mood. Polo G's album THE GOAT echoed everywhere that summer, particularly the songs "Martin & Gina" and "21." Joe tightly rolled a Benjamin.

Holding my breath to avoid making a mess, I pressed the dollar against the table and sniffed the Machu Picchu, sucking every last bit up my left nostril. Tony did the same. Jamming, snorting, drinking, and ripping dabs, we climbed to the stars. If we drank enough, we'd be numb to any comedown, so the beers flowed endlessly.

It was unfortunate that marauding the casinos or clubs was futile. Local businesses had been cursed by vacancy or shitty hours. Besides, we didn't have enough money to gamble with. Instead, our consensus involved leaving the safety of our room to walk southbound on Las Vegas Boulevard. We brought two of the Space Cake blunts and passed them around.

Our pregame in the hotel room lasted for a couple hours, and we left at a quarter to 11. Joe pocketed the snow, and I brought my keys along so we could take bumps. Surely, we'd find a nice, quiet, sketchy location in the Strip to rip a few at.

We flew to Mars through the midnight air, wired from the quadruple fade of alcohol, cocaine, THC, and mushrooms... Or acid, considering Tony popped another two tabs after dinner. None of us had been that stoned since our first days smoking in the seventh grade. We stumbled past Caesars Palace and The Bellagio, seeing double. My balance had come back, but I remained disoriented. Those hallucinations would spell the death of me.

Traveling to Las Vegas is like being sucked into a plush, retro-futuristic madhouse. I dug it and lit the first blunt, humbled by our surroundings. *This town could kill us*, I thought. A city of thieves, gangsters, prostitutes, drinkers, and gamblers that sucks tourists from every corner of kingdom come. Half the city was probably fucking while we roamed those streets.

"I think somebody put crack in these blunts," I said after exhaling.

"What'd you expect, Morrison. They have enough THC to kill Snoop Dogg!" Joe was elevated, riding waves. Me, too. "Look, it's Richard Nixon with a couple of hookers!"

"He's been dead since the '90s, Joe," I said.

"Wait no—" Joe interrupted, "it's a congressman getting head from a camel."

"Where? Which one?" I frantically asked, hoping to catch a glimpse of yet another politician violating their own lockdown rules and engaging in a repulsive act of bestiality.

"Over there, in the lot next to The World's Largest Gift Shop."

I did my best to fight off the hallucinations. "False alarm. It's just a drag queen." Disappointing.

Drugs and alcohol staked claims in our bodies, and the political references were by no means random. The 2020 election lurked right around the corner. One month from our adventure, Joe Biden would receive the Democratic Party's nomination for presidency. Typical of an incumbent, Donald Trump ran virtually unopposed in the Republican Primary, save for a weak challenge from Bill Weld, the former

Massachusetts governor who ran on the Libertarian ticket with Gary Johnson in 2016.

With Trump and Joe Biden poised to throw down in November, none of us had faith in either choice. Our generation was skeptical we'd be accurately represented by a couple of rich 80-year-olds. Contrary to what our forebears believe, Generation Z is more than a bunch of pronoun-obsessed, pink-haired, emotionally unstable iPhone addicts. Our depth lies deeper than the media and our elders give us credit for. We see our world, this world we didn't ask for, exactly as it is. We can't be tricked.

"Who are you voting for, Morrison?" Tony asked.

"I would consider voting for Biden if he wasn't a neoliberal gun-grabber. I have my doubts he'll end the forever wars in the Middle East. To be honest, this neoliberal coalition reminds me of everything wrong with American politics. So, there's another reason, and Trump—well, I don't even need to dive into him. Gonna sit this one out."

"Bold move."

"Not really, if you think about it. Voting's a right and rights involve freedom of choice. Politicians must earn our votes, and if neither candidate deserves them, why the fuck should we give them the benefit of the doubt? Not voting for mediocre candidates needs to be normalized. Y'all familiar with W.E.B. DuBois?"

"I've heard the name, but that's the extent of my knowledge," Tony said in a puzzled voice.

"Wasn't he the first Black person to get a PhD from Harvard?" Joe asked.

"Yup. He wrote tons of books including *The Souls of Black Folk*, which I highly recommend to y'all. The FBI opened a 700-page file on him."

"Jesus, why? He do something?" Tony asked.

"He was a target for the same reason Dr. King and every other civil rights leader was. He challenged the power structure, so they labeled him a communist."

I nodded. "He once said during the 1956 election that he had no desire to vote in it. Why? Because he believed the two-party system gives us only the illusion of choice, that the Democrats and Republicans are two sides of the same coin, and they'll win elections, regardless of our efforts, so I'm not voting. Besides, Biden's winning Illinois whether or not we vote. At any rate, we don't have a two-party system in this country. We have one party, the Corporate Party, with its two vanity-stricken wings."

"The 'Corporate Party,' I like that... And I agree. Politicians are nothing but con men, the fuckin' jagoffs. But how do you think the election will go down?"

"Either the mishandling of coronavirus kills Trump, the same way Vietnam killed Lyndon Johnson 50 years ago, or the Democrats fuck up like in 2016 by painting all Trump supporters as uneducated racists. Hillary Clinton's 'basket of deplorables' comment cost her the election."

"True. The Democrats shot themselves in the foot back in 2016, and I wouldn't be surprised if they did it again. Just wait until this year's race is in full swing and all the smug, cringey 'get out the vote' campaigns start." Joe's warning resonated with Tony and me.

"We'll be hearing those half-assed messages from everybody soon enough. Everybody, from politicians to professional athletes, to Hollywood elites. Basically, a bunch of people who are outta touch. Goddamn, man, I don't even wanna think about it." Tony sullenly shrugged. He wasn't as political as Joe and me but nevertheless understood how phony the game is. He said, "What these politicians and celebrities really mean is 'get out and vote as long as you vote for me or who I support,' it's horse shit."

"Only a free-thinking and informed base of voters can get corrupt politicians out of office, and we don't have an electorate like that in this country. Machiavelli, y'all, Machiavelli. Over 500 years ago he left us a clear message— politics is about power and nothin' else. He died centuries ago... And before him, we had the Roman satirist, Juvenal. No matter how much human civilization advances technologically, our problems always stay the same. They simply wear different masks. So, here we are in the present, still bitching and moaning amongst ourselves, trying to figure out why the politicians cheat us time and time again. They sell us promises, then they sell us out. All for a dollar and some power. But does anybody care about being robbed blind? No.

We're focused on who's railing who in Hollywood. The Roman Circus lives on... Our society is a fucking clown show. We'll pay for it and so will our children."

"It's the doom loop, Morrison!" Joe said. "Both parties want power and support so bad, they'll mislead anybody gullible enough to fall for their tricks. They're damn good at it too. The problem is that they can make people feel like they have to vote for them or give them their hard-earned money."

"The whole system is malevolent. I'm not the most political person, but I can't believe how much bullshit we put up with."

"A Gallup poll said that 25% of voters disapprove of Joe Biden and Donald Trump but I guarantee most of those people will vote for one or the other because they're brainwashed to do their 'civic duty'—voting just for the sake of voting, an ego trip. 'Look at me, I'm helping,'—that type of shit. People love to pat themselves on the back." I spoke passionately because it was the only way I knew how. The cocaine also played its part.

"Shit, Morrison, you're making sense. Similar thoughts crossed my mind recently, and I didn't want to express them out loud. I think it might be better for the country this time around if people don't vote even if it's mail-in. Teach the people in power a lesson. We won't vote for candidates we don't like," Joe declared.

Although disheartened, I couldn't help but persist, "The establishment produces shitty candidates who the masses flock to vote for every goddamn cycle. This tells the party elites that they can run whatever dipshit candidate they want, and we'll take the bait. Are y'all planning on voting?"

"I'm indecisive," Tony muttered, "neither candidate appeals to me, but Trump needs to go. The rest of the world looks at us like we're a fuckin' joke."

"What about you, Joe? You voting?"

"I won't lie, Morrison, I'm still figuring it out. My gut tells me to say, 'fuck it,' but I'm confused on what to do. I lean right, but our options are damn awful. I might grudgingly vote for Trump for the sake of Supreme Court appointees. I don't want them coming for the guns. All in all, there won't be meaningful change until people choose to think for themselves and utilize the resources we have at our disposal. I also think the people will be represented better when us and the Millennials form a larger share of the electorate."

"We're all screwed. At the end of the day, the political class is a club we don't belong to, boys. I don't like what Trump's done to our country, but I don't care enough. Besides, Morrison, as you said... Biden's winning Illinois whether or not we mail in our ballots. Swing state votes are the votes that matter. Political parties fuck everything up. They undermine our whole democracy. The coasts and Middle America are at war. Think of the states as a chain that's slowly but steadily breaking."

"People pontificate that those who don't vote can't complain, even though they're the ones giving these fools power and validating their evil. For them, political participation is simply voting, while doing nothing in between. Every two to four years, voters are upset with one party's leadership, so they vote for a candidate from the rival party. Then they're up in arms over the shitty candidate they invested in, so they vote in the party that pissed them off in the first place. It shouldn't take a rocket scientist to figure out that our election cycles are synonymous with Einstein's definition of insanity... American Democracy is an illusion within an illusion... There is no choice. Nobody's in control," I explained. "If anything proves our democracy is a lie, it lies in the truth that a majority of Congress is composed of millionaires, while most of the general public can't even afford a $400 emergency without borrowing money. Kropotkin said that the rich achieve their wealth from the poverty of the destitute. The culture war between the states is a damning revelation to all of this."

These truths are discomforting, but preferable to any alternatives. Comforting lies mark the origin of our discontent. The two-party system is totalitarian, and if a candidate's gut says to disagree with the party platform on any issue, the party ostracizes them, a shared strategy of single-party regimes. Worsening in the mid-2010s and precipitating into the 2020s, the dire, hopeless stench reeking from Washington has disenfranchised millions, thanks to a smug, out-of-touch neoliberal Democratic establishment and the invasion of the

GOP by demagogues whose most ardent supporters would have you believe they shit gold bricks.

A pandemic, "law and order" candidates, civil unrest, and culture wars—was 2020 a dumbed-down version of 1968? Theoretically, the Populist Right isn't especially evil, considering other political ideologies in the spotlight or worse—the Big Tech machine, the culprit behind humanity's destruction. I'd sacrifice the entirety of my meager possessions to see congressmen and Big Tech CEOs publicly corralled by citizens. Strip the fuckers naked, tar and feather, or feed them to hungry gators, but I digress.

Our political conversation fizzled out and we ventured through the night, drunk and high. The cocaine and THC took over the psilocybin, and our sanity slowly resurfaced, facilitating conversations with ease.

Small groups paraded in the streets under the flashing lights. The place wasn't the same, not as many people as usual. In the absence of stripteases, burlesque shows, and concerts, Vegas suffered from paralysis. Empty poker tables, clubs, and stadiums. However, what can't be controlled can't be controlled. A night out in Sin City is a night out in Sin City, and we enjoyed ourselves.

"This is Las Vegas Boulevard, dammit," I muttered to myself.

Nighthawks play in the shadows; homeless folks push shopping carts and panhandle in the streets. Parents even push strollers, insane enough to expose their small children to the monstrosities of such a sinful place. Debauchery, heathenism, destroyed fortunes, and stolen souls for the children! I'd call child protective services on their asses! Subjecting their children to monsters who call this concrete jungle home appalled me, but parenting isn't my area of expertise.

By this point, the first blunt had long extinguished, and Tony grabbed the next one from his pocket. We stumbled across a parking garage. Aside from a few sports cars, the lot was empty. Tony wandered off to take a piss while Joe and I lit the blunt. "Damn bro, we're really out here. It's like a movie," Joe said, coughing.

"Damn straight, Torres. We may as well be in one. How many of our friends back in Chicago, or anywhere, have done something like this? The world is shit right now, but it doesn't mean we have to go down with it. I see the look on your face and your body language, you're enjoyin' yourself. I'm glad."

"I'm happy we're away from the bullshit. All this control... 'stay home... get a job... vote for me so I can rule you...' Boy, this circus can be sickening at times. The politicians will never produce a rulebook for life. I'm very content out here. No doubt, no doubt at all, the West is the best. I'm alive, but it's sad, thinking about all those who never truly live. They exist, but don't live. And those things are not the same."

"*In Will to Power,* Nietzsche says, 'There is an element of decay in everything that characterizes modern man, but close beside this sickness stand signs of an untested force and powerfulness of soul.' [4]Something exists within us all, Joe, something untapped and beautiful. Something they can't take from us... Our souls, man. They can only take ours away if we surrender to 'em. The human body was made to move, make art, travel, build, and climb. God didn't create us to sit in some fuckin' cubicle for 50 years, gaining weight, stressin' everything 'til death, only to take shit from bosses who would happily replace the employees they, in patronizing fashion, call a 'family' over a minor inconvenience.

"Tolkien wrote in a letter once that nobody is fit enough to exert control over others, especially those who try to do it. In the 20th century, the world chose to get itself into a damn hurry. This young century is upping the momentum, thanks to Big Tech and competition in the work world. Human beings don't belong in a marketplace. People who live in competition cannot exist in harmony, let alone prosperity. Authentic revolution stems from the soul. It's uncomfortable, but we have to overcome our own anxieties to transcend the trivialities of this society. The majority of us won't, but it's not necessarily our fault. We're conditioned to hide our dreams and desires, not to ask questions."

---

[4] Nietzsche, Friedrich, and Walter Arnold Kaufmann. *The Will to Power: A New Transl.* Vintage Books, 1968.

"Self-overcoming is central to Nietzsche's thought. We're on a steady path, I hope. I read Kierkegaard back in the spring during lockdown, and his books are thought-provoking as fuck. He might've inspired the scene in Joker where Arthur says he thought his life was a tragedy when, in reality, it was comedy. He wrote that, when he opened his eyes to reality, he started to laugh. He never stopped. We take ourselves way too fuckin' seriously these days, and it shows."

"Kierkegaard is unbelievable, the OG existentialist, save for Dostoevsky. I need to dive deeper into his work... The fuck is Tony at?"

"There he is," Joe said, pointing as Tony strolled past one of the few cars in the garage—a yellow '18 Dodge Charger. The mind games from the shrooms receded, and it was one in the morning. Joe caught Tony up, informing him that the conversation train was once again in full throttle.

"Here, we saved the last third of it for ya," I told him.

He snatched the blunt.

"What do you think about all this, Tony? We've been talking about philosophy and how post-industrial society depresses people, the usual," Joe said.

"Why am I not surprised? When it comes to society, I'm indecisive, but I've been to lots of cities. I think the world is big and fantastic. The people who run it are ruining it."

"I'm coming across more and more people, folks our age, who're sayin' fuck it—young, middle- and working-class, just like us. Tired of all the bullshit expectations, their parents, and their bosses. Our generation has a chance to do something special and we can't piss it away. We're still so damn young," I said. I've met people our age from all over the country who dream big and are guilty of possessing an all-or-nothing mentality.

This generation has witnessed the hard work of our predecessors get demolished by disaster after disaster. Such an irksome struggle isn't worth it. We intend to choose a different one because most who conform have already begun to die.

"I'm on board with what you mentioned in Grand Junction, Tony. Let's hit the road after our loans are done and

live free. This trip's been a blessing," Joe said, his voice ringing
with hope.

"Hell yeah! And shit, Morrison, you're lucky. You're
getting a head start with your loans. Imagine what we could do
if they weren't a problem? We could stay on the road without
a worry in the world! We could start businesses, become
homeowners, and pursue our passions without having to slave
away for the man. This is like watered-down feudalism."

"Maybe, but y'all will pay them off in no time.
Sisyphus carries his stone."

"Huh?" Tony asked.

"Sisyphus. He's a figure in Greek mythology. In short,
he cheated Death numerous times and tricked the gods.
Sisyphus was condemned to the underworld. For eternity, he
must carry a giant boulder up a hill, just for it to fall down
every time he reaches the top."

"Sounds fucking depressing."

"Maybe so. Camus wrote a series of essays called *The
Myth of Sisyphus*. It explains what he called 'the absurd.' Life
may often seem meaningless, but we have no choice but to
push forward. In the book, Camus encourages us to imagine
Sisyphus is happy with his boulder. I have a copy if you wanna
read it."

"I like the idea. I might take you up on the offer."

"Follow the rabbit hole, son, you won't regret it. The
truth is horrifying, but you'll appreciate the third eye. Your
mind will be free."

"I hope so," he said, killing the blunt. "Let's go back to
the room and get drunker."

"You still got that?" I asked Joe, referring to the coke.
"I'm tryna' rip a bump."

"I do. I can use one myself."

"Facts. It'll help with the walk." I dug the key into the
bag, snorted my bump, and handed Joe the goods. He took his,
Tony took his next. Then we headed back to the boulevard for
additional late-night conversation. We commonly joked,
calling ourselves philosophers, and hundreds of garage smoke
sessions reinforced this notion.

Meanwhile, Joe laughed at his phone—a meme poking
fun at the two presidential candidates. Hannah Arendt crossed

my mind again. In her notorious essay "On Violence," she says, "Humor can operate to challenge the authority of institutions as well as individuals," which is exactly what our generation has done with memes for multiple election cycles. 50 years from now, our grandkids will be assigned essays about how young people in our time used them to cope with the hostile political climate and the pandemic.

Faded but still kicking, we pressed our way back to the hotel. Joe came within inches of barfing all over a fellow pedestrian, and Tony yelled to a drunk girl if she wanted some acid. She said she'd rather rub him down. Her friends jerked her away, saying, "Oh my God, you're so drunk!"

Once back in the safety of our room, Tony connected to the speaker as we prepared for a nightcap with some Miller Lites. "Gimme Shelter" by the Rolling Stones reverberated throughout the room. The lyrics, which reflect the turbulent times in 1969, resonate with our own. My soul left my body momentarily, watching The Stones bring the house down at Soldier Field in Chicago in June of 2019.

A 75-year-old Mick Jagger performed before a sold-out crowd that roared each song. He jumped up and down the stage for over two hours, reinforced by a giant psychedelic tongue glowing from a screen behind him. Keith Richards shredded his guitar, Ronnie Wood strummed the bass, and Charlie Watts killed the drums. My taste for Rock 'n' Roll escalated into an obsession. The Rolling Stones changed my life. Classic rock artists are dwindling in supply, therefore chances to watch them perform are imperative.

A mood was set in the hotel room. We'd suffered an uncontrollable urge for chaos all night, and it was time to drink up a storm. Beyond there, we lost everything in a fog, and somewhere around 2 o'clock, all three of us blacked out.

Hangovers And Hookers

I awoke the next morning on the floor with a throbbing headache, wearing nothing but briefs. A pair of earrings sat next to my head, and on the table sat a tube of lipstick. "What the fuck happened last night? Did we participate in some drunken Vegas orgy?" I muttered to myself.

The time on my phone said 7:15 AM. Joe's unconscious body lay almost lifeless on one of the beds, and Tony had vanished without a trace. *For fuck's sake. Did we lose him?* I tossed on a pair of shorts and walked into the bathroom to find him sprawled in the shower and soaking wet. I tiptoed around a used condom and woke him up.

"I don't remember falling asleep here, but I woke up at 6, freezing my ass off, so I turned on some hot water to warm up," he said.

"Fully clothed?"

"Yeah."

"Goddammit, Tony, you are a fuckin' slob. How are you feeling?"

"Not bad. Sore from sleeping here but fine otherwise. You?"

"Ah, my head hurts. I'll recover after I drink some water and take an Excedrin. Did we have company last night?"

"I'm not sure, but I had an awesome dream... Gross, is that a used condom? The fuck?"

"Yeah... You sure it was a dream, man? I woke up next to a pair of earrings and found a tube of lipstick on the table."

"Jesus, did we call escorts?"

"Not sure, but it looks that way, man. We were belligerent. Let's wake up Joe and see what he can recall."

"Bet."

Waking Joe was rough. He felt even shittier than I did. He tossed, turned, and groaned for half an hour before forming a coherent sentence. Suddenly, he leaped out of bed and ran to the bathroom, vomiting a concoction of whiskey, beer, burgers, and mushrooms. After slowly munching on a piece of bread, popping some Excedrin, and drinking a glass of water, his spirits improved. His speedy recovery stunned me, but overcoming an alcoholic beating is always possible in youth.

Less than 48 hours before waking up that morning, we had tripped our balls off in the Painted Desert. Our night in Vegas apparently continued long after we could soundly remember. So much had happened already, but we had to figure out what the hell occurred deep into the AM. Regardless, there was a sense of embarrassment.

Tony and I impatiently waited for Joe to finish puking. "You see the earrings on the floor and that lipstick?" I interrogated.

"Yeah, you called a couple of escorts last night. I'm not touching that condom, by the way."

"No shit, did I really?"

Tony laughed hysterically in the background.

"Yeah, I'm surprised you don't remember. You and that girl, I think Star, her name was, fucked in the bathroom for almost an hour until Tony broke in on you. You two were loud as hell."

"Wait," I said. "It's coming back to me, I think. Did she have brown hair? Tan? Wearing red lingerie?"

"Yeah! She was fine, you should be proud."

"Proud I paid to fuck?" I sarcastically snapped, wondering how on earth I'd been able to get it up after so much booze and cocaine.

"She was fine. That's all I gotta say."

"True, I wish I remembered it. What about y'all?"

"A blonde girl—Tasha. She was great." Joe's eyes widened as he smirked.

"Tony, you bastard! The hell did you think you were doin' breaking in on us like that?"

"Shit, man, beats me. I was drunk and on drugs just like you. I couldn't remember last night either."

"You two fucked in there after Morrison and Star left," Joe informed us.

"Yessir, I closed the night out!" Tony yelled.

"What went up came down!"

"What a night!"

"And I started it, she rocked my world. Jesus, don't tell me I've fallen for a prostitute," Joe begged The Divine. "Hold up though, we need to check our bank accounts. Who paid? Check the coke too, it'll be fucking disappointing if it's all gone after one night."

"Beats me. Let's check our balances for any surprises."

We each pulled out our phones to open our banking apps.

"The bag's on the table—looks like a lot's left. It's amazing we weren't robbed blind."

"Fuckin' hell, boys. I'm down bad financially," I muttered with my eyebrows raised.

The other two didn't notice any major plummets in their accounts, making it obvious I covered the expenses at the ATM downstairs. "We'll Venmo you."

"This is like *The Hangover*."

"Don't say that, Joe! Are you nuts? Those guys get into disaster after disaster, such fuckery won't be our fate."

"I have a point, don't I?"

"You do," I confessed. "Let's pack up our shit and get the hell out of here. I wanna get some burgers on the E.T. Highway."

"I'll throw the coke into the side pocket of my bag."

"Clutch."

We checked out of the hotel at 9 o'clock, enthralled at the idea of speeding down the Extraterrestrial Highway and arriving in Los Angeles by nightfall. No Monday morning depression for us, just another day on the road. Sure, the E.T. Highway would take us two hours in the wrong direction, but it'd be worthwhile. Driving northbound toward the Little A'Le'Inn and then back to Vegas was our only option, where we'd be westbound to California.

Death, Rattlesnakes, Vacant Highways & Alien Burgers

NO GAS OR SERVICES NEXT 150 MILES, the sign read as we turned onto the Extraterrestrial Highway two hours north of Vegas. America's loneliest road. Pitch-black asphalt sliced through the desert, leading into mountains. Oceans of Joshua trees, rocks, and sand covered the land. A clear midday sky hovered above. We parked and smoked a blunt of my Star Pie. Tony rolled it on the hood of the Jeep. We smoked and cautiously hiked out into the desert.

Area 51 lay on one side of the road, and public land on the other, so we made sure not to hike on the side that would end us in federal prison. The treacherous rocks, hills, prickly plants, and unrelenting heat tested our endurance. Local wildlife also posed a threat. Three high 22-year-old Midwesterners hiking around the desert could result in a fatal disaster involving rattlesnakes. We'd nearly reached the top of a hill when we saw the first one, coiled underneath a rock in its daytime sleep. The creature sat far away, so we held our distance and kept climbing.

At the hilltop, we discovered something eerie.

A grave rested in the sun—a wooden cross, a single poker chip, a lantern, a mini UFO, and a small stone statue of an angel. Words had been etched into the cross.

Dana, in Johnny's heart forever
7/18/2005

We stood there for a minute, studying the gravesite. Joe motioned the Sign of the Cross. Clearly, somebody had died there, so we didn't touch anything. Nature instructs us to respect the land, and in turn, we will be respected; yin and yang shit. To this day, the grave can be found several paces from Highway 375 in the Nevada Desert. Who were these people? What happened? Why such a strange location for a grave? We couldn't imagine and it didn't matter.

The view was nevertheless spectacular. A landscape of desert chaparral and valleys without end. Across the highway, Area 51 looked ghostly. No buildings or signs of military activity. Joshua trees as far as the eye can see. This was indeed a ghostly place. For decades, the government tested hundreds of nukes out there.

"*Memento mori*," the stoics say. It means, "Remember you must die." Death crosses my mind every day. I don't try to suppress it, either. Knowing that one day I will die motivates me to live as much as possible before the final moment arrives. I came within minutes of my last breath on several occasions before my first birthday. Therefore, the crushing weight of inevitable demise is a part of my reality. From the day I was born, it's been a hard road. And a lot of people out there relate.

We backtracked to the highway, seeing yet another sleeping rattlesnake just before reaching the car. Stoned, hungry, and zeroing in on the Little A'Le'Inn, an old diner/motel right off of the ET Highway, our stomachs rumbled alongside "Go to Her" by Jefferson Airplane. There appeared to be a body bag along the highway. The rancid carcass of a cow appeared several miles later among abandoned cars.

"Aliens abducted the cow and sent it back," Joe guffawed. Meanwhile, an asphalt trail took us deeper into the valley toward the distant mountains, which never seemed to get any closer. "This image will be burnt into my head for the rest of my life," Joe said with his hands on the wheel. "The road just keeps going."

"We've only seen three cars since merging onto the highway, and it's been an hour," Tony pointed out. "Morrison, is your phone working? Mine's dead."

"Mine too," Joe said before I could answer.

"Yeah, we're about 10 minutes away. I'll need a charge."

"Thank God, I'm fucking starving." He gave me the charger. "Imagine having car trouble out here."

"We'd be unequivocally fucked. Good thing we got gas in Alamo."

"For real."

"I'm gonna close my eyes until we get there," Tony said.

"The grave back there was fuckin' creepy, same with the dead cow and the crack cars. You think it was a body bag back there?" Joe asked.

"Don't know, don't care, but we've seen strange shit out here. It makes sense, I suppose. Laws don't mean shit in places like this. This is no-man's land. It's like the fuckin' *Twilight Zone* out here."

"You're right. It's off-putting, thinking about dark shit happening in such a pretty place. Don't you agree?"

"Yeah, but the cities ain't any better. I remember last year in Baton Rouge a guy rolled up to a bar I regularly went to with a machete. One hour later, he was dead in a ditch. Two blocks from my apartment. There was also a double homicide two floors above our place."

"Jesus Christ. You've told me about the shit going on there, but fuck, man."

"A hard road, Joe. Life is a hard road."

"Won't catch me disagreeing."

"There, I think I see the Little A'Le'Inn," I said, pointing.

A large grey alien face covered the wall, and a dainty green plastic figure stood in front. Leaving the diner, we saw a lovely girl, a brunette. She wore a white tank top and jean shorts, her skin tanned by the sun. She had a charming face, graced with big green eyes, and a figure that would make any man's jaw drop. She smiled, fully aware we'd fallen victim to her spell—not that we were staring or anything creepy.

She caught our glances. My heart sank deeply into my stomach. A gorgeous woman who will never be more than a stranger to me. What is it, the feeling you get when you find yourself captivated by a beautiful person you'll never see again? Is it mere lust, or something else? I wrote a poem about her while awaiting service in the diner.

An angel here,
the desert there.
Her beauty revealed
with green eyes and brown hair.
Never again to be seen,
for it's time to let go.
Like an ancient sea,
my heart sank long ago.

The anguish that heartache induces can either make or break us. Suffering is a natural process that's thrust upon us from birth, yet we desperately avoid it, but why? Discomfort, trauma, and sadness depend entirely on our reactions to them. Pain is an inevitability, something we have to make room for, and one who fails to do this will suffocate to the brink of defeat. I suppressed my heartache because it would pass.

Inside the diner was dusty, with alien memorabilia, license plates, retro tables and chairs scattered around. A gift shop in the corner displayed shot glasses, mugs, shirts, and other souvenirs. We claimed a table and opened our menus. Within moments, a waitress darted our way with water. She was a thin, frizzy-haired, middle-aged woman. Her shirt read **Little A'Le'Inn, Rachel, Nevada**, bearing the same green alien face we'd seen outside. "Where are you boys from?" she asked with a familiar small-town friendliness, common to the land between the coasts.

I always answer, "Louisiana" when asked where I'm from. It's where I became who I am.

"We're driving from Chicago," Joe and Tony clarified in chorus.

"You've come a long way, what for?"

"Just driving around the West," I told her. "We needed an escape from the nonsense."

"I get it. It seems like these people are blowing everything out of proportion with this coronavirus. It ain't fair for you kids. Wishing you three the best. You boys can't be older than 20."

"We're twenty-two."

"Stay safe on the road, y'all are still really young," she advised in a motherly fashion.

"We will, thank you, ma'am."

A few minutes later, our food arrived. Joe and I requested alien burgers and Tony ordered himself a saucer burger. One bite was all it took—we'd made the right decision. The burger sauce tasted like a strange, unique chipotle flavor, and the fries were superb. Although we'd been strapped for time, we enjoyed our meal in the middle of nowhere, talking about the colossal fuckfest the previous 48 hours had been.

"We've seen some really sketchy shit since crossing the Rockies," Joe chuckled. "Those guys at the ghost town, the grave site, the snakes, this God-forsaken highway... There's terror... As if we'll lose control at any given moment. It's strange and dark but I sense myself becoming addicted to the unknown."

"Damn, Joe. As deep as that is, I relate. There's something about being cut off, vulnerable, and alone that makes your fuckin' blood boil, but inna good way. Your heart pounds and you're alive, horrifically alive. What'd ya think, Morrison?"

"Y'all sum up my thoughts. I don't know if you heard with your eyes closed, but in the car, when I mentioned the type of shit I've seen in Baton Rouge—"

"I heard ya."

"Bet. When that guy tweakin' on the needle—or perhaps bath salts, did what he did... When I hear about drive-bys happening... I can't explain it, but I want to go out more. Our lives are so civilized, so routine, and so orderly, that even irrational violence and chaos seduces us. We risk our health and lives just to feel something." I was shocked at the words coming out of my mouth but meant them from my gut.

"Sheesh!" Tony exclaimed with a grin. "I can't wait to tell everybody in Chicago about the shit we've seen!"

"We've been on the road together for four days... We got a whole week ahead. There'll be plenty more," I said.

"Venice Beach is gonna be nice. It's been a few years, but I love that fuckin' place."

"So many people are affiliated with it. Venice is where The Doors originated, where Arnold Schwarzenegger power-lifted... This is a pilgrimage. The views must be crazy."

"Especially at sundown, Morrison. There better not be any dickhead cops telling us we can't hang out there."

"To Hell with the bureaucrats! We'll probably be okay, Tony. Good vibes."

"Hell yeah. Y'all done with your food?"

Joe nodded.

"Yessir," Tony yawned, bound for a food coma.

"Bet, let's pay and get the hell outta here."

It was only one o'clock, but the drive to Los Angeles would take hours. We backtracked past the dead cow, the body bag, Area 51, and the gravesite and filled up again at a Sinclair just north of Vegas... From there, we hopped back onto I-15, into the Mojave Desert of Southern California, through the border town of Primm. The temperature climbed to 112 degrees, but air-conditioning came to the rescue, and the view was spectacular. I can't explain my love for Joshua trees and mountains other than the fact that I rarely see them, considering I've lived in two of the flattest states in the country.

Large swaths of Southeastern California are known as the High Desert. It's a quiet region of tumbleweeds and humble, dusty towns... Uncharted territory for Joe and me. I'd like to live out there someday. Find an old shack on Skid Row, refurbish the joint, and turn it into a home. Give me a beautiful, quiet place where I can live self-sufficiently like a human being, with guns to shoot and good books to read. I'd befriend the locals, and maybe a nearby newspaper would hire me—wouldn't be a bad base to build a writing career from. If pandemonium ensues and society remains in a state of decadent stupidity, I'll be safe, living an artist's life in the desert.

Gunning through the towns of Baker, Barstow, and Victorville piqued my desires before reaching the City of Angels.

THE PALMS OF VENICE

We arrived in Los Angeles at 7 o'clock, and Tony sat shirtless behind the wheel, flying down the near-empty highway at 115 miles per hour with the windows down. "Elephant" by Tame Impala blasted from the speakers, the vibrations were electric, and spirits were high. We'd finally arrived. Palm trees taller than any I'd ever seen lined both sides of the highway as signs read, **Crenshaw Boulevard, Pasadena, Beverly Hills**, and, at last, our destination—**Venice**.

Once there, we parked a few blocks from the beach on Washington Boulevard. Contrary to the desert heat we'd fried in all day, it was only about 70 degrees outside. Joe put on a hoodie before grabbing his bottle of Southern Comfort.

The sun hung faintly over the darkening mountains. We made it to Venice Beach, excited to smoke one of the four remaining Space Cake blunts and drink some of Joe's Southern Comfort. The palm trees, the sea, and the mountains reminded me of a Heaven I'd never known. Traveling the road together, our reflections guided us down each rabbit hole, burrowing, burrowing, and burrowing further into the void. Nietzsche's *How One Becomes What One Is* crossed my mind, taking it all in. Halfway through the book, he says,

"*A spirit has become free, that which possesses itself again.*"[5]

Watching the sunset over the beach, we stepped closer to understanding—or possessing ourselves again. Neither Joe nor I had seen the Pacific before. Joe's the humblest person you could meet, the oldest of six and so hadn't had the opportunity to travel the way he wanted to. Helping raise a bunch of siblings is tiresome. He's finally began focusing on his own future. I relate to him on these grounds. I am the oldest of

---

[5] Nietzsche, Friedrich Wilhelm, and Large, Duncan. *Ecce Homo: How One Becomes What One Is.* Oxford University Press.

three. Where we'd grown up, parents sacrificed luxury, working multiple jobs to provide their kids an expensive Catholic education. Traveling isn't on the agenda for most people. Putting food on the table is.

Tony, on the other hand, is no stranger to the West Coast. He's been to San Diego and San Francisco. It was his third time exploring Los Angeles, and he couldn't believe how empty Venice was. Thankfully, our concerns about cops barring entry to the beach remained unfounded. Sparse groups strolled the calm, dusky shores, and couples conversed with their feet in the water. The atmosphere was perfect, and I took a deep breath.

The air itself smelled like summer. California is a damn fine state, no matter the criticisms from a bunch of overly political, pseudo-patriotic blowhards. Those one-sided Neanderthals are no different from the phony intellectual leftists who condescend to Southerners. But I'll retreat from political banter. Positive vibrations overflowed the atmosphere and a weird, unfamiliar peace fell over the mountains.

Stoned and at ease, I peered beyond the shore, into the horizon. We had tested our sanity under the influence of countless drugs, visited places unearthly in their beauty, and behaved to the point of recklessness. And here we were, finally in L.A.. A beautiful freedom engulfed us. We couldn't travel any further west in the Lower Forty-Eight. We'd reached the end of the line.

"I can't believe it, man... I'm really here," Joe said to me while gazing at the sea. "A dream—this must be what Heaven's like if there is one. I think it's up there, somewhere."

"Same, Joe. I sure hope so. For the sake of humanity, I hope there's a Heaven. I'm positive there's an afterlife. A gut feeling I got... But it's far away."

"Never thought I'd see this place so empty," Tony said, sounding pleasantly surprised.

"An unintended benefit of the pandemic," I replied.

"I keep thinking about the rez and the E.T. Highway."

"What about 'em, Joe?"

"I always knew there was plenty of desert here in the States. But I had no idea it covered so much of the West. One day, I hope to drive out here and cross into Mexico to visit my family there."

"You've mentioned that before. Are they in Juarez?"

"Chihuahua."

"Gotta be careful," Tony warned. "But all three of us should go."

"That'd be awesome. To be honest, driving it alone probably wouldn't be the best idea. My aunts and uncles there have told me the risks. They said, if I ever want to visit, to let them know in advance."

"Shit, y'all, I'd go. We'd be fine, just have to play it smart. Don't want to end up like those poor Mormons who got butchered by the cartel."

"They're known to do checkpoints on certain highways there," Joe cautioned.

"It'd be a hell of an adventure. Plenty of risks, but we'll be fine if we're smart. We can't drive at night under any circumstances."

"He's right. Nighttime is when the messy shit goes down. The *vatos* don't fuck around."

"Jesus!" Tony shouted. "Enough of the dark shit, have a look around!"

The violet sky mirrored onto the waves, giving way to shades of pink and orange to the north where the sun eclipsed the mountains. We sat under a palm tree to share Joe's bottle and got drunk, talking about the type of things 22-year-old shitheads like ourselves typically talk about.

"I need to fall in love and come here with a girl instead of you pricks," I laughed after taking a swig of the bottle.

"Damn right," Tony replied, "I'll second that. Let's get laid again!"

"Sounds like the life. We'd be some lucky bastards. But I want more than that. I love fucking as much as anybody, but I want something better, something real," Joe clarified.

"Relationships are overrated, but we'll pull through, you deserve to find somebody to love more than just about anybody I know, Joe. I thought I found it once, but it turned out to be a dead end," Tony assured him.

"Alright, I guess I'll go fuck myself."

"Don't worry, the same applies to you too, Morrison."

"A drink to our dreams!"

"You're goddamn right, Torres!" I shouted. "Pass me the bottle."

Joe and I didn't chase after girls too much. We weren't indolent—we merely gagged at the idea of simping. Besides, it was incumbent upon us to build ourselves into stronger men before taking the romantic leap. But we both were single guys and experienced the bouts of pain a single person sometimes must endure—a confession that most men, from a cultural standpoint, aren't allowed to make.

We dreamed of falling in love, and having a hand to hold in beautiful places... A partner whom we could adore, trust, and hold in our arms. Tony had a girlfriend who he dated through high school and into college. Distance eventually terminated their relationship, and he had a harsh time making sense of it. After years of commitment, he wound up in our lonesome boat, singing the lovesick blues.

"Imagine if Chicago was warm enough to have palm trees," I thought out loud, sipping the bottle.

"That would be dope as fuck," Joe replied.

"I can see it right now," Tony replied. "Imagine being at North Avenue in the summertime, hanging out on the beaches with palm trees and the skyline in the background."

"Talk about an alternate reality I wish was real. No cap, during regular times, Chicago becomes L.A. for three months when summer hits. The beaches are packed, Lincoln Park and River North are bustlin', the baseball games, downtown—God, I'm excited for the end of this bullshit."

"No lies detected. But hell, there's no end in sight without a vaccine," Joe said.

"True, you ain't wrong, but they're predicting a vaccine to be ready sometime in the winter—December or January. The ball's gonna be rollin' by next summer, I bet."

"Better be. If not, we riot."

A half-hour later, I stood up and walked to the water. I felt a fullness of heart, and my mind roamed. For thousands of years, my ancestors gazed westward across the Atlantic from their cold island. And here I stood, also gazing westward, but at a different ocean. Overcoming a dreadful illness as a child I won't specify right now, I was grateful to be alive and in the moment. Even if everything were lost, my heart would remain beating, and such a deep emotion is one only somebody who's met death face-to-face can feel.

Why me? Why was I spared? Was it some plan or luck of the draw? Whether it was the bullying at school or the scars across my body resulting in a devastating loneliness—an eternal night without stars. Times came and went where I'd wonder if my survival had been a mistake. Perhaps I was wicked from birth and deserved it all as punishment. Some kids wished my affliction had killed me. But basking in the dark, listening to the waves wash on the shore and the laughter of my two friends disproved such. My love for life grew like a quiet song, progressing into an indestructible melody.

"What's up with him?" I heard Tony ask Joe.

His response was muffled, but I remained in my tranquil state as darkness fell over the Pacific. Standing on azure shores with waves at my feet, I tasted eternity. My head cleared, and if I died there, I wouldn't complain because I'd accepted the trials and tribulations of this life. Everything. All the pain, joy, suffering, ecstasy, prayers, sins, highs and lows. I professed affection for everything. Sheer peace in the atmosphere. I can't accurately describe it. No mix of poetry, songs, paintings, or pictures can ensure justice; it's simply an experience one has to live to understand. I connected to my spirit like never before, and it called my body home, but only for a little while.

"Morrison!" Joe shouted.

"What's up?"

"Getting a little late, let's check in at the hotel."

"Sure, be there in a minute." I cherished my final moments staring into the abyss. I soared, and the swishing of waves made the only noise. The sparse crowds along the shores faded into an intermittent trickle. Slightly drunk from the liquor, a tear fell from my eye as raw emotion overpowered me—a captivating gratitude for the moment, the beauty. I had officially been from sea to shining sea. Kiawah Island, South Carolina in 2012, and Los Angeles in 2020. With a smirk, I backtracked to Joe and Tony, turning around to take one last glance into the dark.

We were faded and set to check into the hotel at 11. It was a few blocks from the beach. Returning to the car on palm tree-lined Washington Boulevard, we quickly ate at a burrito place and checked into the hotel—a German-style building, greeting us with a large sign and a manmade "cove" near the parking lot. Above it, flew several flags—a Union Jack and a French flag, in addition to others. Working the front desk was a chubby middle-aged man with curly red hair and glasses.

And Christ, was he an oddball. He assured us we didn't need our masks but spoke passive-aggressively as if we were morons. Pleasantly maskless, we marched up a flight of stairs to the room and planned to knock out by midnight, since I'd intended to eat mushrooms the next morning. I locked the door with caution since something about the old bastard downstairs gave me the creeps.

"That guy was a piece of work," Tony said, sitting at a desk near the window.

"Yeah, he was an odd dude," I concurred. I changed the subject. "Shrooms tomorrow morning?"

"Shrooms, the beach, what's the weather like tomorrow?" Joe asked.

"Sunny and 75."

"Say less, man!"

"So, we're all in?" Tony asked jovially.

"Yessir! Joe, you got them water bottles in your bag from the gas station?"

"Yeah, you need one?"

"Yes, please."

He tossed me one, and I funneled it down. "I'll be damned if I'm hungover tomorrow morning, but I should be alright."

"I can use one too," Tony said. "What's our plan tomorrow after our trip? We should hit Slab City."

"We'll drive there when we come down and maybe camp out somewhere in Arizona. Have to get up early though."

"True. Joe, are you driving?"

"Either Morrison or me, I don't give a shit."

"I'll drive if I'm not too messed up," I volunteered.

"Perfect, boys, I'm gonna try to catch some Zs."

"Me too, man. I'm beat."

Brendan Heneghan

GHOSTS SPEAK THROUGH MUSHROOMS

We woke up to eat the mushrooms at 8 o'clock. On a normal day, we're not morning people, but that day was no ordinary one. I checked us out of the hotel while Joe and Tony packed the car. Outside the window, they joked and laughed while an old foreign woman verbally assaulted me for not wearing a mask. I advised her to have a word with the awkward employee who greeted us the previous night.

She obliged, and we parked several blocks from the beach, across from the poster child of hippiedom, an individual not much older than us—shirtless, dreadlocked, and carrying a skateboard under one arm. In his van, clothes dangled from hangers above a wastebasket next to a pack of water bottles. It seemed obvious his van was his home and, for all we knew, he'd been parked there for days. To many, this person comes off as a bum. But not us. We admired the lifestyle. What right does somebody stressing themselves out for a paycheck and bills have to cast judgment on this person living rent-free near a California Beach?

None, and any sane person could agree.

As we made our way closer to the destination, other young nomads roamed the streets, who appeared to be living out of cars or no place at all. As fucked up as 2020 was, who could blame them for abandoning bourgeois society for something freer, more relaxed? Moments spent in beautiful places are enough, if you ask me.

Los Angeles was locked in a severe outbreak of coronavirus, but the restrictions and health advisories failed to discourage Californians from enjoying the sun. Nearby, people walked their dogs, rode skateboards, and smoked joints with friends. Venice is a diverse area, reflective of the West Coast's multicultural character. Scores of California girls in their summer clothes roamed all over near the boardwalk, and the same old ache filled my insides. I was reminded of those lyrics in "Paint It Black" by The Rolling Stones.

As much as I wished to shoot my shot, I was coming up on mushrooms, and I'd surely lose my ability to speak clearly. The last thing those girls needed was some high, mumbling fool interrupting their morning. I will forever dream of those muses out West, whose beauty is matched only by the mountains and seas of their home state.

As soon as we made it to the coast, the shrooms mounted their invasion. A bright Tuesday morning sun rose higher and higher as the beach summoned us, somehow emptier than the night before. I counted on one hand the people out walking. Ideal conditions for a psychedelic trip. Sun, waves, sand, and Heaven... A big sky, blue as the Pacific beneath it, spanned overhead, and we smoked a Space Cake blunt to accelerate the hallucinations. Mountains lay to the north and east, and we had a grand time, envious at the idea of people living in proximity to such natural splendor year-round.

It wasn't long until we each diverged in different directions. Tony splashed in the waves, laughing hysterically while they crashed against the shore. Joe collapsed into a frantic rant about a thunderbird in the sky attempting to devour him. I strolled along the beach, enjoying the waves slamming against my ankles. Hallucinations hurled their way in my direction. I glanced down at my arms and legs. My complexion changed, and I felt as if I were flying. *What the hell is happening to me?* I grabbed my phone, opened Snapchat, and didn't see my reflection. This was one intense trip.

"No way," I thought out loud. *The reflection on the camera is of John Lee Hooker. John Lee Hooker? Christ Almighty, am I dead? I've shapeshifted into the old bluesman from Tallahatchie County, Mississippi.* I noticed my voice was his, too. I hummed his popular songs, "Dimples" and "Boom Boom." The sun beamed from the east, and I may as well have been walking through the air. His voice in my head said, "Tell your story. Make some noise before you can't no more." *Am I frightened or ecstatic?* I wasn't sure, but probably both. For five, ten, perhaps twenty minutes, who knows, Hooker's voice in my head repeated the same two sentences.

"What do you mean?" I asked nobody.

No answer from the voice. Meanwhile, a couple about my age approached from behind, their facial expressions making it obvious they thought me crazy. Given the circumstances, I suppose I was.

The trip was spiritual. Did it mean anything or were these merely absurd, pointless hallucinations spawned from psychedelic psychosis? Out of nowhere, a second voice entered. He conversed with Hooker. Almost instantly, I recognized it... Muddy Waters.

"So, we gonna let this boy live?" Muddy asked John Lee.

"Mhm, we gonna let him keep on. He's got some things he needs to do."

"What the fuck?" I exclaimed. "Are y'all deciding my fate?"

"He's got some shit on his plate. That's for damn sure," Muddy observed.

"He loves the road. The boy hopes to live by the road. You live by what you die by. Who knows how long he's got. He's lookin' for answers."

Hooker's words chilled my blood.

"Answers only lead to questions, my mother told me," Muddy said.

"This is true, my friend. He'll have to find his way on his own."

Silence for a moment. The voices fizzled out.

As desperately as I pleaded with the Lord to restore my sanity, I begged Him to let the madness last a moment longer. By far, this was the strangest experience I'd encountered.

A seagull screeched in the distance, gliding toward the open blue. I looked at my reflection in the phone's camera. *I'm me again.* I remained tripping balls. The waves breathed. The grains of sand, too. I was hopelessly shaken by what the two blues artists had said. *Is death approaching? Will we crash out in the desert somewhere only for buzzards to devour the flesh from our bones?* I couldn't tell if the voices were condemning my soul to an untimely demise or inspiring within me a path of redemption. I preferred option B, but death is not the enemy. We all will leave this life at some point, but I'd like to experience the world, read a few more good books, and hopefully write a couple before I check out.

Reality hit me.

I was alone. I turned around to grasp how far I'd walked. The guys were nowhere in sight.

I marched in the direction I came from and sojourned for an unknown period of time. The waves and sand on my bare feet and the sounds of the ocean were the only things keeping me from tumbling into a full-blown panic. I had a poor conception of time, but 11 o'clock must've been drawing near. *Most people at 11 o'clock on a Tuesday morning are at work*, I thought. *I'm tripping my dick off on a beach.*

After what I estimated to be 15 minutes, I located Joe lying in the sand.

"Look, I'm making snow angels!" he said with childlike innocence.

"You won't believe it, man, I became John Lee Hooker," I boasted. "I heard his voice. Muddy Waters too. They were talkin' with each other."

"The shrooms got your head fucked up. What were they saying?"

"You're telling me... You're the one making snow angels in the damn sand! To address your question, I won't tell you what I heard. It was scary stuff. I'd rather not repeat it. I'm glad to see you though, I'm out of it. This trip's intense."

Tony wasn't in the water. "Where the fuck is he?"

"He was over there a minute ago. What time is it?"

"A quarter past 11."

How long was I gone? I asked myself. *Where's Tony? Did something happen? Cops found the car! Fucking pigs. The oinkers discovered the car and arrested Tony for God-knows-what.* Were we about to stumble across a "Florida Man" headline about him on the news? This appeared to be the only possible solution, and we were next.

Counterculture icon Abbie Hoffman wrote, "The L.A. pigs are matched in their brutality only by their fellow hoggers in Chicago and South Africa."[6] Rodney King poses as a grotesque example. They'd hunt us down like a lion hunts a wounded wildebeest. Finding Tony was absolutely imperative. We were brothers out there and the most important rule of all is never leave a brother behind.

For a half hour, we combed the beach without luck. Calling his phone proved futile, considering we tried three times—each effort leading straight to voicemail. *2,000 miles from Chicago, and this shit happens...* After what felt like an eternity, we abandoned the beach. Just as all hope drifted away, somebody nearby screamed, which messed with our heads. We couldn't understand a word until we inched closer to the source of commotion.

It was Tony. He stood under a palm tree near Pacific Avenue, warning pedestrians that the British were coming. People merely laughed and continued on, aware of psychonauts like us being a regular species in those parts.

"What are you guys waiting for? Redcoats are all over the place! The Revolution never even ended. Are you guys just gonna do nothing?"

"Tony!" Joe yelled.

Shy and timid, I followed him, experiencing disasters of my own floating around upstairs.

"I thought you boys got killed! Let's get out of here, these fucking Brits are on every street corner."

"We called you like three times!"

"Oh yeah, I forgot to charge my phone last night."

"Makes sense..."

"Morrison became John Lee Hooker."

"I have powers." I grinned. "I'm hungry, let's get some food."

Around noon, we stopped at a taco place a block from the beach. Orbs and halos zoomed around us on the way and, once again, I clutched my sanity for dear life. Tony remained on edge about the Redcoats, babbling on about America secretly remaining part of the British Empire. The woman behind the counter resembled a combination of a witch and Jabba the Hutt. Her nose grew two feet long. She nearly jabbed me with it.

---

[6] Hoffman, Abbie. *Steal This Book*. Pirate Editions/Grove Press, 1971.

I ducked, yelled, and cowered, trying to get a grip. Never before had I hallucinated as much as I did in Los Angeles.

"Your friend okay?" she asked, pointing at me.

"He's fine," Joe said. "He had some rotten seafood last night. It makes him act weird."

"*Uh-huh*," she replied skeptically.

"I'll be fine, as long as you don't stab me with your nose," I warned her. I couldn't think straight or keep my damn mouth shut.

"What?"

"Sorry, he's a little sick. We'll order now," Joe said.

"Better not be coronavirus, I have diabetes."

We ordered our meals, ready for a break.

"Morrison you need to relax, man, drink some water," Joe instructed as we tore into the tacos.

"True, I'll be violating my own drug survival advice if I don't hydrate."

"I'm starting to get it together," Tony assured us.

"It's my turn to drive."

"You're up for it, Morrison?" Joe asked.

They both exhibited uncertain facial expressions.

"Yeah, I'm about to come down and I haven't been stoned in over an hour. I'd never suggest driving y'all if I felt I could put us in danger, y'all know that. We'll eat, hydrate, and sort everything out."

I timidly munched on a chicken taco with both green and red salsa at my disposal, desperate to sober up. Word of advice to anybody enjoying a day at Venice Beach... Treat yourself by visiting Tacos Por Favor. It's no more than a couple of blocks from the beach, and it won't disappoint. Whether steak, beef, or chicken, those tacos can't go wrong. My mouth waters at the thought of them.

"We're trying to camp out somewhere tonight?" Tony asked.

"Yeah, we should aim for someplace in Arizona," I suggested.

"We have to go see Slab City."

"Goes without saying," Joe said.

I nodded. "We're exposing ourselves to the other side."

"What'd you mean, Morrison?"

"Think about it. The guy we saw earlier living out of his van, the Navajo Nation... The West is different, there are lots of people who live in ways not common to the norm."

"True. It's definitely leading me to question a lot of things... How we live, our values, and even how the government treats people. The tribes out here are forgotten people, especially by the average person."

"Say less, Tony. We learn about the bullshit between the pilgrims and Wampanoag as if everything's kumbaya. Do either of y'all even remember learning about the Indian Wars? The Apache, the Lakota, and their resistance to the government? It took a civilization with unmatched firepower, manpower, and technology hundreds of years to finish subjugating civilizations without equal means. Not to mention disease. The resistance was legendary."

"That's what the schools should teach," Joe said. "I have Indigenous blood in my veins. Apache. Although I'm positive my ancestry is more Spanish. My roots lay south of the border, and I'm damn proud of it."

"I remember you mentioning that before," Tony said.

"Yeah, it's a value I hold close. My great-grandpa grew up on the San Carlos Reservation and left to marry my great-grandma, who was on her way north from Chihuahua. They raised my grandpa in Laredo. At 16, he hopped a freight train to Chicago and met my grandma in Pilsen. Never mind all that for a minute. I'm stoked about Slab City."

"That's one hell of a story, man. I bet we'll find a few folks similar to the character we saw earlier," I said.

"Oh, for sure. Today's off to a good start. I tripped balls but this food's helping me sober up."

"Last time I had a trip like this one was when we were at the apartment in Iowa City," Joe laughed.

"Oh my God, the fuckin' walls were moving. We were seeing faces in 'em!"

"I remember asking if you saw them, too. When you said you did, I was like, 'Fuck, this is a ride.'"

I succumbed to jealousy, overhearing their recollections. "Wish I was there, but I'm sure I was in Louisiana under the influence of something at the time."

"Knowing you, Morrison, I bet it was whiskey, weed, a psychedelic, and some sort of upper."

"Fuck, Joe, you know me too well. Baton Rouge is wild enough, and I spent an ungodly amount of time in New Orleans. Y'all know how it goes."

"Ah, I'd love to sit here and talk, but we gotta hit the road," Joe eagerly snapped.

"Dispo first," Tony growled.

"True."

Tony under no circumstances will refuse a dispensary.

We took a ride to a dispensary on Lincoln Boulevard. I stayed in the car while the other two walked across the street to buy some more weed. They returned several minutes later, and Joe came back with something interesting.

"Look at this shit, man. THC pills in a tin container. Pop 'em, and they get you high. There's a lot in here. We can give them a try later."

"Dope, I'm about it. What'd you get, Tony?"

"An eighth of Chocolope and an eighth of Purple Punch. Stuff was expensive."

"Shit, son, a high roller!"

"Damn right, may as well while we're in California."

Restocked on our—by no means dwindling—weed arsenal, we merged onto I-10, headed away from Los Angeles. The skyline slowly disappeared in the rearview. Our stay lasted less than 24 hours, but we did our best with limited time.

In hindsight, I'm proud of our West Coast shenanigans. The prior night, on the westernmost point of the Lower Forty-Eight, I reached a peak, and the memory reigns supreme. I'll see the Pacific again.

My trip eased as I drove down the highway and, by 2 o'clock, the fringes of the L.A. area had fallen behind us.

THE PIGS OF FREEDOM'S LAST BASTION & A SILENT NIGHT

The sun scorched the ground beneath it as I gunned us back through the Mojave Desert. "Refugee" by Tom Petty and The Heartbreakers played loud. Slab City is three hours southeast of Los Angeles, and we had to be in Flagstaff to set up camp for the night. Pushing 95 on the interstate refreshed the vibrations, and we ached for the next adventure, having come so far, visiting places we'd never seen and doing things we'd never done. Our freedom triumphed under the sun.

Oceans of Joshua trees endlessly reached to God. We drove through the towns of Palm Desert, Indio, Coachella, and Mecca until, at last, we coasted along the shores of the Salton Sea by 4 o'clock.

"The Salton Sea looks like a dope place to hike. We have to be getting close to Slab City," said Tony, his NASA T-shirt full of sweat.

"We're 20 minutes away," I said.

"When we come out here again, we definitely should camp out along the shores," Joe suggested.

"No objections here! The water is so blue, too bad we can't drink from it."

"Such a Tony thing to say."

"What'd ya mean?"

"You're totally the type of guy who would say something like that."

"True, Morrison, you're not wrong."

"Those palm tree forests were something else, y'all."

"Yeah, back in Thermal?"

"Yessir. I didn't expect to see palm tree forests in the middle of the desert. They must be growing fruit there or something."

A bumpy, dusty road guided us closer to Slab City when a sign read, **Caution: Reality Ahead**. It looked like an old phone booth with aliens painted on it. A few yards away, another said, **Welcome to Slab City, the Last Free Place in America**. Designs in shades of yellow, red, purple, and black covered it. Behind it, were two painted Eyes of Horus. Beneath the eyes, a painting of Scooby-Doo and Snoopy entertained us. Scooby was chiefing a joint and Snoopy was laughing at him. I theorized that Scoob probably chewed into Shaggy's stash.

Dirty clothes and a frightening number of needles decorated the dirt around the booths. My stomach turned, thinking about the unending evidence of opioid abuse we'd witnessed, making the crisis all too real. A couple guys from our own neighborhood had been taken by the icy, remorseless needle long before their time was supposed to come.

Mainstream media outlets, fueled by sensationalist journalism and clickbait headlines, ditched the issue as soon as more people started dying from coronavirus. The media loves when people die, and authentic journalism is receding into the dust. During the final week of June, I read an article entitled, "How you can safely celebrate the Fourth of July during a pandemic." I regret wasting five minutes of my day. *Thank you, spineless journalist, for regurgitating messages from faceless, ambiguous authority figures. When Christmas comes, I will be sure to seek your permission to spend time with my friends and family.*

I understood old Dr. Thompson's bitterness toward his fellow journalists. He knew what was coming.

Disturbed by the heroin needles, we passed Salvation Mountain, another famous landmark. The artist who worked around the area was devoutly religious and his art, inspired by the Divine. Atop Salvation Mountain is a tall cross, and below it, in a big red heart, read the words, **God is Love**. It's surrounded by painted rocks and boulders—contrasting shades of blue, purple, green, and pink. The artwork around Slab City enhances the area's peculiarity. Salvation Mountain provoked thoughts about God. In *Brave New World*, there's mention of being able to hear Him in solitude, and the masses believing what they're conditioned to believe.

Post-Columbus American civilization has been puritanical, training the masses to serve God according to the power structure's interpretations of Scripture. But, in the present, the roles have reversed. We exist in a transitional period between two eras—one favoring faith, the other abandoning it. Human beings tend to blame God for the evil inflicted by the Devil. Combine this with the hustle and bustle modern civilization deifies, and an empty, nihilistic concoction is created where soon, I fear, all will be lost for our species.

We are the least religious generation in American history.[7] My views on this trajectory are mixed. Joe's Catholic. And so am I. But we both strayed since churches closed down in March. For a while, faith had been our last hope, and we desperately clung onto whatever was left of it. Even Nietzsche loathed the death of God, arguing that, in a Godless world, the masses would flock to something horrible.

Was the setting sun a metaphor for the loss of God? Our youth?

I don't know. I was high and driving us into a haven for anarchists and outlaws in the middle of the desert with infinitely more questions than answers.

The dusty dirt road we drove on led to another dusty dirt road for a few minutes, and we arrived, greeted by folks living out of their cars, RVs, and tents. Witnessing a community of people living free and distant from civilization empowered me. What drove these people to Slab City? What did they do before then? Was their decision to stay there permanent or temporary? Some were obviously retirees. They looked like gritty, hippie versions of Dale Horvath from *The Walking Dead*. The three of us had been familiar with Slab City, and lots of people are, thanks to the film *Into the Wild*.

---

[7] "Gen Z Is The Least Religious Generation." *PacificStandard Magazine,* 2019.

Situated near the Salton Sea, the commune is in the middle of the Mojave Desert, hardly an hour north of the border. Concrete slabs left behind from what once was an Air Force base during World War II were converted into living spaces.

Shortly after the war ended, the government abandoned the area and left the slabs behind. By the '50s and '60s, outlaws, hippies, and drifters of all sorts made the place into a commune—hence the name *Slab City*. Its reputation as "the last free place in America" is particularly what attracted us.

"I didn't even think places like this existed anymore," said Joe. "It really is free. There's no cops or laws here, Pat?"

"Nope. None whatsoever. There's courtesy rules since it's a commune but, by and large, people here are allowed to do whatever they want, granted they don't hurt nobody. Some are criminals wanted by the law. We shouldn't be fazed, though. They come here for escape and to lay low. Causing trouble's against their interests. I'm gonna live out here someday."

"Take us with!"

"Count on it, Tony."

"We'll make it out here again; the land is surreal. The sand, the mountains, the Joshua trees... We'd have each other's backs just like we do now," Joe remarked with excitement.

Most of our visit in Slab City was silent, aside from Tony's Kid Cudi playlist providing background noise. We explored the commune for an hour. People hung clothes to dry, smoked on lawn chairs, and sold or traded fruits and vegetables. Never had any of us seen what's essentially a community of anarchists mutually agreeing to live peacefully outside the eyes of the law. Trailers, tents, and cars were the primary dwellings. Apparently, more people flock there for the winter. Spending the night was tempting, but it was incumbent upon us to cover as much ground as possible. With evening closing in and almost 400 miles between us and Flagstaff, our trek was far from over. We doubled back to CA-111, turning a corner littered with tires next to a yield sign.

Gaining speed on the highway, we assumed smooth sailing, and Tony ripped the dab rig. The Border Patrol station broke our illusion. The highway had been reduced to a single lane—leaving us no choice but to drive through it. What was a Border Patrol station doing an hour north of the border? This was a horrid, unanticipated obstacle. My muscles tightened as a shovel-chinned agent stepped onto the road, motioning for us to stop.

"Tony! Put the rig down. Put it the fuck down! These pricks are feds!" I yelled. No fucking way I was getting pulled over in that desert with a car full of Schedule I and II drugs. If they found them, those nazis would charge me with a DUI, place my friends under arrest, and our lives would be fucked. Years of college education down the drain... Good luck finding any type of livelihood with a felony drug trafficking charge and DUI on the resumé. Time to brainstorm some get-rich-quick schemes before getting released back to the outside.

Sure, weed is legal in California, but the troglodytes in Washington haven't legalized it at the federal level yet. If this bastard caught a whiff, he'd have probable cause. Add to that the cocaine, mushrooms, and acid tucked in our belongings.

"Shit, shit, okay!" Tony said, placing the rig at his feet and underneath a blanket.

We pulled up, and I put on my best face.

"Are you boys American citizens?" Shovel Chin asked.

"Yessir," I replied.

He peered at Joe and Tony, then back to me. "You look young to be driving out here, I'll need to see some IDs."

We handed him our identification, and he inspected them carefully. He was the type of pig to cross his Ts and dot his Is. *Is this it? The noose, tightening around my neck? Will we go to sleep tonight behind bars?*

After a lengthy 15 seconds, he handed back our IDs and waved us through.

Relief.

Too many law enforcement officers fall in love with power. It's a borderline inevitable consequence of the job. They pull you over, and you behave confidently but with a light smile, showing you're not a threat... Keeping your mouth shut is duty number one. The Fifth Amendment exists for important reasons, and shutting up is the surest method of protection against self-incrimination. Never give the bastards a reason to escalate the situation. You drop whatever trace of an accent you have, to speak as clearly as possible. If you're really pressed and going down no matter what, highlight the wonders of their jurisdiction and exaggerate your contributions to their economy. Don't kiss ass—subtly inform the pig you're a citizen, *same as him.*

The Jeep ran low on gas a few miles down I-10. Luckily, we spotted a Chevron south of Joshua Tree National Park. I merged onto the exit and pulled into the filling station.

Joe and Tony rushed into the convenience store to purchase pods, beer, snacks, and water. "Fuck, my mask!" Joe ran back to the car to grab it. We'd all had similar moments between Chicago and L.A.—or we'd say, "Shit, where's my vape?"

I opened Maps to observe our location. I-10 connects Jacksonville to Los Angeles and launches through New Orleans. Louisiana... It had been a couple of months since graduation, and I missed my Southern home. I was fully aware of the uptick in coronavirus cases there and it wouldn't be as open as usual, but maybe some of my friends in New Orleans had moves for us. I texted Clara O'Reilly, a dear friend of mine who lives there. I asked if she'd be available at all later in the week.

Maybe we'd have a chance in Hell of partying in the Big Easy. Clara's a love child: a kind and beautiful person. I had the pleasure of meeting her when I started at LSU. If she had anything going on, us guys would be in luck.

Moments later, Joe and Tony returned, and we continued burning rubber.

Around 8 o'clock, we still had lots of ground to make up. We wound through cliffs, canyons, and open desert. Mountains surrounded us on all sides. The sunset shone, immaculate, beaming on us from the West. A roadrunner darted across the interstate, but sadly no coyote followed. Shades of blue, purple, and orange painted the sky while the sun slowly disappeared behind the mountains. Polo G's "21" played on repeat for what felt like the millionth time, but we didn't care.

A sign on I-40 read, **8 miles to Needles, 72 miles to Kingman, and 221 miles to Flagstaff.** I remember thinking, *Thank God we're less than 20 minutes from Arizona.* By 9:30

darkness fell over the land, and we had passed through Kingman. I stopped there for food once in 2017.

Driving through the desert at night is a perilous endeavor. Bends in the road come suddenly. As fast as I like to drive, I had to tread a line to keep us from dolphin-diving over a cliff like the O'Doyle family in *Billy Madison*. There's little trace of life between Kingman and Flagstaff, nothing but barren badlands of cactus, tumbleweeds, and mountains. As far as animal life, there's mountain lions, coyotes, and rattlesnakes.

Joe and Tony were zonked out, and the music ended. I drove, listening to the low engine rumble and the occasional bump in the road. Here and there, Tony would let out a snore. Arizona's a big state and, for the second time that day, the car needed gas, so we stopped in Williams, arriving at the campsite shortly after one in the morning.

I woke the guys to get the tent ready and unload our sleeping bags. We built a fire, and I packed my one-hitter with the last of the Star Pie. Joe had half a pack of cigarettes, and Tony bought a twelver of beers at the Chevron—I tossed him a few bucks. Tony grabbed his speaker from the Jeep and queued his classic rock playlist, starting with, "The Weight" by The Band. A damn fine song and it set a tranquil mood as we drank and smoked under the stars.

"A hell of a day, boys," Tony announced, dragging the one-hitter.

"We did a lot," Joe said, sipping his beer.

"24 hours in a day ain't enough," I chuckled.

My companions had a point. 12 hours earlier, we shamelessly wreaked havoc in Los Angeles and made fools of ourselves. We saw the last free place in America and drove over 500 miles across the desert. By the hair on our nuts, we escaped the clutches of the criminal justice system. Although not as overwhelming as the ones we saw near Monument Valley, the stars of Arizona spanned forever.

I remembered my text to Clara and checked my phone. She had replied an hour earlier, informing me of a housewarming party at her new apartment in the French Quarter on Friday. *Be still, my beating heart*, I thought. *We have a party to look forward to.* A road trip hitting Vegas *and* New Orleans would be of legendary proportions.

"Y'all tryna go to Louisiana? We can stop by the apartment in Baton Rouge, rest up, and then go to New Orleans," I recommended with a yawn.

"Let's do it, I've never been there or really anywhere in the Deep South before," Joe said as his eyes sparkled.

"I've never been to New Orleans either but, I gotta say, Morrison, I've seen your Snaps. It looks like a crazy time. I can only imagine what type of shit goes on there," Tony replied. "But wait... You're graduated, you still got the apartment?"

"Yep, but the lease is up early next month. My boy Fish is riding it out because he doesn't wanna move back to Mississippi. It's Tuesday. We can get there in two days easily. And damn right, you can only imagine what goes on there. When I was 18, I saw some drunk-asses having a threesome in an alley in the French Quarter. I'll never be able to unsee it. I've witnessed other shit, too. Lots of fights and lots of swindling. You gotta be on your guard for pickpockets. We ain't got much to worry about, though. The streets won't be anywhere near as crowded as usual."

"Fucking hell. Sounds lawless—" Tony's phone rang. "It's Mike, I'll see you guys in the tent."

Mike's his brother.

"Word," I said to Joe. "We can hit the road early in the morning, but where should we stay tomorrow night?"

"West Texas?" he suggested and lit a cigarette. "How long would a drive to West Texas be?"

"Probably 10 or 12 hours. We'd need to go a little deeper into Texas though, since it's such a massive state."

"You're right. We could stop in Odessa or somewhere. It'd be at least 11 hours but isn't something we haven't done already on this trip."

"Cool, sounds like we have ourselves a plan. How are we lookin' on drugs? I have a few tabs of acid and maybe enough shrooms for two more trips. We're still stocked up on grass. Do you have the coke?"

"Yeah, we probably have about half of it left."

"Good, we'll want it in New Orleans."

"For sure," he said, fixating on the fire. "Want a cig?"

"Why the fuck not? Did you take those THC pills?"

"I took some a few minutes before we got here. I won't lie, I'm pretty baked. You want to give 'em a try?"

"I would, but I'm already stoned. It'd be a waste. I'll take some tomorrow before we get to Albuquerque. I'm tryna eat at the hotdog place from *Breaking Bad*. I bet it'll slap high."

"Damn, I didn't even think of that. We'll be passing through Albuquerque on the way to Texas. Take these." He handed me two of the THC pills, and I put them in my Levi's.

"It's wild, we're already heading back east. But the journey is far from over. Wait until y'all spend a night in New Orleans. We still have quite a bit of sand to eat between here and the bayou."

For a few minutes, we drank and smoked in silence. Tony must've disconnected from the speaker when his brother called. Crickets, nothing but crickets, and the crackling of the fire sang in the night. Our discussions and thoughts in the dark of night brought out the best in us. Darkness humbles the soul, and in the pale glare of the moon, encourages us to recognize both our insignificance and our potential.

Western sky, moonlight glare, and pine trees covering a land elevated thousands of feet above sea level brilliantly converge and impose their mystery on the traveler, the outlaw, and even the common tourist. Joe and I understood each other as if we could speak without using words.

"What's your worst regret as an older brother?" Joe asked.

"Wow... One hell of a question... But I know the answer since it's haunted me for much of my life..."

"Tell me about it if you're comfortable."

"It has to do with Jerry... I'd knock his ass into next week all the time when we were little. Sure, he deserved it sometimes, and he'd even pick fights with me, but I was so much bigger than him. I got carried away. Too excessive. I did too much, you know? Shit's haunted my conscience for as long as I can remember. We're close now, and I love him to death, but the guilt persists. Ain't gonna lie."

"Have you two spoken about it?"

"Yeah. We even laugh about it, but it's a monkey I ain't been able to get off my back. What about you?"

"Hmmm..." He paused. "Well, the first thing that comes to mind is the way my youngest brother, Ricky, always mimics what I do. He learned how to do laundry from me. I even got him doing pushups. It's rewarding. I played an important role in their growth. So, to answer my own question, my biggest regret is when they see me doing something wrong. Sometimes I'd fight with my parents in front of all my siblings. Other shit, too. It weighs on me, the same way your regrets weigh on you."

"I couldn't have put it better myself, but I guess it's counterproductive to worry about the past." I continued ripping the cigarette.

"True, I mean... We can't forget what Epictetus said. There's no worthwhile reason to be anxious about shit we can't control."

"Facts, Joe, it's easier said than done, but the stoics are worth listening to. It's an important thing to improve on because gettin' worked up over trivialities... Think of Nietzsche and self-overcoming..."

"Full circle... Amazing... How it all connects."

"That's what philosophy is. Every thinker builds off their predecessor's ideas, transforming and molding concepts into their own unique vision. Think of how Camus used existentialism to create absurdism."

"You're spot on, and my mind is fucked. I'm really stoned," he replied. "I'm calling it a night. Lots of driving tomorrow."

"No cap."

Our time in the desert left us dirty and scrappy. Our clothes, the car... Everything but our youthful enthusiasm for adventure. We must've slain a million insects. The Jeep Patriot was a far cry from the shiny ride it had been a week before. High as I was, I grabbed the revolver from the glove compartment and placed it safely in the tent, pointing away from us.

Paranoia got the best of me.

My mind wandered as I lay awake, reading a few articles on my phone about protests and demonstrations splitting the country wide open. Anarchy dominated Portland and Seattle, which I didn't mind—chaos frightens powerful folks and the bootlickers who defend them. People who achieve throbbing erections for order and control in defense of the establishment's wishes.

I again must draw a comparison between the present and past. As it was 50 years ago, the country is torn between warring factions, one of which rallies behind "law and order" while the other challenges the status quo. In the meantime, the cycle seems unending:

SEATTLE (*WaPo*)—In the four days since the Seattle Police Department vacated its East Precinct building and a leaderless congregation of activists established the police-free "Capitol Hill Autonomous Zone"—or CHAZ—across four blocks outside, the largely peaceful demonstration has forced activists and city officials to grapple with questions of accountability, leadership, and what comes next.

A rapper showed up there, allegedly distributing rifles to people and media outlets had a field day calling him a "warlord." Watching a rabid swarm of right-wing politicians on TV order the mayor of Seattle to "take back" the area was peak comedy. CHAZ disbanded on July 1st but, nevertheless, the media blew up over it, and Seattle remained an enormous disaster zone. Upon its end, CHAZ looked nothing like it started as a unified front declaring war on police brutality. Violence reigned. Rape and murder claimed lives. Needles littered the parks and streets of Capitol Hill. A complete and total degeneration of ideals and behaviors.

The civil disobedience sent a clear message. It revealed the horrors that too many people suffer from in a society priding itself on privilege. Chaos doesn't fall from the sky, it's the offspring of injustice. It's stoked like a fire and will continue to burn until relief appears in some shape or form to the downtrodden.

I reread the text from Clara. New Orleans would be a demented, depraved, and amazing time. During Mardi Gras, weeks before the pandemic locked society in a chokehold, I lost track of my friends while drunk and drugged out on uppers. The Bacchus Parade moving down Saint Charles Avenue raged all around me as pushers advertised their products. My fellow college students fought like warring chimpanzees, punching, and throwing up at each other.

Old buildings and homes decked with columns reminiscent of Greece or Rome shone brightly in the dark. Beads, trash, empty beer cans, and broken bottles littered the streets. Lawless, the city was, but I craved the wild vibrations. I'd rather enjoy the thrill of being afraid than let it drag me to Hell. Between the memories and relief of having a place to go in New Orleans later in the week, I fell asleep.

A Farewell To The Desert

Eight in the morning...

Joe sat behind the wheel, restless, listening to "Run to You" by Bryan Adams. Up in the mountains, the elevation popped my ears, riding through the forests. The Coconino National Forest surrounds Flagstaff. The clusters of conifers and evergreen pines form a sharp contrast to the desert. We coasted along the edge of the Grand Canyon, taking in the cool morning, but by the time we hit Winslow, the heat sweltered, and we were back in the desert, cruising down Historic Route 66—a drive I made back in 2017.

Red sand, field fencing, and shrubs spread for miles under a sky of intermittent clouds. The only major towns, Winslow and Gallup, lie between Flagstaff and Albuquerque. You'll find multiple reservations throughout the region—Diné, Hopi, Anasazi, Zuni, and Ramah peoples call the isolated region home. We spotted a few Anasazi families selling beads, jewelry, and other hand-made products from roadside stands in the heat near Holbrook, Arizona.

"How the hell do people make their livings like that? It's over 100 degrees!" Tony shrieked. "I respect the grind."

"The country's different out here," I replied. "People do what they can to get by."

"I don't know what the solution is," Joe said. "But from what I've seen, from what we've seen... Out here, we've basically forgotten the people who called this land home before any Europeans. The reservations are remote and there's no opportunity. There's a reason my great-grandpa left."

"Truth. The government nearly wiped out an entire race for power. A way of life was smothered. Now we're a country of narcissistic materialists who wouldn't last a day without Netflix and running water. It's regrettable that such an unfit, depraved population has inherited and spoiled a continent once populated by hunters and warriors. There is absolutely nothing Western civilization has to offer that Indigenous people want."

Tony replied, "I wonder what the country would be like if the feds left the Indians alone. Let 'em carry on with their traditions... But I know why it wouldn't fly... They did all the forced removal and shit for the same reasons politicians today are a buncha pigs, and that's as you said, Morrison. Power. Control."

"Pursuit of power is inherent in any hierarchical civilization. It's probably why societies always end up so fucked. Every single thing the ruling class does, even if they claim it's for public safety, benefits them in one way or another. Whether or not it's at our expense."

"True shit, Joe. One day you have a republic, then the next, you're being ruled over by liver-spotted fascists. A fucking geriatric plutocracy! The political and corporate elites are a bunch of fucking cockroaches. We *are* living in a dystopia," I said. "Neoliberalism is a cancer that claims to be the peak of humanity's potential. It's all a fuckin' lie."

His eyes widened. "Jesus, man. You're right. We have dystopia in our movies and TV shows and books. But now they're in real life. Our civil liberties are limited, and in most places right now you can't even go to a bar. The media is bullshitting us with headlines about what activities we can and can't do as if we need their permission, and everybody's going along with it, but not us."

"Well said, my friend. You too, Tony. Every society needs its black sheep... Conscientious objectors who possess the courage to say, 'No, I refuse to comply.'"

Our conversation fizzled out, and the music took over—"Long Tall Sally" by Little Richard emanated from the speakers as a sign on the highway read, **Welcome to New Mexico.** We lost Little Richard in May. I popped the THC pills to kick up a buzz in memory of Little Richard... He'd smile on us from the kingdom in the sky, guaranteed. Feasting at the Dog House high and experiencing the world of *Breaking Bad* sounded ideal. Meanwhile, gaunt green shrubs, sandy hills, and rocks flew by as we passed Gallup, Grants, and Laguna. Wire fencing and herds of cattle completed the picture.

Somewhere around Laguna, the pills hit me. We steadily closed in on Albuquerque, and I morphed into a zombie in the passenger seat. Then the munchies hit. "DNA" by Kendrick Lamar played in the background. Tony got high in the backseat, laughing at memes on Instagram, and Joe was silent with his eyes on the road and hands at the wheel. Psychonauts zooming through the desert, we sold our souls to vice, and anything went. The 505 was right around the bend.

I had been to Albuquerque once before—a strange city. Spanish missions, balloon fiestas, hiking, and tons of crime— over half a million people live there, and *Breaking Bad* accurately portrays its dark underside. During my first visit, packs of junk fiends marauded downtown. It was a Thursday night, and everything had closed by 10 o'clock. *What the hell kind of city is this?* I recall thinking. Albuquerque proved more welcoming the second time around. The sun was out, and a few people strolled along the street, going about their routines, running, going to work, or enjoying a sunny day.

Upon our arrival at the Dog House, we captured the table where Jesse Pinkman anxiously ate before a drug deal. The building itself gives retro vibrations, and the dog sign glows at dusk. Iron bars guard the windows. A masked teenager with bags under his eyes took our orders in a frustrated monotone. I could tell his bosses had sentenced him to the opening shift. Five minutes flew by, and our orders were ready. We sat outside in the 102-degree heat to save gas, but the shakes helped cool us down. We tried to scarf our chili dogs. If there was a prayer of arriving in Baton Rouge the next day, our stop in ABQ had to remain brief.

"This chili dog is gas... How's your vanilla shake, Morrison?" Tony asked with chili dripping from his chin.

I felt like we were eating lunch at summer camp in 2005. "Pretty fuckin' good. The hype around this place is makin' some sense, I can't tell if it's because I'm high or what. The dog and the shake really complement each other."

"I think you're onto something. But just wait, they'll fuck up your stomach."

"To be honest, chili dogs and shakes aren't the first things you'd think would go well together, but here we are! The risk of temporary digestive discomfort is worth it, but a few hours from now, I might not feel the same way. How much longer 'til we reach Odessa?" Joe inquired.

"Probably seven hours," I replied. "I'll see what places I can find for us to stay on my hotel app."

"Bet. Let's stop at Walter White's house," Tony suggested.

"I'm down, but we'll have to drive past. We got miles to make."

"Sounds good."

The White residence from *Breaking Bad* is on Albuquerque's East Side. We drove past it on the way out. The property was fenced off, making evident the current owner's desire for privacy. We kept our field trip swift because we had to check in at the Marriott in Downtown Odessa by 11.

I-40 cuts through the mountains of Eastern New Mexico. From there, it spills into a series of smaller highways through the plains. The first signs of dusk set in. Joe drove all day, so I took the wheel. The pandemic crossed my mind, specifically my hatred for masks—I don't like wearing one and equally despise seeing other people in them. The sight makes my skin crawl, a consequence of spending vast periods of time in the hospital as a child. Despite making a full recovery, CAT scans and other hospital visits were mandatory. They terrified me as a small boy. Some of the earliest memories involve being surrounded by masked doctors picking away, and pinning my limbs to the table while I screamed, "Why, Mama, why do I have to do this?" The air ran thick with a chemical smell. To this day, the scent of ammonia is nauseating, and the sight of masks makes me uneasy.

In a civilization ruled by crooks, the gravest sin is not becoming one. Freedom of association proved expendable during the lockdowns—this isn't to say I'm a flag-waving pseudo-libertarian, but the government's abuse of power is a perpetual concern. Freedom of association's abolition arrived two decades after the right to privacy had been obliterated under the Patriot Act, begging the question—which civil liberty is next to be thrown to the wolves? Each government action was done for some murky sense of common good, and utilitarians are creaming their pants just thinking about it. "Common good..." What a stupid farce of a phrase. Nietzsche agrees because, if something's abundant, chances are that it's expendable.

I'm highly skeptical whenever a powerful person references the "general welfare" or anything regarding the public's well-being. Individual vs. Society, Max Stirner's philosophy... I loathed the upcoming election and had no intention of voting. What the fuck were we doing? Who was there to vote *for* instead of *against*? Why did a collective of East Coast governors find it humane to throw COVID patients into nursing homes? Perhaps I'm asking an excessive number of questions, but when authority breaks down, violence is invited.

"Thinking of voting for Trump?" Joe read from his phone. "The microphone access overheard me, it's aware of my right-wing leanings."

"Shit happens," I laughed. "Algorithms are fuckin' creepy, man... I'ma take a rip of the one-hitter. Those pills wore off a while ago. Could you toss it to me?"

"Sure thing, I forgot I had it. Make no mistake, they knock you on your ass." He returned to the subject. "I've been thinking about our conversation from earlier... About the current state of affairs in the world... We're obviously living in a dystopia... Basic freedoms are heavily restricted, a disease is killing people, the country is flipping the fuck out, and huge numbers of people actively want to vote their rights away. Big Tech's figured out everything about us, man. These fucking devices are more familiarized with our habits and routines than our own friends and families and every app is designed to make us addicted to cheap dopamine. What's next?"

"Right on, Torres. Big Tech and social media are draining us of our humanity. Those campaign ads are propaganda. The constant commercials thanking first responders for doing what they're paid to do are propaganda.

When restaurant owners in the neighborhood advertise free food to cops—once again, propaganda."

I handed Joe the one-hitter after repacking it with leftover kief.

"Propaganda is a word that should be on the tip of everybody's tongue. It's funny, you mentioned restaurants feeding cops, as if most of them aren't overweight as it is."

I coughed and snorted at his remark.

"The statistic is 80% via the FBI. They conducted a study and found cops are more likely to die from heart disease than on the job. Protectin' and servin' themselves a Big Mac and a large fry."

"Dude, stop, you're making me laugh too hard. My jaw hurts from all this roasting."

"Damn incompetency, Joe. I am befuddled by the assholes in charge of our lives. Just Google '40% of cops' if you really wanna hammer a nail into the Thin Blue Line coffin. What right does some normal-ass person who spent a few months training in the damn academy have to tell anybody what to do? Every person should be their own first responder. I have a six-shooter. My response time is 2,200 feet per second. Somebody attempts to hurt me or mine, the rat'll get smoked."

The familiar aggressive passion flared inside.

"I respect the outlook. There was a time when most Americans shared a similar thought process of liberation from state control. Today, a scary number of people seem to want the government to protect them. It's disheartening. We're quickly becoming a society of people who don't have any idea how to be individuals. They're mindless herd animals who sacrifice their dreams and desires to serve companies run by the worst fucking people on earth."

"The rugged American is going extinct, and the funeral is right around the corner. Social media, late-stage capitalism's service-based structure, among an immeasurable number of components, are executing the human being. And it's only a matter of time 'til the process is complete."

"Bleak shit," he replied. "But it's honest. Fuck the Machine, bro."

"Of course we're discussing this shit while driving through Roswell," I chuckled.

"Even weirder is all the shit about UFOs being spotted in recent years. The government's actually taking them seriously."

"And all we do is create fucking memes about it! Kierkegaard's message is clearer now—reality is hilarious... Depressing, horrid, and grotesque, but hilarious," I guffawed to the point of convulsion.

"Fuck," he replied, "rabbit hole after rabbit hole... Goes on forever, man."

"The void is infinite, I must admit. Turn up the music. I'm in the mood for some Rock n' Roll."

The sun slowly faded over the flat golden landscape. Around Roswell, sporadic ranch houses dotted the horizon. *Who would've thought a little town like this could possibly have extraterrestrial visitors?* There's no shortage of conspiracies regarding what happened in this lonely region of the New Mexico Desert during the 1940s. Much like Area 51. Had the mystery of Roswell occurred today, the frenzy would be unthinkable in the era of fake news, QAnon, and mass misinformation. Most of us remember the failed attempt to storm Area 51 in the fall of 2019. Unsurprisingly, people showed up, and Uncle Sam sent them to federal prison.

Our reflections about social media and propaganda exacerbated the weirdness. Somewhere during the 2010s, young people left Facebook in droves. A Pew study found Americans between the ages of 50-64 were more likely to use the app than ages of 18-29. Social media is rife with misinformation, ego trips, and toxic political debates. Of course, young people aren't immune to fallacies or partaking in hostility, but coming of age alongside the internet has allowed us to navigate social media with greater proficiency than our elders.

Research shows older Americans are increasingly susceptible to believing in fake news stories *and* likelier to share and regurgitate the messages. Devastating days of reckoning await any citizenry which allows politicians, celebrities, and social media influencers to shape their views while thinkers and artists go broke—where algorithms cater to people's beliefs, reinforcing confirmation bias, and widening the divide. Civil discourse has been reduced to a screaming match between strangers, most of whom are dullards who let other people think for them. We've completely lost our sense of community *and* individuality, nearing the fatal epoch where nothing's left at all but Nietzsche's abyss staring back at us as a reminder of our devolution.

"How much longer until we reach Texas?" Joe asked. Tony snored in the background.

"About 40 minutes; it's half past seven."

"To think we woke up in Flagstaff!"

"We've done an absurd amount of driving on this trip. It's good practice."

"You getting tired?"

"Somewhat, but I ain't sleepin' 'til we're in Odessa."

"I'm ready to burn through Texas tomorrow."

"Me too. We'll have to proceed with caution though, cops in Texas don't fuck around, from what I hear. The last thing we need is getting pulled over in some bumfuck town. I'm not trying to have any *Easy Rider*-type shit happen."

"True," he said. "But we'll be fine, we got really lucky at the Border Patrol station back in Cali."

"Yeah, no shit, man. Tony almost got us pinched."

"Yeah, yeah, don't be a dick," Tony growled, emerging from his slumber.

I turned the volume dial up—"Castles Made of Sand" by Jimi Hendrix.

"I fuck with this song," Tony said, jolting upward.

"It's a classic," Joe said. "How was your rest?"

"Worth it. I feel great. Where are we?"

"About a half hour 'til we're in Texas," Joe yawned.

"Bet, we should pass out as soon as we get to Odessa. There's nowhere we have to be until Louisiana. Lots of driving tomorrow."

"He's right," I said. "We'll check in by 11, sleep 'til seven, and then gun it for Baton Rouge. It's Wednesday, and I have a party for us at an apartment in the French Quarter on Friday night."

"For real?" Joe questioned, his eyes springing to life.

"Yessir, a friend of mine recently moved into an apartment on Bienville Street. That's a block off Bourbon. Her name's Clara. We graduated back in May. She was one of my first friends I made in LSU. We celebrated my 21st together on Tchoupitoulas Street two years ago. Clara's a gal who knows how to have a fun time so be ready to throw down."

"Let's go!" Tony yelled. "Looks like we'll be flying through Texas tomorrow."

"Choppa-what?" Joe chuckled.

"Tchoupitoulas," I repeated. "I get it, dude, the names of some places in Louisiana can be a battle to pronounce."

At last, we rolled into Texas via Bronco. Fire on the plains. A chunk of time left until Odessa. The sun's final rays eclipsed behind us over the dark, dry land. Lantern lights glowed invitingly from porches of small cattle ranches. Headlights from cars westbound to New Mexico provided the only other light. *Here it is again*, I thought, *the eeriness of driving in dark, barren places, still far and away from all familiar parts of the country.* And yes, an uneasiness lingered along but, close beside it, a strange peace. Paradoxical, I suppose. We ventured through the night toward our destination, quietly listening to music until we reached Odessa shortly after 10 o'clock— excellent timing. This allowed us to hit the rig for a few minutes before checking in and calling it a night.

Our free roam proved a sobering revelation. The death of the Wild West is an illusion, a lie we're sold to prevent us from seeking what's out there. Long after the last Native rebels surrendered their guns, long after the cattle rustlers were jailed, long after cities tarnished the mountains, the land lives on. And with an ambitious pair of eyes, you'll find it... The great wide open. The flame hasn't died.

"Farewell Great American Desert, we shall meet again!"

Part Two:

The South

Brendan Heneghan

BIENVENUE EN LOUISIANE

We crossed into Louisiana sometime around 3 o'clock. After Texas, the eastward drive rejuvenated us. Longleaf pines surrounded the outskirts of Shreveport, and I-49 was by far the greenest highway we'd seen since the Rocky Mountains. Enough roadkill to feed a Cajun cookout bordered the roadside... Armadillos, possums, and deer. Outside of Natchitoches, we spotted some wild pigs at the roadside.

"Is that a family of boar?" Joe asked, pointing out the window toward the pigs.

"Yeah," I answered while glancing over, "they're a real problem not only in Louisiana but all across the South. Here and in Texas with the proper licensing, you can hunt those sons of bitches year-round."

"Let's get a license and hunt some dinner," Tony joked.

"Yeah, hunting boar with my revolver... Wouldn't that be something? Just joking. That would be an awful idea."

I imagined a wild pig charging me as I unloaded on it with my six-shooter. Sure, my piece is a .44 and capable of putting a baseball-sized hole in a person, but nothing is guaranteed in a wild place. Maybe I'd climb a tree, empty the cylinder, reload it, and dump another one into the tusked monster just to be safe.

"Let's grab food soon," Tony suggested.

"In an hour or two," I replied. "We'll stop downstate, closer to Baton Rouge. Can you manage?"

"Yeah, I'm straight. I'm not starving but getting there."

"Joe, what about you?"

"I'm fine. We should wait 'til we're further south."

"Bet. Y'all ever had any Louisiana cuisine?" I asked.

They both shook their heads.

"There's a place down in Krotz Springs we can hit up."

"You lived here for a few years, so I don't doubt it's good," Joe told me.

"Krotz Springs is a bit east of Opelousas and Lafayette. It's along I-90 on the way to Baton Rouge."

"What typa food they have down there?" Tony asked.

"Po' boys, boudin balls, gumbo, cracklins, crawfish pies... The list goes on and on."

"What the hell are boudin balls?" Joe giggled.

"So boudin is a type of sausage. Boudin balls have pork sausage, which is called boudin, rolled up with rice and all different types of seasoning balled up with a fried exterior. At Billy's, the breaded exterior reminds me of how Wendy's chicken strips smelled. They're fire. Got a bit of a kick, too, but nothing overpowering. The ones I get have pepper jack in the middle. My mouth is watering just tellin' y'all about it."

"Shit, let's give Billy's a try," Tony said.

In a nick of time, we barreled through Alexandria, which is widely considered the borderline between North and South Louisiana. The ethnic and religious character north of it is different, making the cultural rift a sharp one. Baptists to the north, Catholics to the south. Most of the friends I made at LSU grew up in Metro New Orleans or between there and Baton Rouge. However, a sizable number came from the Shreveport area and frequently dealt with South Louisianans calling their hometown "East Texas" or most damning of all, "South Arkansas." From an outsider's view, this may sound comical, but the depiction is accurate. Dixie transforms into an empire of Papists in the land of Cajuns and Creoles.

We reached Lafayette and Opelousas after battling a torrential downpour for 15 minutes. Joe pressed on the hazards because visibility had been so poor. But as quickly as the storm struck, it ceased, and the dark clouds gave way to sunshine peeking through the treelines of bayous heading into Opelousas. By the time you enter the Lafayette area, you're deep into Cajun country. In some of the smaller towns like Arnaudville and Porte Barre, signs on shops might read *"ici on parle Français,"* alerting potential customers that French will be spoken in their establishment.

The French language has a long history in Louisiana, and people still speak it there, but far less these days. A series of legislation a century ago damaged the language's status, forcing English to become the dominant one. Teachers beat children or forced them to kneel on corn kernels if caught speaking French. I've conversed with old Cajuns who were familiar with the practices. However, a resurgence has been underway since the laws changed.

We pulled into Billy's in Krotz Springs. "Lover of the Bayou" by Mudcrutch on the radio completed the picture. Inside, the other two examined the menu. Boudin balls with pepper jack for me. I'd craved those lovely concoctions since graduation. Joe mimicked my order, and Tony secured himself a bag of seasoned cracklins.

We consumed our Cajun feast on the hood of the Jeep and stayed hydrated on ice-cold bottles of water.

"Where has this been all my life?" Joe asked with a mouthful of boudin ball.

"You like them, huh? God, I've missed these dearly. What about you, Tony, how about them cracklins?"

"They're fire. I've never had anything like these. You want one?"

"I sure do, thanks. Take a piece of this boudin ball."

He snatched it. "Fuck, this is good. We need to come to Louisiana more often."

I smiled. "When I'm living in an apartment in New Orleans after my loans are paid, y'all are welcome to visit."

"We'll take you up on it. No cap, I'm holding you to it! There's so much more, too. I've never had gumbo or crawfish."

"In due time, Tony. Have y'all ever seen *Easy Rider*?"

He shook his head.

"Parts of it," Joe replied. "Probably the first half hour."

"It's from 1969, one of Jack Nicholson's first movies. Peter Fonda and Dennis Hopper play the main characters, two bikers involved with the counterculture. They finish a drug deal in the desert, not far from where we're coming from. Their goal is to make it to New Orleans for Mardi Gras, and as rebels, small-town America doesn't take too kindly to them. They run into trouble along the way, but when they make it to

Louisiana, there's a scene or two filmed here in Krotz Springs. Monument Valley's in it too. You'd like it, Tony."

"Sounds like a dope movie; I gotta watch it."

"The Library of Congress has a copy of it, it's considered so important. I'm sure you can stream it."

"Looks like I have a movie to finish." Joe smirked.

"You should, man. My dad hyped it up when I was a kid, and I've been a fan of old movies and Westerns for as long as I can remember. *Josey Wales, True Grit, Duel at Diablo,* all—"

"I gotta question," Tony interrupted. "I know we're tryna take it easy tonight—"

"Nobody said that!" Joe laughed.

"Let me finish, dipshit. Morrison, what are the bars looking like in Baton Rouge?"

"Ah, not much of a different story than New Orleans. The college bars opened up for a little while but closed again at the end of June. We'll just kick it at the apartment. Tomorrow, we go balls to the wall. Take no prisoners."

With our bellies full, I drove the final portion of the long haul. We coasted by hole-in-the-wall restaurants, Dixie flags, casinos, oil rigs, shotgun houses, and old Catholic churches. Sugar cane fields stretched along the way. Virgin Mary statues and crosses guarded country homes, reminding us of South Louisiana's massive Catholic population. Huey Long, Louisiana's Populist, Depression Era governor lied about having Catholic grandparents in exchange for votes in southern parishes, and it worked—hook, line, and sink. He preached to a raving crowd about rising before dawn and hitching horses to take his grandparents to Mass as a boy, despite being a Baptist. Asked behind closed doors about having Catholic grandparents, he allegedly answered, "Don't be a damned fool, we didn't even have a horse."[8]

---

[8] *Lapham's Quarterly.* "Huey Long Fabricates His Past."

It wasn't long until the Capitol Building pierced the sky as we thundered into Port Allen to merge onto I-10. It reminds me of the skyscrapers from the '20s and '30s and is the tallest capitol building in the country. We crossed the bridge into Baton Rouge as I queued "Big River" by Johnny Cash—the stereo version. To some, Baton Rouge is damn awful, and to others, it's Heaven. But to most of us, the relationship is defined by a love-hate dichotomy. All lines are hopelessly blurred. You spend a night there, and it's the Wild fucking West.

I'd smoke on my balcony nightly. At times, I'd unintentionally catch a glimpse of people in the midst of hot, steamy intercourse through their windows. X-rated content. Not to mention the violent reputation the city has. I already spoke of the drive-bys. If you walk out of a bar at two in the morning, you'll sometimes find some sloppy honkey sprawled on the ground with empty pockets, covered in his own vomit. Or perhaps two people shamelessly fucking along the street. Every now and then, corpses pop up near the bars, and students are swamped with a barrage of safety emails. All hail the timeless architecture, massive antebellum columns, and shotgun houses, haunted by each passing generation. I called this place home for three years. The little city on the big river is etched into my memory forever.

We arrived just past 7 o'clock. Fledgling sunlight reflected from puddled streets and sidewalks, thunderstorms common to Southern summers. Rows of shotgun houses blew past us in the ghettos between Downtown and campus. A group of little kids in wifebeaters chased each other on a front lawn, pelting one another with water balloons, triggering a brief yearning for my childhood. Joe had never traveled to the Deep South, so a wave of awe flew over him.

"Welcome to Baton Rouge," I announced like a flight attendant. "Y'all want to stop at a liquor store before gettin' to the apartment? Some booze for a little bit will give us a fine night of sleep."

"Sure," Joe replied. "I can go for a twelver."

The case we bought in Arizona was reduced to a couple of beers.

"Damn," Tony moaned, "may as well get buzzed while we're here."

"I don't think I've seen a place go from so rich to so poor ever in my life," Joe observed. "But this is a very nice city. I'm surprised."

"Ghosts of the past. The Mississippi Delta region between Memphis and New Orleans used to be the richest place on earth. Italy's economy didn't reach the Confederate States' GDP 'til the '6os, a fucking century after the war. Obviously, this was a slave society, but the wealth gaps haven't gone anywhere," I explained. "The cradle of American slavery was in the 'Black Belt.' It stretches from South Carolina to Texas, through central Georgia, Alabama, Mississippi, and Louisiana. The enslaved outnumbered slaveholders by insane ratios."

"Makes sense. It's so different here. Feels different, looks different, same goes for the food. Don't take this out of context, man, but there's so many Black people. You can tell you're in a radically different part of the country," Joe replied.

"We ain't on the Northwest Side anymore, y'all," I said. "To this day, many towns in the Delta are 80-90% Black."

"No, sir, we aren't," Tony answered. "My family and I've taken trips to Mississippi, Arkansas, and Georgia before, but, from what I've seen, Louisiana is very different."

"It's the Catholicism brought by French and Spanish colonialism. The KKK never got a foothold in Southeast Louisiana for that reason—loads of French, Irish, Germans, and Italians... They couldn't stand the Irish, and Italians flooding off the boats and bringin' with 'em their tainted Catholic theology. We Irish Catholics were considered pagan. In Louisiana, we saw refuge." I craved giving history lessons.

"Very interesting," he replied.

We pulled into a Circle K a block from campus on Highland Road for the booze. Louisiana's drinking laws are among the laxest in the country. From drive-thru daiquiri shops to abundant liquor stores, one can always embark on a booze binge. You can slam a whiskey bottle while casually walking down the street during Mardi Gras and wake up three states away, wondering how the fuck you got there. Public drinking is a rare freedom. Not in those parts.

I purchased another bottle of Jack Daniel's. Joe bought his twelver of Miller Lite, and Tony copped some local rum—three young and reckless pseudo-intellectuals contributing to the Louisiana economy. An excellent public service. A constant hankering for alcohol thunders through my veins, like any other Irishman captivated by his own misery. We hopped back into the car, and I introduced the boys to campus.

Live oak trees lined the streets, and their long branches wound through the evening air, like dark arms reaching from the soil, fertilized by corpses of the enslaved, Irish laborers, and Civil War soldiers. Everywhere I've ever traveled to in the South, I've sensed ghosts. I wouldn't expect anything else from an old region with such an ugly past. The sun sank below the bell tower on the parade grounds across from the law school—a Roman-style building with large columns atop the steps. LSU's architecture was inspired by Italian Renaissance cities. I turned a few times, eventually riding along Nicholson in order to show the boys Tiger Stadium, the crown jewel of this top-tier American University. Purple and gold beams of light glowed from the stadium, and the yellow letters spelling L-S-U shone gloriously.

"We gotta catch a game down here," Tony said, breaking the silence. "How many did you see last year, Pat?"

"Every home game except Texas A&M."

"I can't even imagine the atmosphere," he said.

"LSU fans have literally caused an earthquake."

"Are you for real?" Joe asked.

"Mhm, look up the 1986 earthquake game. The fans got so rowdy that it caused an earthquake. Registered on a seismograph."

"I was at an Ole Miss game two years ago, but I bet it's a fuckin' wild time here."

"What I would give to have watched Joe Burrow throw a bomb into the end zone," Joe said in a dreamlike tone.

"It's a sight to see, I'll tell y'all that. One of these years, we'll tailgate. The SEC football tradition is unparalleled by any other sports culture in this country." My bias towards the Southeastern Conference showed too obviously, but the vibrant wave of LSU winning a national title my senior year left me riding high.

Three minutes after touring Tiger Stadium, we pulled into the parking lot of the apartment complex. The white 2017 Jeep Patriot was still dusty as hell from the sandy land we had come from. Dead mosquito splatter-coated the windows. I ran my finger along the side of the car, leaving a pristine white streak. It was a quarter to 8, but the temperature still bordered 90 degrees, the air repressive and humid. Tony laughed about hopping in the car and heading back out to the desert.

4,000 miles. We'd roamed the country for 4,000 miles. Less than a week before, we'd hiked through the land of the Diné, our heads full of acid. We'd come full circle. The shrooms were almost gone, but more than enough acid remained. About a gram and a half of Watts' cocaine sat at the ready for New Orleans, along with an eighth of California weed.

I fumbled through my mess of clothes and drugs to find the keys. I never remember where I leave them, but out of instinct, I keep them close to my wallet. Back in Krotz Springs, I texted my roommate Jack "Fish" Henderson, alerting him of our arrival. We call him "Fish" because he drinks like one. The man is my trusted friend, a brother more or less—same as Joe and Tony. We were randomly paired before moving in. He'd spent his whole life in rural Mississippi and speaks with a slow drawl but, like me, he gained a South Louisiana twang. He's never been proud to call Mississippi home for as long as I've known him. I can't say I don't understand his distaste for his home state, because it's a struggling place. He needed more. The same way I didn't want to cast myself among the ranks of Chicago's neighborhood barflies. Jack too was an outsider and had no desire to stay put. Our hearts ached for something better.

ARRIVAL AT THE FORTRESS

When we walked through the door, we found Jack sitting on the couch, indulging in some home-cooked gumbo. I'd dearly missed that aroma. The complex always smelled of weed and food, a welcoming combination. Well, aside from the occasional smell of piss and feces, thanks to the careless scumbags who let their dogs shit in the halls.

"What's up, my brother?" I shouted.

"Morrison," Jack began with a mouth full of gumbo. "Good to see you, man. Y'all been driving all day, huh?"

Better Call Saul played on the TV.

"Damn right. All the way from Odessa. These are my boys Tony and Joe. We've been friends since we were eight."

"Nice to meet y'all. Make yourselves at home," he said, getting up to rinse out his bowl.

"Likewise," Tony answered, relieved. "I've been in this state for four hours, and I can already tell it's a different type of place."

"Morrison introduced us to boudin balls," Joe added.

"Damn, y'all really got a good ole Louisiana welcome."

"Yessir," I said, "we'll go back out after we put our stuff away."

Joe and Tony followed me into my room to unpack. Once settled, I kicked them out to wash up. 15 minutes later, I waltzed back to the living room.

"Is it cool if I hop in your room? I feel disgusting and gotta shower," Tony asked me.

"Of course, do what you gotta do. There's a towel ready."

He leaped out of his chair and vanished behind the door.

I glanced toward Jack. "How've you been, man?"

"Okay, given the circumstances. The highlight of my day is going to a job I don't like to deal with stuck-up strangers. Last week... Tuesday... I thought it was still Monday. Probably because I went to work, slept, and went straight back. The other day, I found myself staring at the wall, thinking about when we first moved here three years ago, and how optimistic we used to be... I felt sick because there's no light on the horizon. The repetition's getting to me. I don't wanna go back to Mississippi, but at least it's some type of change. But who knows how long until that gets old. I'll get sick of it after a fucking week, probably less."

"Lord have mercy," I shrieked. "We need to get some booze and drugs into your system ASAP."

"I'm fixin' to lose my mind. Been drinkin' every night... It's one of the many mindless activities I do to keep busy around the apartment. Maker's Mark Monday night, a twelver of Twisted Tea Tuesday, a bottle of red wine Wednesday, and who knows tonight," he chuckled. "By far, the funnest thing to do is get drunk with Dalton, go to the levee, and hit golf balls at barges floating down the river. But I've developed a passion for cooking. I bet y'all smelled the gumbo the second y'all got in here."

"Hell yeah, it was glorious. It's nice to hear you've found something to work on during this nonsense."

"It's the best thing anybody can do. The biggest lesson I've learned from COVID is that nothing ever goes the way we hope. Trump's flopping on North Korea and Afghanistan, the country's on fire, and COVID patients are being thrown into nursing homes of all places. Who the hell even knows what's next? ...The best I can do is focus on me."

"I've formed a similar outlook. I started writing again during the spring lockdowns. I'm anticipating building off the poetry and essays I've jotted down."

"Keep it up, Morrison. There's one great way to cope with bullshit—and that's self-investment."

"I can't believe the amount of alcohol you two drank, holy shit," Joe interrupted, awestruck at the collection of bottles crowning the kitchen cabinets. There must've stood a hundred empty bottles. Whiskey, rum, vodka, and tequila: all trophies rewarding years of liver damage.

"Doesn't even count the breaks from school in between," I proudly clarified.

"It's safe to say that we're all a bunch of functioning alcoholics," Jack bragged.

"Speaking of which," I said, fishing the whiskey bottle from my backpack. "Who wants a shot?"

"Please," Joe said.

"Fish?"

"Pour me one. I've been studying for the LSAT all fucking day."

"By the way, Jack, do you mind if I fix myself a bowl? I'd do unspeakable things for a fuckin' bowl of gumbo."

"Of course. There's plenty to go around. I can't imagine how badly you gotta be craving some since you moved back to Chicago and all."

"You have no idea, my brother..." I cracked the bottle of Old No. 7 and poured some into an alien shot glass I purchased at Little A'Le'Inn. An uncanny level of excitement swells inside me when loading up on intoxicants. When free to do so, I deviate from the mechanical realm of sobriety to escape into a funnel of booze and drugs. *Don't be anxious, don't feel guilty. Roll the dice and accept your fate.* "Jack," I gasped as the whiskey warmed my insides, "we're goin' to New Orleans tomorrow. You tryna come along?"

"I'm down. I actually don't have work again until Monday, but since y'all are driving back up to Chicago, I'll come in my own car and meet y'all."

"Bet, we have ourselves a plan. Clara's throwing a housewarming party at her apartment tomorrow night. Should be a damn good time. She told me Shane, Dre, Raven, Dunkel, and David would slide."

"I actually heard about that, let's do it," he said.

"What are we doin' tomorrow night?" I asked him.

"We die!" He shouted, dumping the shot into his mouth.

"Damn right!"

"It's cool y'all ended up here. It's a pleasant surprise. April and May were terrible. Cases stayed pretty low for a couple months, but the virus has been getting bad here lately, and lots of shit shut down again."

"Good thing we have a house party," Joe said with a sigh of relief. "What about tomorrow during the day? Will we have any luck with bars at all?"

Jack paused. "Probably not, but you're in Louisiana, son, they'll give us drinks to go. We'll be good."

"Bet, good thing I have a couple of locals here."

Tony returned with some nugs and a cigarillo to empty out. He demanded a shot after spotting the empty glasses on the counter, and I happily obliged. Gotta keep everybody on the same level. We drank in the living room for a while. I left my speaker at the apartment during spring lockdown and connected to play some tunes. "Break On Through" by The Doors echoed to every corner of the apartment. The music moved from Greta Van Fleet and CCR to Post Malone and Juice WRLD. After an hour, Jack retired to his room. Poor bastard burnt himself out.

Tony rolled the blunt with his Chocolope, and we discussed the plan for New Orleans. We concluded that we'd drop acid during the afternoon, trip in the French Quarter, and gravitate towards heavy alcohol as the day progressed. Clara usually returned home from work around 5, so she said we could come over after. She'd long been eager to meet some of my Chicago friends. Her apartment sat across from a jazz joint called Arnaud's.

"She's all done," Tony said, running the flame of his lighter underneath the blunt to dry it out.

"Let's smoke out on the balcony," I suggested. "Y'all will love the view." It was midnight and we had been awake for almost 18 hours.

"You weren't lying Morrison," Tony said, sparking the blunt. The balcony overlooked a lazy river, a pool, and several palm trees. Synthetic adobe walls and terra-cotta rooftops surrounded them, reminding us of the Southwest.

"I'll be honest," Joe said with a smile, "I didn't expect all these palm trees. But I guess it makes sense. We're at the bottom of the country."

"Believe it or not, Baton Rouge is further south on the map than L.A. and San Diego. If we were to head straight west from here, we'd end up in Mexico."

"I'm looking forward to tomorrow," Tony said. "I wonder how New Orleans compares to Vegas."

"It won't be as wild because of the pandemic, but something I've learned living down here is that New Orleans will always be New Orleans—pandemic or no pandemic. Vegas is a wild town, make no mistake about it. But it barely even existed until the '50s. Both places are havens for sin... Gambling, drinking, drugs, prostitutes, strip clubs... But the Crescent City has more flavor. It blows Vegas outta the water. The history is out of this world."

"I am amazed at the giant circle we've driven in... Chicago... L.A.... Here... I keep saying the same shit, but it's impossible to hold back my thoughts." Joe sounded magnanimous as he reflected. "For my entire life, my schedule's been school, work, and helping raise my siblings. Being on the road like this, I think I've found a sense of liberation foreign to me. There's something about the absence of obligations and looking at what the world has to offer that frees the spirit. It makes me think of *Meditations*."

"Ah, Marcus Aurelius. Dwell on the beauty of life, watch the stars, and see yourself running with them," I replied, quoting the Roman Emperor.

"I haven't read *Meditations* yet—bits and pieces, but I've been meaning to get to it. The amount of phrases we hear every day that come from it is unbelievable."

"How? The Caesars are your ancestors, Tony. You got some catchin' up to do!"

"Morrison, you prick! I will, don't you worry!"

He was onto something. Long before the phrase, "Live every day as if it were your last" appeared on Tumblr and artsy Instagram posts, those words had been etched into eternity by one of the greatest Caesars that Rome ever knew. Few people know their source. It's true modern humans usually fall short in utilizing the infinite amount of information at our fingertips. Folks like us challenged the narrative though, one book and one adventure at a time, grateful for the classics like Homer, Cicero, and Plato—the vast universe of ancient wisdom.

My personal rabbit hole found its genesis with Homer. Studying the ancients poised me to journey into modern philosophy. The wretchedly eye-opening words of Nietzsche exposed me to existentialism and, ever since, the catastrophes happening all around compel me to either rip the hair from my scalp or laugh uncontrollably like a Chicago alderman does after conning a bloc of voters into electing him. I credit Nietzsche, Camus, and Hunter S. Thompson for my sanity and madness. Existentialism is the philosophy of our time.

I don't believe there are any answers in systems constructed by men, and we have no choice but to find our *own* purpose during this decay. In totality, I am a humanist. I believe in our species. But the power-hungry will always control, and even the most glorious of revolutions result in a repressive bureaucracy, loaded with demagogues bent on lining their pockets. The Caesars and pharaohs had their gold and our presidents have their green American dollars.

American society is riddled with monotony, and the pandemic only made everything worse, thanks to lockdowns. Sheltering in place led us to believe our lives were nothing but repetitive, rudderless accidents without meaning. Joe hinted at this. Fish implied the same earlier that night. Existentialism is a potential remedy for these problems. Perhaps civilization is a hopelessly corrupt Philistine temple built on conformity, but it's our duty to find the human dignity within us to carry on and figure out precisely what makes us unique.

Albert Camus wrote that absurdity can hit anyone right in the face at any time and at any place. It's our choice, how we react to the absurdities of this nihilistic era. Joe and Tony understood this. For 21st Century Nietzsche junkies like ourselves, the usual course of conversation led from philosophy to politics or vice versa. Political conversations in our time are inescapable. Whether in Chicago, Louisiana or among my English friends in Argentina, this is our reality. The world has grown fat on shallow opinions warped by demagogues who preach utopian visions from ivory towers.

I once again wandered in my own reflections, higher than Mount Everest. The view from the balcony relaxed us, and the stormy skies of July in Louisiana had disappeared. The night grew clear, and all was well for the time being.

We had long finished smoking the blunt and hammered into Tony's rum bottle. The conversations lived on well into the night, talking in strange, obscene languages. When you drink hard, you talk hard, and that's just how it is. Our night ended around one o'clock. Joe slept on the couch, and Tony ate floor. I collapsed into my bed to chip away at *The Dharma Bums* by Jack Kerouac. I hadn't been able to read as much as I hoped on the trip so did so until I dozed off.

Run Through The Bayou

I woke up to the alarm, sweating my balls off. After showering, I walked out to the kitchen to make some green tea. "Waking up the right way is imperative," I muttered to myself. "You need to be in tip-top shape for the beating you'll put your body through today."

Jack had already risen and quietly fixed himself breakfast—the apartment smelled like bacon and hash browns.

"Wake up, fuckbrains," I said to Joe, shaking him awake.

He rubbed his eyes. "What time is it?"

"Half past 10. We should try to hit the road by noon."

"For sure, I need to get ready."

"We should get Tony up and going," I said as he peacefully slept on the floor in my room. I almost trampled him while getting out of bed.

Waking the crazy Italian wasn't difficult. He easily regained consciousness and was ready to "attack the day" as my father says. A deviously hopeful energy kicked and contorted inside, something I always experience visiting New Orleans. The Crescent City casts a spell on you. It puts you in a trance. You're captivated by the city's Southern charm and unpredictability. The combination is perfectly poetic. New Orleans may be considered our nation's most European city, but it embodies American grit more than anywhere else.

Tony jumped up off the floor. "Gotta say, I'm amped about today."

"Just wait until we're there, drunk and trippin'," I said with a serpentine smile. "Hey, Jack, you tryna' drop acid?"

He paused. "To be honest, man, I've been told some fucked-up stories about acid. I don't know..."

"Well, we have a bag of shrooms if you want some of those. They're typically more mellow. Although I personally have never had a bummer on acid."

"Sure, why not... I've never tripped before, but mushrooms seem better than acid-based. I'll try 'em."

"I'll toss you some in a bit. Take 'em shortly before you start driving. It won't take more than an hour getting to New Orleans, and the shrooms will kick in by the time we're parked and in the streets. Be warned though, they taste like shit."

"I'll wash it down with a roadie." He smiled, opening the fridge and pointing to a case of beer. Jack is a devout Michelob drinker on top of all the whiskey and wine.

"That's the spirit!" I roared like a high school kid who convinced his crush to go to prom with him.

"I gotta bring my rum," Tony said, cradling the bottle like an infant. "I'm gonna get ready."

"Me too." Joe followed suit.

"Well, shit," Jack sighed, "I may as well. I still have to shower."

I waited on the couch, ready to go, and peered over at the Robert Johnson photo hanging in the kitchen. Then I glanced at the tin "Battle of the Blues" poster hanging to the left with pictures of Muddy Waters and Howlin' Wolf. **Club Paradise - Memphis, Tennessee**, it read. Memphis would be our stop after New Orleans. It's tragically underrated—a blues city far grittier than the Yankee mecca Nashville's becoming.

Not that I have anything against Nashville, it's a booming place and a damn playground for anybody over 21. But I've always avoided places the masses flock to. My first time going there was at 13. Obviously, I couldn't partake in any of the alcoholic debauchery, but the barrage of bachelorette parties kept my adolescent self horny and entertained.

On the contrary, I had a history of reckless alcoholic madness in Memphis. During senior year of high school, my father and I were kicked out of a bar there. Since I'd forgotten my fake ID in Chicago, we decided to wing it at a Beale Street juke joint. He bought the drinks and discreetly passed them to me while watching live music. After downing a couple beers, the bouncer caught onto our game and kicked us out. At least he let me keep the beer I was in the middle of. We drank for hours at a Grizzlies game earlier in the night, so I was plastered. We even had to stop in an alley so I could blow chunks—mere months before I'd start college and become in love with drowning in whiskey bottles.

While pondering on Tennessee misadventures, Tony walked out of my room, dressed up in the nicest clothes he had with him—a Baja Llama T-shirt with a Joshua tree and cactus on it and chino pants. *Good luck wearing those chinos in the heat, my friend.* We hadn't anticipated partying in New Orleans, let alone stopping there. As a result, Joe and Tony had to fish around for fresh clothes. I was lucky. My wardrobe remained intact from the spring.

"Morning blunt?" Tony offered.

I nodded.

"Joe and Jack should be all set any minute," I said as he emptied out a cigarillo to roll.

He glanced over at me. "Aside from that alley orgy, what else have you seen in New Orleans?"

"Fuck, where do I even begin? My first time in New Orleans was 2016. Our senior year of high school. I saw a grown-ass man wind up and deck some poor girl in the face. Young as I was, I wanted to castrate the motherfucker. During my first Mardi Gras back in 2019, I saw a lady's weave fall off of her head into a pile of green horse shit and, during the national championship earlier this year, I was with some friends on Bourbon Street and we saw a crackhead bobbing his head back and forth, with his entire face covered in blood, yelling, 'Fuck 12.' Those are actually the lighter stories."

"Fucking hell, Morrison. Are we gonna die today?"

"Nothin's killed us yet on this trip, and I doubt a day in New Orleans will. But even if we do in fact die, this week would be as good a week as any."

"True. I've been thinking though, man. What's our plan tomorrow? Memphis? It's a long way back to Chicago, and I gotta be in Iowa City on Monday."

"You read my mind, Tony. I was thinking about hitting Memphis while sitting here. Have you ever been?"

"Once when I was little. Not old enough to really experience it, but it seemed like a cool place."

"I got drunk there once a few years ago, but it's a fun town. Very bluesy, very old school. You'll like it. Joe, too."

"Bet. Another city to add to our list for the trip."

Jack emerged from his room, wearing one of his best LSU polos and a clean pair of Nikes.

"Have some bacon and hash browns if y'all want," Jack insisted. "I made a lot."

"Say less. We have a long day ahead of us," Tony replied, taking up the offer.

I snagged a couple of bacon strips.

Finally, Joe entered the kitchen, carrying his bags. "We all ready to go?" he asked excitedly.

"Yessir, have some breakfast if you want some," I recommended. "We also rolled a blunt."

"I'm okay. I imagine we'll be getting food in New Orleans at some point, but I'll partake in the smoke."

Tony sat on the couch, gobbling up his hash browns and bacon.

"I'll ride with Jack," I said. "I'm stupid enough to trust y'all with the car."

"I'll drive," replied Joe as he ripped the blunt.

"Sounds good. We'll finish the blunt and drop the acid." Joe passed me the blunt, and I inhaled a couple of hits. "Want some of this?" I asked Jack.

"I've driven drunk, but never high... But we're going to New Orleans so fuck it, sure." He adjusted his glasses with one hand, extending the other for the blunt.

Jack's hunger for vice on that fine Baton Rouge morning impressed me. Make no mistake about it, the man is a heavy drinker and, on occasion, he did smoke with me. At a Halloween party in 2019, he drunkenly banged on the doors of nearby apartments, shouting obscenities in a prison jumpsuit.

Fish Henderson has his occasions where he goes nuclear but not in a threatening or dangerous way. Drugs usually aren't quite his thing, so I was pleasantly surprised by his behavior. This was his first chance to cut loose in a very long time, and I suppose that the old city on the bayou is one of the only places in the country where he can be convinced to take psychedelics. New Orleans is a city without innocence, and there's no haven for sobriety in such a dastardly place.

We each grabbed our bags and loaded the cars. Joe and Tony hopped in the Patriot. Jack and I walked down the hall, into the parking garage, and over to his car—also a Jeep—Michelobs in hand.

"You have 'em?" Jack asked me, referring to the mushrooms.

"Yessir, here you go. Eat 'em and chase with the beer. I have to warn you though... You're not on an empty stomach... Might want to wait a little while."

He paused. "I didn't eat much. I think I'll be fine. I'll eat some now and more when we get there."

"Cool, I got your back if you need me," I said, swigging my bottle of Jack.

"Here goes nothing, bruh," he said, shoving the mushrooms into his mouth and quickly chewing. He instantly cracked a beer. "You weren't kidding. These taste like dog shit." He chugged the foamy Michelob.

"They do, but the taste won't last. Here, take some of this gum."

"Much better. Let's drive to your boys."

"Let's go."

We whipped the car down a level in the parking garage to the Patriot. Joe and Tony waited there with the engine running and the windows down.

"Y'all ready to go?" I asked cheerfully.

"Yessir!" Tony exclaimed as Joe nodded.

"Hold up," Joe paused, "gotta drop the acid."

We were thankful for the reminder. I retrieved the bag of LSD and handed out a couple tabs like candy.

"Jack took the shrooms already."

"Goddamn, we're in for a ride," Jack laughed.

"Just follow us on the way in and we'll find a parking garage Downtown or near the Quarter," I instructed Joe.

"Bet."

Jack peeled off out of the parking lot, and we cruised along Parker Boulevard, bypassing campus, with the other two trailing us. Across the sidewalk, inmates from the parish prison labored in the summer heat, their navy-blue jumpsuits stained with sweat. July humidity wafted through the air, and the temperature fired upward.

"Still haven't gotten used to it yet," I said, peering out the window at the inmates.

"Same here," Jack replied. "You don't see prison labor in Meridian like the Delta."

His remark raised my eyebrows. "You don't see this at all where I grew up in Chicago."

"I guess you can say slavery was never abolished... The Thirteenth Amendment allows enslavement as a punishment for what the State considers criminal behavior."

"True, and it's no coincidence that the War on Drugs was waged as the Civil Rights Era drew to a close."

"The government straight up said, 'Not so fast, Black people,' and made sure to reverse any progress. I'm confused how my right-leaning contemporaries fail to realize that systemic racism is a product of big government. Just look up the 1985 Philadelphia Bombing."

"It's hidden in plain sight, man. People just listen to what their media sources tell them. They act as if acknowledging systemic racism automatically makes them a 'dirty liberal' or something. Implicit bias leads to bad results."

"Facts, Morrison, but I don't see it getting better. These protests and riots in many ways are justified, but they'll die down eventually, and the bullshit's gonna keep happening."

Jack's a principled conservative, a well-read political communications major who graduated with me. He aspires to be an attorney. Understandably, it's shocking to some that a gun-toting Southern Baptist from rural Mississippi holds progressive views on racial issues, but this is a big country, and regional politics isn't monolithic. People like him are examples of how far things have come in the South, but there's plenty of darkness yet to be removed.

It's not uncommon to see prisoners toiling in the sun all over Baton Rouge. While an undergrad, I did some landscaping around town, and inmates from the East Baton Rouge Parish Prison frequently had lunch in the facility's break room. I've spoken with several, and a sizable number of those poor bastards were condemned to spend years, decades, or even their entire lives behind bars for non-violent crimes.

Every single prisoner I met was Black. It's no coincidence that numerous Southern prisons were once slave plantations. Some are the largest in the South. Angola comes to mind. Otherwise known as the Louisiana State Penitentiary, it's about 40 miles upriver from Baton Rouge.

The prison earned its namesake because Angola served as the primary country of origin for the area's enslaved population during the Antebellum Period, and it is a contender for the most violent maximum-security prisons in the nation. I doubt its inmates ever leave rehabilitated. Back in Illinois, a Black man is more likely to see the inside of a prison than a university. [9]The incarceration rates plaguing this land of the free undoubtedly stem from the current racial caste system, and without overt racism on paper, millions fail to see this fascist nonsense for what it is. In failing one of our communities, all are failed in return.

Lord have mercy... Bats out of Hell... I'm recollecting the pictures and footage of that nazi kneeling on George Floyd's neck for almost 10 minutes. The look on Floyd's face, the cries he made, spitting and screaming for help. The terror in his eyes was nausea-inducing. Footage of militarized police patrolling neighborhoods, firing rubber bullets at people standing on their porches in Minneapolis, it appalled me. Pseudo-tough guy cops abusing their power. These scum have no appreciation for the Constitution they swear to protect.

Since 1997, our beloved Pentagon has sold billions of dollars' worth of weapons, vehicles, and armor to local police departments between Providence and San Francisco. This practice is known as the 1033 Program. These things don't happen in a free country. How can anyone possibly believe we're free? Had Goethe's ideas become reality? [10]

Amid its ongoing war against citizens, the law enforcement community would have you believe *they* are the ones who face mounting injustices and are "not allowed to do their jobs"—rhetoric of extreme peril. In 1968, segregationist Alabama Governor George Wallace said the police had been

---

[9] Alexander, Michelle, and West, Cornel. *The New Jim Crow: Mass Incarceration in the Age of Colorblindness.* The New Press, 2020.
[10] "None are more hopelessly enslaved than those who falsely believe they're free."

"handcuffed" by the Supreme Court. Half a century later, the same rhetoric remains alive among "law and order" politicians and the weak and misguided masses who fawn over them.

On the outskirts, we drove past patterns of old houses, massive estates, and former plantations—ancient classical buildings with massive columns engulfed by live oaks and decorated with Spanish moss. The ghosts had returned.

Eventually, Baton Rouge fell behind us, then Prairieville, Gonzales, and Laplace. Shortly after passing through Laplace, we cruised on the I-10 bridge along Lake Pontchartrain. The lake's on one side, marshes and bayous on the other. Trees topped with eagles' nests kissed the cloud-covered sky as the sun faintly peaked through; a pleasant sight, unfortunately tainted by chemical plants off in the distance. The portion of Louisiana running between Baton Rouge and New Orleans is called "Cancer Alley" because of overwhelming levels of pollution, and residents frequently suffer from poor health, which I learned while reading *Strangers in Their Own Land* by Arlie Russell Hochschild.

Jack knew this, too. Our friend Dalton grew up in Destrehan, Louisiana, which we'd drive through before entering Jefferson Parish. Cancer claimed the lives of his uncle, a cousin, and three grandparents. Several childhood friends of his lost their parents. Blood-sucking politicians persistently pander to these corporations for "jobs," unaware or indifferent that they're effectively killing their constituents.

These greedy nerds would nuke the Rockies and drain the Great Lakes if they found it profitable. There's already an island of trash floating through the Pacific Ocean twice the size of Texas. Sociologist C. Wright Mills is turning in his grave. But what can I do about it? What can anybody do? I must revert to the fauna and wildlife of Southeast Louisiana.

Bayous south of the highway rested—stoic and silent— the ancient trees submerged in brackish water, crowned with eagles' nests and Spanish moss under the sky. How many alligators basked in the sun or remained submerged in nearby water? Louisiana's gator population is in the millions. Sharks regularly swim in Lake Pontchartrain or wind their way up through the swamps. Some friends of mine have told stories of gator-hunting which is an activity I intend to engage in someday. Gator meat is a fine delicacy.

I fixed my eyes out the window when there it was—New Orleans' skyline. It's a strange thing, driving into the New Orleans area. In the blink of an eye, you go from the sticks to densely populated blocks of houses in Kenner and Metairie. Traffic in Southeast Louisiana along I-10 is a massive shitshow, full of bumper-to-bumper traffic and accidents for miles. Luckily, that wasn't the case that day, since it was 11 o'clock on a Friday morning during a pandemic.

Out of nowhere, Joe and Tony pulled next to us in the left lane at 80 miles per hour, staring us down. I recognized their challenge. We drag-raced back in high school on a daily basis. Tony wildly cackled and yelled at us to eat their dust. The Jeeps were neck and neck. The opening of "Misirlou" by Dick Dale & The Del Tones emanated from the speakers.

"Ay, Fish, these douchers wanna race. You need that change?"

A pile of quarters, dimes, and pennies sat in the cupholder.

"Hell no, why?"

"Watch."

Our speed increased to 90. I hung out the window and chucked a handful of change at Tony.

A direct hit. Ballsy, especially since they're driving my old man's car. They lagged for a few seconds but regained ground immediately.

"Rubber, man! Burn that rubber, boy!" I yelled to Jack.

We could've crashed the Daytona 500.

"I am, bruh! I drag-raced all the time in Mississippi. I have my methods." Both his hands gripped the wheel, his vape locked in the left. "They're bogus!" he bellowed as Tony threw a hail of pennies at his clean ride. "Morrison, grab another handful, your boys are in for a goddamn war!"

"Affirmative, chief!"

I whipped another handful of coins at Tony, and it did the trick. Joe fell victim to fallout. We bobbed and weaved around a few cars with a couple close calls.

"A hundred!" I blared.

"What?"

"Push a hundred, man, burn 'em out!"

"Man, I'm too fuckin' high for this!" Jack pressed his foot on the pedal. 90...95...100...105... "Yessir! Yessir!" He cheered as the other two fell behind.

I hung my head out the window. "Eat shit, you pricks!" I shouted, struggling to hold onto the tabs under my tongue.

They laughed hysterically in the Patriot.

"Oh, man, whatta ride," I said to Jack. "Glad those idiots didn't crash!"

"Hell, man. I hear ya."

We fired into New Orleans, enthralled by victory, when Jack queued "Come & Go" by Juice WRLD. I motioned the sign of the cross. Jarad Anthony Higgins was perhaps the most iconic rapper to ever come from our generation—a true artist who lived as he died. His dark lyrics and honesty about substance abuse and mental health drew Jack and me in, the same way they captivated millions. It's a powerful thing, connecting with an artist's music so closely... You can't help but feel as if the song was written *for* you. You're given an escape—a rare strength—just enough to push through the horrors and hardships of life, whatever they may be.

I thought about attending a Juice WRLD concert after the pandemic until I remembered he was dead. And he had been since December of 2019. Feds conducted a sweep of his jet when it landed at Midway Airport in Chicago. To avoid getting caught, Juice shoved the Percs in his mouth, which led to his untimely demise. You really don't know what'll happen when you get up in the morning. He had awoken in Los Angeles ready to head home to Chicago, but never left the plane alive. Thanks to the War on Drugs, a master artist and voice for this generation is gone. Dead at 21. To this day, nobody's taken his place.

Generational gaps in music are a bitch. Back in the '60s and '70s, older generations loathed the rock music their children listened to, the same way they loathe rap today. What music will young people listen to when I'm advanced in age? Music my generation will despise with the utmost intensity? I hope we break the pattern because it does nothing but divide.

Some older people claim rap is too violent even though they loved Johnny Cash, who sang about shooting a man in Reno. I'm a Cash fan, but the example is noteworthy. I thought deep and hard as the music reverted to Classic Rock. Cemeteries on the highway guided my thoughts elsewhere.

New Orleans cemeteries are notorious for resting corpses above ground. They're everywhere and compliment the city's ghostly vibrations. It's Halloween year-round. Stone statues of the Virgin Mary teemed with crucifixes, saints, and mausoleums shaded by live oaks. With the Lizard King's voice screeching in the car, we penetrated deeper into city limits, cruising down palm tree-lined Canal Street Downtown. New Orleans is akin to Vegas only in the realm of vice and retro architecture.

The French Quarter plays a role. It's been with us for hundreds of years. But Downtown New Orleans is endowed with a plethora of hotels and businesses built in the '60s. We drove past the old Walgreens, the classic streetcars, and down a few blocks, taking a left onto Peters Street to park the car. I sent the parking garage's location to Tony as we pulled in.

PSYCHEDELIC

DISASTER

A diverse assortment of inexplicable odors lingers throughout New Orleans, depending on where you are in the city. Or is it an aroma? Nevertheless, the French Quarter has a musty old scent, bearing traces of alcohol, Creole cooking, and horse shit... It changes block by block. Words are half-measures in describing the old city.

"How are you feeling?" I asked Jack once parked.

"Nothin' yet. Still a bit stoned. You sure these shrooms ain't bad? I'm not feeling anything." He ate the other portion I gave him.

"I am, just give 'em some time. You're bigger than me so they might take longer to hit you." Jack's 6'2, so the drugs would take longer to affect him than my 5'10 lean as a damn 2x4".

"Cool," he said.

"That's what everybody says, the drugs ain't hittin' the way they're supposed to, then BAM! They're trippin' balls. Be patient. There's still a bit left in the bag if you need 'em."

I was already on my way up and grateful the playlist changed to upbeat Doors. With a head full of LSD, thoughts of mortality are a quick way to land yourself spiraling into fits of fear and drawing all sorts of unwanted attention.

The other two strolled out of the Jeep Patriot, and I could tell they were coming up. Joe let out a relieving sigh as he shut the car door, and Tony told me the stuff had hit him. I threw on the pair of Aviators I'd worn throughout much of the journey. They complimented my leopard-print Kenny Flowers button-up.

"Fuck, this stuff is hitting me," Joe said. "I'm glad I'm out of that car."

"Same. Time to get started." I slugged whiskey straight from the bottle and chased it with a sip of water.

"Most places are closed for indoor service, but there's all sorts of spots we can stop at on Bourbon," Jack said.

"Y'all haven't even had daiquiris yet," I said, teasing my Midwestern brethren.

"We got everything?" Joe asked.

"We can come back here later to get whatever we need... When our heads are screwed on a bit better, because this come up is kicking my ass." I swigged some more Old No. 7. "Here, drink some. It'll help reduce the anxiety."

"Hold up. I'mma get my cigs," Joe said, patting the pockets of his shorts. He went back into the car, fumbling around before reappearing with the pack of cigarettes. "Got them. I'm good. I also have the THC pills."

"Word, can I cop a couple?"

"Sure thing, there's plenty left."

"Gimme some, too," Tony begged like some seven-year-old who missed out on trick-or-treating.

"Somewhere between space and time, our ancestors are either horrified or laughing at us." Jack nervously chuckled as we strolled onto the street.

"How's it going?" I asked him.

"These things are hitting. I think I'm fucked up. I feel really weird, like I'm tired but I'm not. It's almost out-of-body. All of a sudden, this is really intense. I'm not sure if I fuck with it."

"That's how it goes, especially your first time," Tony reassured him. "It gets better. The come-up is the roughest part. You'll be smooth sailing in an hour."

"I hope man."

"Just consider it an adventure within our adventure, but in your own head. The tribes out West believed psychedelic visions made them stronger at the end of the trip. After all, you're with us and we're experienced with this shit."

"I know. I trust y'all," he said in his slow drawl.

"Whata ya know?" Tony blurted out, "It's Bienville Street."

"Perfect. The garage is at Peters and Bienville. We know exactly where to go. Bienville will take us straight to Bourbon."

I was Louisiana's answer to Odysseus, guiding my friends through the old streets. Although coming up on acid, I was aware I must be somewhat present upstairs or else the city would certainly do us in. How long until another episode like the one at Venice Beach? How much time would it take for one of us to wind up howling at the top of our lungs and running stark-naked through the streets like a rabid hyena?

I couldn't tell. There was no possible way. The best course of action involved finding a place to eat before roaming the old city, all of us mired in psychedelic trances. There were four of us. We'd make it out in one piece if we stuck together. Although it had been midday, we already were in awful shape. We finally settled in the French Quarter.

"What the fuck?" Tony shrieked. "Is Mitch McConnell walking out of that strip club?"

"No fucking way," Jack muttered.

Gentleman's Touch Male Strippers, the sign read, and sure enough, an old White guy stood near the doorway, but it was not Mitch McConnell. "It ain't him, Tony. Besides, can't you see the place is closed?"

"True, Morrison, I'm out of it," he answered, reaching into his pocket for his vape.

"Let's head this way," I suggested. "We'll walk a few blocks up and grab some Willie's."

"Willie's?" Joe asked.

"Willie's Chicken Shack—good ole Louisiana fried chicken. The locals roast you if you tell 'em that's what you decided to eat in New Orleans but, believe me, the chicken's gas. There's one a couple blocks up."

"Bet," he said.

Jack remained silent, humbled by the wars in his head.

"We'll pick up some Willie's and take St. Ann to Jackson Square to recollect ourselves." I referenced our location on my phone to the best of my abilities, but the sun was hot, and the acid mercilessly cooked my head. *What would be more fried?* I thought. *My head or the chicken we're about to eat?* Meanwhile, all four of us dripped with sweat—I felt glad I sprayed on some Dolce & Gabbana and was aggressive with my deodorant two hours earlier.

"Sounds like a plan," Joe answered.

We doubled back up Bourbon Street and, all around us, the routine picked up steam. A few bucket drummers serenaded the streets, but the vendors who usually hover around with boxes full of edibles and pre-rolls were nowhere to be found. The smarter cops turn a blind eye when it comes to drug activity in towns like New Orleans. They know damn well most people around them are engaging in illegal activity, and it helps their city garner money to pay their salaries.

Somewhere behind us, someone played the traditional New Orleans saxophone beat. Sparse groups waded in the street as we pushed through. This was not a typical day. There hadn't been such a thing on Bourbon Street since March and, grief-struck when reality hit... It would be a while until I'd find the New Orleans I'd love again, but my inner optimist stopped me. We'd see that New Orleans later on at Clara's...

I've wandered those French Quarter streets under the influence of almost anything imaginable that doesn't involve a needle. As a result, I've developed a subconscious familiarity with the city's cobblestone streets and sidewalks, a familiarity I knew only in Chicago and Baton Rouge. A lifetime could've passed since leaving Chicago eight days earlier. A lot had happened, not including the additional mess we'd found ourselves in. Sweaty, hot, and tripping balls, we had to pave our way out of despair.

Our condition horrified me. I horrified myself. A couple of hours until Clara's party... *You can do this, Pat. Steer the ship, carry on through the psychosis and repressive heat long enough to survive... 5 o'clock is the magic hour...* We couldn't go to her place yet, because she'd be at work. Our only course of action involved sticking to the plan.

"Shit! Shit! Fuck, man, they're all over me!" Jack blurted, hollering into a frenzy of psychosis.

"What's wrong?" I asked. "What's all over you?"

"These bugs, Morrison, they're all over me, what the fuck?!" He performed a frantic jig and ran in circles.

"Jack, relax, there are no bugs," Tony said.

Joe stood there, speechless.

"Goddammit, Jack, you'll bring the whole damn pigpen on us. Calm down, there isn't anything on you!" I had to be stern.

"Nothing?"

"No, take a breather, just breathe, man," I suggested. "It'll help. Deep breaths through the nose."

"I'm feeling pretty fucked, I'm not gonna lie. The buildings look hazy, and the streets are moving. I'm dizzy."

"All good, bro, we'll get our chicken, drink some water, and sit down."

He adjusted his glasses. "Fine, fine. I ain't tryna get us in trouble with no cops. I guess it's just these damn shrooms fuckin' me up."

"We found Tony on the streets of Venice, yelling to people that the British are coming," Joe reminded, trying to reassure him.

"This man thinks he's Paul Revere and shit!"

"Fuck off, Morrison, let's just stick to your dumbass plan," he retorted.

"I suppose getting some damn chicken is too much to ask," I snapped. "There it is, at the corner of the next block."

Walking into Willie's off the street provided temporary salvation. We desperately requested water to replace what we'd been sweating out. In five minutes, our chicken was ready, and we ditched Willie's for Jackson Square. Dining indoors wasn't an option. We took it to Jackson Square. Balconies, potted plants, and flags surrounded us. Anyone who roams those streets will notice hundreds of flags all over the Quarter, a reflection of New Orleans' multicultural heritage.

At last, we arrived at Jackson Square after passing up the Place d'Armes Hotel. Straight ahead, the statue of Andrew Jackson glinted in the sun, his horse leaping in the air, hat tipped in victory. President Jackson is a controversial figure and for damn convincing reasons. His sins against the Indigenous American remain an open wound in our country's history. He developed a nasty reputation as a particularly cruel slaveholder and dueling man. However, history is complicated.

The Big Easy was expected to fall to the British Army, and Jackson's military prowess prevailed at the Battle of New Orleans—the city's finest hour. Outnumbered, poorly trained, and outgunned American forces led by Jackson and fearless Jamaican and Irish troops, they decimated the experienced British Army. Shortly after, the Treaty of Ghent was signed, effectively ending the War of 1812. With Saint Louis Cathedral right next to us, the square looked glorious. We cut through the park, past palm trees and hedges to sit and eat our chicken.

"How are y'all feeling?" I asked my three companions.

"Better," Joe said. "The high is starting to stabilize. There was some vasoconstriction an hour ago, but it's gone."

"I'm better," Tony said, dragging his vape. "Morrison, pass me the whiskey."

I obliged. "Jack, how about you?"

"I'm a bit nauseous, but it was worse back on Bourbon. Otherwise, I'm doing fine. It's still weird though, I can't explain it, but it's as if I think more clearly now. It's nice chillin' in an open area."

"Makes sense, you're accessing parts of your brain you don't use otherwise. Shrooms make you wanna spend time in open spaces, not confined."

"Who else wants some of this?" Tony offered, holding the bottle. "Jack?"

"I'll swig some."

"Pass it to me next," Joe boomed, diving into his food.

"They never give you enough sauce," Jack complained, tossing his empty packet of Willie's Sauce back into the bag.

"Reverend Henderson, you are a preachin' up a sermon," I chuckled in an exaggerated Southern accent—not that I needed to try very hard. Having called the fine State of Louisiana home for three years, I absorbed the accent. My friends up North teased me for having a twang, and some people from Louisiana figured I was from the New Orleans area until Chicago would casually come up in conversation.

"You guys were right," Joe said, sipping the bottle. "This chicken is *fuego*."

"We told you, bruh!" Jack laughed.

We concluded our feast, bypassed the Cabildo and turned on St. Peter Street. Pat O'Brien's and several other vacant bars and businesses depressed the mood. Self-inflicted wounds. My emotions stirred up an uneasy sensation while observing the current state of New Orleans, and the world at large. Where is the light at the end of this dark road? For how long must we cower in a self-destructive storm of pitiless fear? The worst thing about an unjust world is the pipeline from apathy to nihilism. I refused to let this vex me because, all in all, I'm always happy on Bourbon Street.

Navigating those streets in the middle of an acid trip wasn't easy and the walls, trees, and streets moved in strange patterns. *Lord, have mercy on my wretched soul!* By then, the whiskey had hit me violently. To the left of Cats Meow is Fat Tuesday, a well-known spot for daiquiris. Jack and I advised Joe and Tony what to order since we both had consumed enough daiquiris over the years to kill Janis Joplin twice. A rush of anxiety hit me as two cops patrolled past us.

They'd sense something's up and shoot us in the back like lame horses. There's nothing those corrupt cavemen would love more than to throw some helplessly intoxicated out-of-towners behind bars. They'd force us at gunpoint to show them the Jeep, where our drugs would be found. "Stop it... Stop it... Get your shit together," I told myself. "These yellow-belly lawmen ain't got a chance in Hell of catching us." One of the best ways to quell psychedelic anxiety among strangers is by repeating to yourself that, to them, you're merely another person. They are entirely unaware of the chaos unleashed inside your head. This realization always helps soothe me, and I've spoken to other people who've tripped under similar circumstances and said the same thing.

I scanned the weather app on my phone. It was 92 degrees, and waves of humidity increased the heat index to 110. We'd reached the hottest point in the day. I sipped my water, and the boys were visibly refreshed by the daiquiris in their hands. The acid, while potent, mellowed as liquor flowed in my veins and brightened my spirits. Here I was in one of my favorite places with friends I considered brothers—a similar feeling to the one I tasted while stargazing in Monument Valley. The pandemic may have turned New Orleans into a shadow of its self, but we wandered its streets drunk, tripping, and stoned without complaint. We were lucky to survive such an absurd start to the day and had a party to look forward to.

REFUGE AT LAST

At 5:00, I texted Clara, alerting her of our arrival. A half-hour later, she invited us to swing by. All day, we'd sojourned through the French Quarter, dehydrated and obliterated off a number of substances. Meanwhile, we ventured down Rampart Street and along the fences of Saint Louis Cemetery No. 1, which would've prompted thoughts of terror, death, rapture, angels, and demons, but alcohol dominated the acid, relieving me of psychosis.

Our peace dissolved when a group of guys approached us. They wore bright-collared shirts and khaki shorts. As our paths crossed, one of them fell under the impression that Joe tried to pickpocket him. They seemed classic examples of the inebriated Neanderthals typical of the French Quarter. They all wore Sperrys. The stereotypical mold of these characters was all too real. Some people can't booze, and it shows. Such individuals should never come to New Orleans, but *they do in droves.*

One of them, a cock-nosed rat wearing a pink polo shirt with slicked hair shoved Joe, who retaliated by pushing back and telling him to go fuck himself in broken Spanish. Four on four, and my blood boiled. My heartrate increased, sobering me up. One of the bastard's friends yanked him back, and I gripped Joe's shoulder... Not to restrain, but to say, "I'm here and ready to curb stomp whoever lays a finger on you."

I've visited New Orleans dozens of times since senior year of high school, and never has there been a time when somebody hasn't tried fighting me or my friends. We aren't confrontational people, but we're not afraid to use our fists. After all, Tony and I boxed together for years in the old neighborhood. Boxing is a gentleman's sport, and its ethics dictate a fighter mustn't be violent unless threatened.

"Fucking hippie faggots!" yelled the prick in the pink polo as they parted ways with us.

I couldn't take it, I had to speak my mind. "I'll staple your nuts to your forehead, you piece of shit!"

Jack went old school Mississippi, yelling, "I'll knock your teeth out, boy, you gon' get yusself hurt now!"

To my surprise, our yelling match didn't escalate the situation, and we moved further down the hard road, aching for relief. We ventured back into the French Quarter, taking Bourbon Street to Bienville. I instructed Clara to meet us outside and when we arrived, sure enough, there she was. Her blonde hair was up in a ponytail and glimmering in the sun. She looked like an actress from 1950s' Hollywood and damn charming as always. Her rose-shaded building stood four stories high and had a seemingly infinite number of balconies. Lanterns lit both sides of the front door.

"Patricius Morrison, you Irish motherfucker," she squealed, wrapping me with her small body.

"It's been a minute," I chuckled. "How've you been? You're teaching here, right?"

"Yes, they condemned me to teach summer school, but I desperately need money. It's good to see you, Jack."

"The pleasure is mine," he replied.

"This is Joe Torres and Tony Cerrone. We grew up together in Chicago."

"Welcome to New Orleans! How do y'all like it?"

"I had no idea places like this existed. All day I've wondered what the actual fuck is going on," Joe emphatically replied.

"Same here," Tony concurred. "People casually walk up to you, asking if you want blow." He relayed our near-fight in the French Quarter.

"We've been tripping all day and we're drunk as hell, to be honest," I bashfully conceded.

"*Shocker*. Well, come on upstairs and meet everybody. We're getting everything started."

"Is there *anybody* Jack and I know here yet?" I asked.

"Not currently, but the crew will pull through within the next couple of hours."

"Oh, nice, I haven't seen 'em since spring."

We followed Clara up the stairs to the second level and into the apartment. Her place still felt spacious. It's probably a better idea to throw a colossal banger *before* transporting all the valuables in. Several friends of hers conversed around the kitchen counter adorned with almost every type of liquor imaginable. I caught Clara walking down a hall into what appeared to be her room. Meanwhile, her friends were curious about my companions and me.

"What aw they doin' heeya? Do they know Clara?" I heard one ask in a soft, angelic Southern accent. Music fired from a large set of speakers in two corners of the room—"Wow" by Post Malone. We struck up conversation with the girls and made ourselves comfortable. We had long run out of whiskey, so half a dozen liquor bottles was a welcoming sight. Suddenly, Clara returned and quietly placed a pill in my hand.

"This what I think it is?" I asked.

"M-D-M-A," she whispered, emphasizing each letter. "I took some five minutes ago. Be discreet, I don't want the whole party asking for some. I picked it up after work."

"Good thing I haven't had any whiskey for a couple of hours." Molly dehydrates you quicker than the desert heat. "How much do I owe you?"

"Nothing, we're square. Let's have some fun, *mi amor*."

"Thank you for this," I said in a flattered tone.

"You know me, Pat. Always up for a fun time." Her blue eyes sparkled as she spoke.

I admit without shame that Clara is extremely beautiful.

"Y'all can help yourselves to whatever you want on the table." She motioned to the other three.

"Thanks for having us."

"You're welcome, Tony! A friend of Pat's is a friend of mine." Clara led me to the bathroom so I could take the molly in peace. There're a few doors in the hallway, but she led me to the first one. I shut the door and glared at my reflection. *What am I turning into?* I thought. *I'm alive... More alive than ever, but I'm a damn fiend. Weed hardly classifies as a drug these days, but acid, shrooms, cocaine—bottle after bottle—and now I'm fixing to roll, fixing to die. The edge is in sight, and the only question is whether or not I'm going over.* The acid peaked long ago, but the subtle head games persisted. I was not in the clear. "Shut up and take the damn drug," I said. "...You'll survive as always and with a story to tell..."

I swallowed the pill and chugged a full glass of water. It was imperative to proceed with caution. Molly is unrivaled, by far, the scariest drug I've ever consumed but a blast. I rolled at a party during my final semester and threw up half a gallon of water. The same thing happened while visiting Illinois State at a Fourth of July party in 2019. Dehydration can drain the life from your body, but, if you puke and rally, victory is possible.

The MDMA sprawling through my system allowed me to bounce back stronger than before, and those days proved massive successes—ecstasy for hours, distinct to the drug. You're captivated by a deep affection for everyone and everything. It makes me want to call my mother and tell her I love her. I want to profess affection for my friends. I want a stunning angel of a woman to place her lips on mine and tell me she adores me. I want to dance like a fool under the moon without a fuck to give.

Sure, the first half hour would be a trip to the Circle of Hell that Dante never wrote about, but the waters would calm. Like psychedelics, an MDMA come-up is the scariest part. In 2015, I attended Lollapalooza, the massive annual festival in Grant Park, headlined by the world's most popular musicians. Grant Park... Where a bloodbath in 1968 led to split skulls and savage police violence... What could possibly go wrong? My friend Tommy O'Shea popped molly on the Blue Line. By the time we got off at Clark and Lake, he had lost his eyesight. Bastard was blind as a bat.

"Morrison, I can't see," he said, to which I replied, "What?"

He extended his arm, and I grabbed it. "I can't see a thing," he repeated. I thought he was joking because his eyes were wide open, but he insisted that he couldn't see, so my duty entailed leading him through the crowd of sweaty, violent, puke-covered teenagers. Poor fool would've been helpless otherwise. The condition is called nystagmus, where your eyes move rapidly without your control—a normal side effect of molly. It's nothing serious, just frightening and it doesn't usually last long.

I stood by the sink, still staring at myself in the mirror, stuck in thought, half-mad from the LSD. *What the hell are we? What the hell am I? Some blue-collar alcoholic drug addict from*

Chicago, turned Southern man? Sure, I accomplished a feat nobody in my family had ever achieved by securing a college degree. However, my conscience said I was sliding into decline. I suffered horrible bouts of self-loathing.

This trip put our bodies through Hell. I wondered if I was going off the deep end and why. My spine tingled, and the hair on the back of my neck spiked up. I've felt it before, the horror of impending doom. We had reduced ourselves to booze and drug-fed animals, caught in a worrying chasm between hedonism and the fear of God.

Peering into the depths, our madness wasn't without method. We admired the desert's unspoiled tranquility, but our adventures in Vegas, L.A., and New Orleans coincided with chaos—stemming from bitterness toward an unjust civilization nearing collapse. But when we looked at society, we saw a joke... A dark hole defined by decline and disconnect, growing increasingly stupid. Bland and uniform. Lunacy and erratic behavior are the law of the earth itself. In the mirror, my face looked as if it were melting like an ice cream cone on a hot day. Backing away from the mirror, I left the bathroom to rejoin the group. Trouble would hunt me down soon enough.

Everybody else happily drank around the granite counter, and the guys were slugging shots of clear alcohol. Tequila cranks up the party, behaving as a stimulant, but vodka reminds me too much of a damn hospital. Tony raised his glass. "To a good-ass night!" he cheered.

We conversed with our new friends for a while. We were the only guys at the party. Striking conversation was easy, given our adventures out West. The acid receded, which strengthened my confidence, but sobriety wouldn't last. Jack had long come down from the shrooms but was drunk as a fish, living up to his nickname. The girls were lovely, their skin and hair in natural shades of every color. Being there with my boys, the air teemed with opportunity and zealous excitement—not simply because of all the pretty Southern women—but because I enjoy meeting individuals who have stories to tell.

My blood boils fantastically when meeting deep, intelligent, and open-minded people who ride the fringe. They live fast and young, carrying with them the mantles of their dreams. Torches aflame in the night. Wherever they come from, whoever they are, I fall madly in love, aching to learn more. Even the darker stories seduce me.

One girl, wearing a green shirt and bellbottom jeans, mentioned how her great-grandfather, a bootlegger, shot five people at a French Quarter saloon. My own family has a similar story I was about to share until Tony walked up, holding the keys to the Patriot.

"I left my rum in the car, some weed, too," he said.

"Ugh, fuck. The coke's also in Joe's red bag," I replied.

"Ah, I almost forgot. Fuck."

"Let's go," I groaned. "Hey, Clara! Clara!"

She hurried over. "What's up, babe?"

"We're heading to the car to grab some booze and more drugs. Be back in 20."

"Okay, be safe! Call me if anything happens."

"Got it."

We rushed out the door, heading straight for the parking garage on Peters when the molly took hold. My body temperature steadily rose, and the effects came on at a rapid pace. *For the second time today, you're coming up, you degenerate piece of shit.* Like Jack, Tony was hammered from the concoction of whiskey and daiquiris, in addition to whatever demon drink they'd been shooting around the counter. He, too, rode the undercurrent of his acid wave.

A 10-minute hurry to the car—impeccable timing. Tony seized his rum. I secured the cocaine and one-hitter. Then I froze. Night was falling, and I was still a little shaken up from the brawl we'd almost gotten into. I opened the glove compartment to grab the Smith & Wesson. After a few seconds of contemplation, I swung the backpack around my shoulders, tossing the gun into the front pocket. Back to Clara's apartment. I felt uneasy, guilty about bringing a gun to her place, but she's a Southern girl who grew up around them, and I figured we'd be better safe than sorry. A poor excuse, I'll admit, but an avalanche of drugs deteriorated my decision-making skills.

Vae Victis

The molly pounced on me like a panther on a rabbit. I was sweating profusely and had lost control of my eyes. But at the same time, the terror invigorated me. *I'm invincible.* However, gravity dictates that what goes up, must come down. We strolled along Royal Street and there they were... The preppy douchebags we almost rumbled with hours earlier on Rampart Street. They crossed toward us, and the Quarter was vacant in the sun's absence. Not a soul in sight, thanks to pandemic restrictions.

"Look who it is!" the asshole wearing the pink polo said to his friends.

"Fuck," I growled to Tony, "not again."

"Be ready for anything," he replied.

"I don't care what happens. We'll show these lame fucks that they're messin' with the wrong guys."

They rushed over to us. "Where's your tough-guy friend who tried pickpocketing me?"

"How many times do we gotta tell you, he wasn't putting his hands in your pockets?" Tony scolded.

"You better watch how you talk to him," slurred another one of the douchebags, a tall string bean in a turquoise-collared shirt. They weren't from Louisiana. Their voices gave them away.

"We're not trying to get in any trouble," I said, attempting to stay calm. My heart pounded, and I perspired as the molly conquered all logical thought. Four-on-two odds are not preferable. Communicating with privileged, egocentric maniacs is an exhausting battle, let alone reasoning with them. The window was closing.

"This one's sweating," said the string bean. "You scared, you little shit?"

"No need for problems," I hopelessly replied, clenching my fists. "We can part ways, and nobody gets hurt."

"There's four of us and two of you. I can tell you're a bitch, you look like you're 14," he said, shoving me.

Fuck this. I dropped my backpack, realizing there was only one way to avert the crisis. My eyes widened. "Push me one more fuckin' time. I fuckin' dare you."

When I was in the sixth grade, my father gave me the rundown when it comes to fighting. He'd lived on the streets of Chicago after getting booted from home at 16, when my grandfather died. American cities back then were savage and brutal. In the '70s, the streets were *not* where you wanted to be, and, consequently, my old man learned a lesson or two. He taught me how to hurt somebody if they pushed me, and the technique is useful since most fights begin with a shoving match.

The string bean maneuvered in for a second shove and, with his momentum hurling forward, I gripped him by the hair and plowed my knee into his face. Daddy's money in the pink polo drunkenly swung at Tony, whose boxing instincts kicked in. He ducked and cracked the guy across the mouth—a textbook jaw shot. The bastard spit out a tooth as the string bean returned to his feet, his mouth pouring blood.

I decked him in the face again when a sharp, piercing pain struck my back.

We held our own, but the enemies had been too numerous. After a brief struggle, the bastards overpowered us, and we were on the ground, getting kicked and spit on. String Bean pulled a knife.

I covered my face and reached for my backpack. *They are going to kill us.* I flung my piece from the bag and viciously pistol-whipped him across his ribs.

I turned off the safety, cocked the hammer, and darted away with Tony.

I spun around to point it right back at the tall string bean, holding it at my hip for discretion.

To my amazement, our commotion drew zero attention.

Among the enemies, two were largely unscathed, but the string bean and Jordan Belfort-wannabe in the pink bathed in his own blood. "Gun! He's got a gun!" one of them gasped.

"What the fuck did I tell y'all? This is what happens when you think you can treat motherfuckers however you want! The world don't work that way!" I yelled. "Y'all better get the hell outta here. Them gators outside of town are hungry, and they ain't gonna leave evidence!"

"You won't use that," said Daddy's Money.

"I don't think you wanna find out," Tony snarled. "No witnesses. Let it go."

"You stupid motherfucker, we're from Chicago and, I swear to God, I will smoke you if you don't piss off! I will personally shit-fuck you with the barrel of this .44! Go! Get outta here!" I growled, my eyes wide and fierce.

"Let's go, dude, it's not worth it," one of them said—a stocky individual wearing a Red Sox shirt.

"Look at his eyes, he's on something. I don't like the look of this guy. We should go," said another.

"*Vae victis! Vae victis!*" I taunted them in ancient Latin for "woe to the vanquished."

They slowly backed away, petrified. I'm pretty sure the fat one in the Red Sox shirt wet himself.

A heart attack was imminent, and I perspired from head to toe. I tightly gripped the gun so it wouldn't slip. Bouts of nystagmus hit me, and my eyes flickered back and forth uncontrollably. The whole ordeal felt like an eternity, but it had been no more than a couple of minutes. Once a reasonably safe distance away, I pushed the hammer down, safety back on, and retired the gun into my backpack.

Was some booze and a little cocaine too much to ask for? This is exactly why you don't start trouble with random people. The stranger is capable of anything, but common sense is a pitiful fallacy, posing serious consequences for the arrogant and unprepared. Those drunken frat boys, likely from some East Coast state, had no idea they'd picked a fight with an armed and rolling drug fiend alongside his degenerate companion. When the Irishman and the Italian are fighting on the *same side*, the opposition is in a tremendous heap of peril. Especially if they've spent half their lives in a boxing ring.

Tony suffered a cut around his eye and some bruises on his arms. I was bruised up, but we were alive. Despite our gritty appearance and body aches, we walked on air hurrying back to Clara's. We embodied outlaws and reveled in our victory.

A few minutes later, Clara answered the door with a puzzled expression on her face. "The fuck happened to y'all?" she asked timidly. Her pupils replaced all traces of blue.

"We got into a fight, but we're okay."

"Well, come on back to the party, I have bandages."

"Thanks."

The party had tripled in size during our absence. David Bolton glanced over to me from across the room, and I grinned foolishly, giving him a nod, to which he responded by mouthing, *What the fuck?* He wouldn't be shocked. His ancestors were kicked out of Ireland for fighting.

Clara grabbed a bottle of vodka from the counter and motioned for us to follow. Alongside her was a short Asian girl, gorgeous, with long, wavy hair and big, brown eyes. She wore a Playboy crop top. "This is Vanessa. She's in med school at UNO."

"It's a pleasure meeting you under these circumstances. I like your shirt," I said.

"Yeah, you too. And thanks! Does it make me look glamorous?"

"Yes, it does."

"Tell us what happened," Clara commanded like a concerned mother.

Tony finally opened his mouth. "We saw some guys earlier today. They thought Joe was trying to pickpocket one of 'em. We almost scrapped right then and there until we defused the situation. So, on our way back from the car, we see 'em again and, this time, it's four-on-two. They crossed the street and immediately tried fighting us. We did everything we could to avoid it, but they wouldn't stop. We held them off for a bit, but there were too many of 'em. Not a fair fight."

Clara's expression exhibited horror. "So, how'd y'all get away?"

"So, we took out a couple of the bastards, but they overpowered us. I thought we were fixin' to die, so I pulled my piece on 'em."

"You pulled a gun on them?! Y'all have a gun with you?" Vanessa asked.

I did my best to sound reasonable. "We just traveled across the country, and I wasn't about to do it unarmed. I really didn't want to bring it, Clara, but I'm high as hell right now, and it seemed logical."

"I don't give a shit about the gun, Pat, I'm just glad y'all made it back okay. Why didn't you call me?"

"You know, I tried asking the fellas to give me a minute for a phone call but, for some reason, they wouldn't let it fly." My sarcasm couldn't be worse.

"Lord Almighty, Pat, always in some type of danger. But I know you didn't start it."

"Hell no, we didn't."

"What a bunch of jackasses," Vanessa said, "but you get a lot of those in New Orleans, and they come from all over."

"How's the drug?" Clara asked me. "I can see you're sweating a ton, obviously in part because it's hot out there and you were just in a fight."

"It's intense. I haven't been in control of my eyes for probably 20 minutes, but I feel like I can run through a wall."

"What's he on?" Vanessa asked with concern.

"Acid and molly," I replied. "And I've been drinking whiskey all day."

"Oh my God, are you insane?" she asked while patching up Tony.

"We're on vacation. Clara, could you please toss me some water?"

"Of course."

"Thanks, you're actually the best." *Thank Heaven for this woman*, I thought.

"I do what I can, Pat," she said, making her signature goofy face, crossing her eyes, and sticking her tongue out.

REDEMPTION

I thanked Vanessa for patching my wounds. She appreciated the gesture, and I impulsively hugged her—tightly. Getting taken care of by somebody in the depths of an intense roll elicits a pure, all-too-human affection. I told her that people like her in the medical field saved my life...

"It's my passion," she replied before heading out for a much-needed beverage.

However, one struggle ended, and another began. A concoction of chicken, whiskey, and stomach bile fired its way up my esophagus and I darted into the bathroom. I unleashed it all into the shitter.

"Oh fuck, he's throwing up, I'll leave this on the desk," Clara said outside the door. Tony muttered something inaudible, probably an "okay," and they both cleared out into the fray.

"Why do you do this to yourself?" I chuckled while wiping my mouth clean. *Going to strange places, huh?* I swished some mouthwash and spit into the sink. A tide of questions swept over me. I recall in April of 2019, a hooker on Bourbon Street spotted me getting blitzed with my dad, and laughed that he raised a monster and, apparently, she was right. Aren't we all monsters somewhere deep inside? We shouldn't deny it. By confronting the beast within, self-awareness peaks higher and higher. As flawed beings, the soul's journey has no ceiling. The trip manifested all the debauchery I'd engaged in for a decade... A savage peak, one I'll perhaps never meet again.

Leaving the bathroom felt like emerging from a bomb shelter. I slowly sipped the water, swished some mouthwash, and sprayed on some additional cologne I kept in my backpack. You can never go wrong with a couple strong sprays of Dolce & Gabbana. All alone, I inspected the gun I'd aimed with lethal intent only a half hour ago and, after spinning the cylinder, I didn't know whether to laugh or cry. My high, stupid-ass hadn't even reloaded it before leaving the car. I chalked it up as another lesson and, by the grace of God, there was no price to pay for the mistake, aside from a couple of cuts and bruises.

I guffawed at my foolishness and headed back into the party, reborn. After all, it was only 9 o'clock. In the middle of the living room, Clara was performing a strange, primitive dance as she confronted a roll of her own. "Animals" by Martin Garrix fulfilled the picture, and more partygoers poured in. Tony, Jack, Joe, and David conversed a meager distance away—their demeanor expressed mortification, guilt, and a hint of laughter.

"He did what?" Joe exclaimed before turning around to face me. "You pulled your piece on those guys?"

"They pulled a fucking knife! And I just realized—while sitting in the other room—it wasn't even loaded. I must've fired all six shots back in Colorado."

"You dumbass," Jack hollered.

My actions were so irredeemably foolish I couldn't even begin to defend myself. A crisis occurred, decisions were made, and they had consequences.

"What if a cop saw you?"

"I don't know, Joe, and can't tell, but there weren't any nearby. And I don't care to think about what would've happened. We—"

"The street was empty. Step out on the balcony, I bet you won't find a single person out there," Tony interrupted.

"Torres, man, I actually thought they would kill us, and I was tripping balls. I was fucked up. We held our own and mangled a couple of their faces, but the fuckers overwhelmed us. It was two-on-four, for Christ's sake. We've all heard of drunken fights where someone ends up dead, often unintentionally. It was either us or them, and I chose us."

"Y'all are really lucky," Jack said sternly. "But I'm glad everything went okay. Hopefully, they didn't go to any cops. They strike me as a few of them Back the Blue-types. Bootlickin' Yankees."

"I doubt it," Tony sighed. "They were fucked up, and they started it. I bet they had drugs on them, too. Besides, they had no idea where we were going."

"Where did it happen?"

"On the corner of Royal and Bienville, a few blocks away. Right near that old restaurant where we watched the Saints last November, Fish. We'll be fine."

"We should've been with you," Joe said guiltily. "You wouldn't have had to resort to that on your own. We easily could've taken them on."

"You best believe we would've whooped 'em," Jack chuckled.

Joe turned toward Tony. "You get your rum?"

"Yessir, but it's in the freezer. It was really warm from sitting in the car all day."

"Nice, we'll check on it in 30 minutes."

"I have the blow, though!" I howled.

"Good to hear, Morrison. I can use some. I'm pretty drunk and a kickstart would be nice," Joe replied.

"Let's go to Clara's room, there's a desk in there."

We navigated through the ocean of bodies toward the hall. With four years of college experience under my belt, I've developed a keen eye for the coke room. Every party has one. A lone bedroom where scruffy mobs of guys and their girlfriends file into, all credited to their desire for the uplifting high that white powder provides. I've snorted off all kinds of surfaces... Buck knives, fingers, desks, tables, floors, and books—the proudest of which was a copy of *Fear and Loathing in Las Vegas*. The Gonzo King's ghost smiled upon me.

Yes, one could say I've witnessed and participated in awkward situations and rituals known only to those who are insane to live. We huddled around the desk where my wounds had been tended to minutes before. "We'll cut it up into a few lines. Jack, you want some?" Joe offered.

"Fuck it. May as well, it's been a minute though."

Meanwhile, David leaned against the doorway. I was guilty, having put off saying hello for so long, but I'd been preoccupied explaining the disaster on the street. He wore a Colt .45 holstered at his hip, and my guilt over packing heat dissipated.

"David, how the hell are ya, brother? How's the crawfish farm?"

"I'm alright. Been chipping away at this whiskey all night. This summer's been a drag, but I'm hangin' in there. Believe it or not, the crawfish business has been solid. With everything closed down, people are having hella crawfish boils. Can't shut those down. The governor would be committing political suicide. I've seen your stories on Instagram. It looks like y'all been having one hell of a road trip."

"That's one way to put it. You have to hit the road one of these days, man."

"I drove out to the Carolinas last summer, and it was a blast. I love the mountains. I actually have a plan to hit all the national parks out West after I graduate."

"Fuckin' do it, David. You'll remember that trip for the rest of your life. Any national parks that you got in mind?"

"Oh, yeah. Yellowstone, Yosemite, and Joshua Tree are the first. There's so many options to choose from."

"We drove along the exterior of Joshua Tree a few days ago, before making our way here. It's gorgeous out there."

"I bet. It must've been hot as balls."

"115 degrees."

"Damn, I should go during the fall or winter."

"Bruh, you're from Alexandria, Louisiana. You're used to humid heat. You'll be fine."

"I guess, but I'm trying to get outta here. I want to move to the Carolinas or Colorado."

"Can't go wrong with those options. But tell me about that piece you got there on your right hip. A Colt?"

He cautiously released the piece from its holster. "Yessir. A .45, government edition. Hollow points. I usually don't like to keep a round chambered because I at least wanna warn someone before blastin' 'em with that big of a round."

"No matter where you shoot some bastard, they ain't gettin' back up. I've witnessed those things blow up a watermelon. I've done so with my .44 Magnum as well."

"Fuckin' right, Morrison. I actually started to alternate my round in the clip. First shot is a hollow point, and the second, a full metal jacket. The first round is always intended for a visible target. The full metal jacket's there in case they're behind a wall or door."

"Them hollow points do more damage, but those full metal jackets will go through anything. I dig your strategy, brother, I'm takin' notes."

"Be my guest, I'm glad I can help—"

"Morrison, we got 'em all set up!" Tony shrieked.

"I'll be right there. You want some cocaine?"

A look of intense contemplation flared across his face. "I have a drug test on Monday. I can't even smoke right now, it blows."

"I feel that, man. Well, don't mind if I do."

Tony handed me a rolled twenty, and we snorted our lines. I gummed the remaining residue, grabbing the bag as Clara stumbled inside, holding a bottle of tequila.

"What've we got goin' on in here?" She muttered like a mother does after catching her son cursing up a storm of racial slurs in an Xbox Live lobby.

"You want some?" I asked her as other guys scurried back into the party.

"Do I? Give me the dollar."

"Hold up, I'll dump some of this stuff and give you a line." I poured out a modest pile and cut it with my driver's license. "Cocaine Blues" by Johnny Cash fired from Joe's phone. "Here you go, Clara."

She hungrily railed the line. "This is really good stuff, where'd y'all get it?"

"Vegas. We had some left over and weren't sure where we'd go after Arizona, so we decided to come here. That's when I texted you."

"Well, I'm glad y'all decided to come to NOLA. I missed you, Pat."

"I missed you too, Clara. I'll say, our adventures never disappoint. You're the reason I was able to spend my 21st in this city. When I mentioned it to my friends in Chicago, I became the envy of the neighborhood."

She made the same old goofy expression she makes when flattered or embarrassed. "I do my best. But tell me about your trip! Joe mentioned the three of you had an awesome time in the desert and in Vegas."

"Mhm, but those are only a couple of things."

"Hold up one minute. You need a drink. I'll be back."

"I'll come with. You wanna talk on the balcony?"

"Sure, my dear."

I stuffed the bag into my pocket and followed her through the hall into the kitchen, and she poured a red solo cup two-fifths of the way up with Wild Turkey, finishing it off with heavy ice. She warmed my heart because friends who understand your drinking habits are a rare blessing. I thanked her once more for the hospitality and, from there, we settled on the balcony. I recanted what we'd done. The horrific ecstasy of my shrooms trip through the Rocky Mountains, the lessons we learned in the Land of the Diné, our reflections and political discussions in Vegas, and the psychedelic disaster in Los Angeles.

She listened attentively as she always does, an increasingly rare but attractive quality in this technology-driven world. Within minutes, the conversations gravitated elsewhere.

"You seeing anybody?" she asked. Clara's the type of girl who goes straight for the throat in conversations, another quality I admire.

"Nah. Just Valentina, the girl from Argentina I was with in Cordoba. She came to Baton Rouge to see me in February before the pandemic, but she's gone now. I really liked her," I sighed, sipping the whiskey. "What about you?"

"There's a boy. He's working, established, and actually has an idea what he wants to do with his life."

"Hell, I love to hear it. Y'all gone out at all, or is this still in its infancy?"

"We've gone on a couple of dates around town. Nothing's official yet. But I can tell he's different from most guys. He's actually interesting."

"What's his name?"

"William."

"Well, I'm wishing the best. For both of you. I would say he better treat you good, but I have no fear. You are a strong Irish woman, Clara. Hell, a tough Southern gal, too. That's a lethal one-two combo right there."

She laughed.

"Do you feel passion when y'all are together?" I asked.

"For once in my life, I do. It's scary. The past couple of relationships I've been in never came close, and I'm glad it finally seems to be here."

"Music to my ears. You deserve all the love you can get, Clara, but remember this. Never can there be love without passion," I said, reaching into my pocket for the one-hitter.

"I'm not sure what it is about you, Pat, but you have a way with words. A way most people don't. You have a beautiful soul, and I want you to know that. You changed your major, what? Three times? What do you plan on doing?"

"I'm nothing special, Clara. I take the love I've been given and do what I can to pass it on. I'm really nothing special, simply a drugged-out college graduate who is terrified of the future, and according to the views of some people, 'doesn't want to work.' But something will happen eventually. Out in the desert, I learned a lot about myself. All three of us did. Away from endless tides of busybodies, I found music in the silence. I'm gonna be a writer. As a little kid, I wrote stories all the time and, somewhere along the line, I stopped.

"I've written a couple hundred poems since the pandemic started. I think I have a good direction to go in. I only need to act. I'm also eyeing law school somewhere down the line. Not necessarily to be an attorney, but for another option or credential, if you will. Or maybe journalism, like Hunter S. Thompson or Joan Didion. In the meantime, I'm getting rid of these student loans. Without debt, I can go wherever I want. Maybe I'll be the homeless king of Venice Beach or the desert. Something about waking up in L.A. and falling asleep in Reno one day, and then another town the next sounds edifying. I can only imagine the people I'll meet and the places I can see. I learned at too young of an age that I can die at any time, and until the hour of my death comes, whenever it may be, I'll know I lived a full, free, and adventurous life. It's time for the outlaws to come home."

"I think you'd be great at whatever you set your mind to. You mentioned passion a minute ago. You have tons, don't ever lose it. I'll always be rooting for ya. Whatever you leave to the world will be something special. You have a beautiful soul, Patricius."

"And I'm the one who's good with words? I feel the same about you, too. You're creative, you're smart, and you're gorgeous. Your heart is a rare one, Clara. And mine sings whenever we're together. Thank you for the kind words. They keep me going."

She pulled me close and wrapped her arms around me.

"You want a hit of this?" I asked, motioning to the one-hitter.

"Of course, I was waiting for you to make an offer!"

I packed the weed and gave her the lighter. "Shit, Clara, *taking all my damn drugs from me!*"

"You jackass, this is my damn apartment. I spotted you on some molly!"

We cackled hysterically and, in the midst of our heart-to-heart, I nearly forgot about the coke in my pocket.

"Let's do a bump."

"I'm always up for it, you dingus," she replied, making a squeak-like sound she frequently makes when giddy.

We both are well-connected to the children within us. I summoned the keys from my left pocket and dug into the bag. "Here you go, be careful," I cautioned, handing her the key.

She took a big snort, not leaving behind so much as a speck of white and handed them back. "Don't mind if I do."

I plunged the key into the bag, took my bump, and followed with a swig of whiskey.

"Well, I'll be heading back inside," Clara said, getting up with her drink.

"I'll be in there soon."

The temperature soared in the 90s all day but, in the moonlight, it cooled and developed into a fine summer night. I was happy. The night air pressed gently on my face. Balconies across the street and flickering lights outside their doors complimented the mood. The molly remained potent, but I stabilized, meaning it was time to drink again.

We established an uncommon connection from the day we met, Clara and I. It's a pure, natural love and understanding that's hard to sever. When you find those people, hold on for dear life because, no matter where you are, you're home whenever they're around.

I thought about my friends. My family. The world around me. We're losing something as human beings. The downward spiral planted itself in the 20th century and is rapidly accelerating in this one. Civilization mass-produces people for a workforce that too often forces us to compromise ourselves to an intolerable degree. We surrender our dreams for less, for survival, and they become ashes and dust alongside us. Our best solution to this dilemma is to dream big. A depressingly high number of people find their livelihoods meaningless, according to a variety of research I've read. The school-to-work pipeline was something I dreaded falling into. Many academics and nutritionists argue this sedentary way of life is primarily responsible for the poor health among people not just here in the States but across the West.

There's nothing *wrong* with following the straight and narrow path, but too many people are left behind. Not everyone can conform to a lifestyle in service of neoliberalism. Thus, a premise of the English Existentialist Colin Wilson's masterpiece, *The Outsider:* "The Outsider is a man who cannot live in the comfortable, insulated world of the bourgeois, accepting what he sees and touches as reality. 'He sees too deep and too much,' and what he sees is essentially chaos."

More paths are needed. We possess more control over our destinies than we're conditioned to believe. There's no need to sell our everlasting souls for the almighty dollar. Every person, at some point, should say, "I am *me*. And I will be who I am." The bourgeois machine, through the apparatus and its infinite levers, drains the creativity right out of our heads. It is plentiful inside of us as children, where we are less anxious and paranoid. It comes from our minds and souls, only to be snuffed out as we journey into adulthood.

The system teaches us to subdue our natural instincts. Surrender your autonomy in your prime, they tell us, don't explore the world or value your health. We live in a madhouse where hordes of people are degraded into zombies who think nothing, feel nothing, and see nothing beyond their smartphones, TVs, and careers. The free American is a dying animal. I can't help but be tormented by the insane horrors of this monotonous order. We fear Orwell's world, but it's Huxley's we're living in.

The pandemic worsened these horrors into freefall. I've heard of *CDC* reports claiming that more than a quarter of people between the ages of 18-24 considered killing themselves at some point between March and August of 2020[11]. Long before the massive winter surge of the virus to boot. The CDC also reported that three-quarters of young adults struggled with drugs or mental health at the time. Three-quarters! I don't prefer anecdotes when establishing a point, but there's no reason to doubt those numbers based on personal observations. Obviously, the pandemic played a role, but society has been sick long before anyone had any idea about COVID-19. Decadent trends gained tremendous steam throughout the 2010s. And the pandemic, gasoline on the fire.

The party raged inside as I smoked on the balcony, enslaved by my own mind, as usual. The dark, empty streets below rested silent. A meager four months earlier, a different story would be told. I turned on "White Rabbit" by Jefferson Airplane. It's a favorite of mine because of its message, exposing the naïveté of parents. Using *Alice in Wonderland* as a metaphor and Grace Slick's powerful voice, it scolds authority for telling reality-bending fairytales to children, only to slide into a fucking panic attack when those kids grow up, succumb to curiosity, and indulge in psychedelic drugs. Jefferson Airplane's music was as revolutionary as the era itself. Nothing beats blasting *Surrealistic Pillow* while going 95 on a desert highway.

As the song drew to a close, Joe drunkenly stumbled onto the balcony. He held Tony's rum bottle. "How are you feeling?" he asked.

"Feelin' alright... I'm wired. The acid is negligent at his point. I'm still rollin' a bit, but I have a steady buzz going. What about you?"

"Wait, you're rolling?" he asked with a surprised grin.

"Yeah, Clara gave me some molly shortly after we showed up. I was on the come-up when those pricks tried jumping Tony and me."

"I can't even imagine how you must've felt. You stuck up a bunch of frat kids while rolling with an unloaded

---

[11] Leidman, Eva, etc. "COVID Trends." *MMWR Early Release*, Jan. 2021.

gun." He laughed hysterically, and I couldn't help but join in. "I'm drunk and wired," he said, answering my question. "Wanna smoke?"

"I'll never turn that down!" I packed the one-hitter and handed it over. He ripped it clean, and I took mine while Grace Slick's howls tripped us out.

"Play 'Somebody to Love,'" Joe requested, and I obliged.

Out of the sky, childhood nostalgia captivated me with its warm claws. Joe and Tony also gave in to yearning for a time gone forever. It's an inevitable consequence of traveling with lifelong friends. Either the best or worst conversations begin with the phrase, "Remember when."

"Remember when we climbed that really tall tree near Olympia Park as kids, and that random guy ran out of his house and yelled at us to get down?" I asked him.

"Hell yeah, I do. We could see the Sears Tower and the whole city."

"Yeah, you almost fell but I moved my leg against the branch to break the fall."

"Damn, man, I remember. It was a beautiful day, too, not a cloud in the sky. We were like nine or ten maybe? Man, I loved those summers back then."

"I tell ya, Joe, before that miserable scumbag ran out of his house to yell at us, sitting on top of that tree was one of the most peaceful, ecstatic moments in my life. The only other times I've felt anything remotely close to it were on this trip."

"Amen. These have been the best days of my life. I understand our journey's not over yet. We can do a hundred more road trips and bring along whoever wants to come with."

"Tara and her friends want to come with us next time. Nicole's been Snapping me about it, too. There's interest."

Tara's my sister.

"We can get a whole caravan!" The enthusiasm in his eyes was contagious. "I can't wait until our student loans are paid off. We'll have nothing holding us back."

"Truth, Joe. I'm serious when I tell y'all I'mma just say, fuck it, and live out of a car and write after my loans are paid and I have a little money saved. I've been writing some poetry since the pandemic started, but I want to do more. I'll go back to the desert, live at Venice Beach, and travel the country, along the oceans and over the hills and mountains, writing nonstop. I will be free."

"Dude, we're down."

"Sounds like a dream. Y'all sounded excited when I hinted at the idea back in Slab City. If all three of us can do that, it would be amazing... Can I get a swig of the rum? My drink's empty."

"For sure." He poured the golden nectar into my cup.

"I anticipate and loathe the future, Joe. But even if life's meaningless, we'll carry on. I'll make my own damn purpose, and you will, too."

"Existentialism helped save my life, Pat. I was in some really dark places during the lockdowns. All I did was go to class from home and answer people's dumb questions working at Costco. You know, I've been familiar with the stoics for years, and I first read Nietzsche last summer, but I hit the ground hard since the pandemic started."

"Relatable. Granted, I started the classics years ago, and read my first book by Nietzsche around Christmas in 2018. *Human, All Too Human*. But, like you, Joe, the pandemic had me pursue the existentialist rabbit hole. And it sure as fuck is one hell of a rabbit hole."

"Our questions about the world remain unanswered, but there's a clarity the philosophy gives you. You're at peace, and all of a sudden, you realize it's okay to ask those questions about life, about society, and the world we live in as a whole. It's okay to feel like shit sometimes."

"Well said, my brother. We wouldn't be the people we are today without these books. I look around and can see something amazing in every little detail. A tree branch, a snow-covered mountaintop, a grain of sand, or tall grass blowing in a breeze. Part of it definitely comes from the fact that I'm not supposed to be here, but all these books and experiences add up. We're becoming who we are."

"You're right for the most part, Morrison. But you're wrong about one thing."

"And what would that be?"

"You *are* supposed to be here, Patricius. You survived all that Hell for a reason. You're alive, and I'm happy as hell you are. This world is better with you in it."

I choked up. Nobody's ever told me something so incredible. A tear streaked down my face. "Bring it in, you bastard. I guess I am supposed to be here after all. I really am in this bitch, huh?" I placed my arm around his shoulder and, with a heavy heart, looked to the sky and said thanks to Whoever's up there.

"You wanna do a line?" he asked.

"Sure."

We organized two lines on his phone, snorting up every last bit. By now "Not to Touch the Earth" by The Doors screeched from mine. I focused on Joe. He had a strange, melancholy expression. The same one on mine, too. We were a far cry from the starry-eyed, blue-collar Catholic school kids we grew up as. At one point, all three of us were altar boys.

How did we get here? We grew up in the 2000s and rode our bikes to the park free from phone screens. We chewed on boxes of candy and bags of beef jerky. Back in those days, the sun shined bright, and summer lasted forever until it didn't. Our innocence is buried in a past that won't return.

My journey led me through years of Catholic masses, anointed by gospel choirs in young adulthood, and transformed by psychedelic existentialism. The metamorphosis had neared completion. For the entire journey, we behaved like lunatics—a drug- and alcohol-guzzling Ed, Ed, 'n' Eddy. Nietzsche says, while avoiding the monsters of existence, we must see to it that we don't become monsters. Have we made monsters of ourselves, behaving so savagely? To some people, we certainly did. But to others, we were nothing more than young Americans, reckless and cutting loose during a difficult time.

Here it comes. I'm rambling on about something deep, something I don't quite understand. Perhaps this problem is a byproduct of growing up in a country, a world, dominated by people who take themselves too seriously. In combating the wars of being human in a chaotic world, the best we can do is laugh, because any other reaction will kill us quicker.

"BLAAAAHHHHHHH WOOOOHHHHH!"

"The fuck?" I asked, not knowing whether to laugh or leap into action.

"Let's check it out, it's coming from inside."

It was Shane. He was whooping and hollering next to his boyfriend, Dre. They became trusted friends of mine during my final days at LSU. Two thrill-chasing guys from South Louisiana. One White, the other Black. And they fell in love. You're *always* in for a fun time when they're around. Dre brings a careless, laid-back vibe because he's constantly stoned. Shane, on the other hand, will drink whatever alcohol is in front of him. And he'll do any drug. Sometimes he's defeated and will knock out like a log within an hour. Other times, he'll throw back a gallon of booze and smoke until the break of dawn. You never know what you'll get with him, and it makes him a hell of a guy to be around.

"Shane, don't wear yourself out now, boy, it's only midnight!" I yelled from across the room.

"Holy shit, Morrison. Clara told me you were here. Where the fuck have you been?"

"On the balcony, ripping blow and drinking whiskey."

"Damn, in the leopard-print, too. *Pat Morrison doing drugs? I'd never imagine!*"

"You know me well, Shane. Where'd Dre go?"

"He's rolling a blunt by the counter. You want in?"

"I'm good for the time being. I smacked the one-hitter a bunch outside. Will y'all be smoking again later?"

"I'm almost positive."

"Bet, homie, let's do a shot."

"Hell yeah!"

We strolled to the counter and poured some Ole No. 7 into a couple fresh glasses. "We should do a toast. We haven't drank together in a long-ass time. Dre, you say hello to Pat? He was on the balcony this whole time."

"Let's drink, I know you'll gulp any shot like water, Morrison," Dre said.

"Yessir, let's drink! Raise 'em up, fellas!"

I'm unstoppable.

"To good times and better friends!" Dre shouted as our glasses clinked and warm whiskey burned our throats, throwing us further into a frenzy of bottomless intoxication.

"Lord Almighty, I've missed you fuckers."

"We've missed you too, man, you should come down more often. Dalton and Kenzie miss you. So does El Paso Jessie. Everybody in Baton Rouge right now does."

"Damn, Dre, I wish they were here. I talked with David earlier. He says the crawfish farm is doing well in spite of the pandemic."

"I'll talk to him. We should get a crawfish boil going next season!"

"I'd drive, fly, run, or crawl down here for a crawfish boil, Shane." The aroma of spices, shrimp powder, and the red mustache the seasoning always leaves on my face elates me. "By the way, have y'all seen Jack?"

"Not recently," Dre said. "I saw him with Vanessa probably a half hour ago."

I grinned. "Good for him. I'll see the bastard when I see him, I guess. What about Raven? I was told she'd be here."

"She worked late. I called her and she left Baton Rouge at 8:30. She'll be here soon."

"Bet. She's always a ton of fun. I miss her dearly."

"We're gonna head outside to smoke this blunt. Are you sure you're good on it?" Shane asked.

"Yeah, I'm gonna stroll around and drink more. Enjoy the smoke, y'all."

I abandoned the comfort of the kitchen counter. Everywhere, people screeched. Polo G's voice raised the damn roof. Clouds of smoke from vapes, cigarettes, and joints wafted through the air. Bottles rattled and clinked. Pure, uninterrupted disorder. Everybody was high. Everybody was wasted. The fleur-de-lis on the wall above the TV shone like a lonely star, and I was happy to be there. Tony double-fisted a couple of Coors Lites on the couch.

Beautiful women in bellbottom jeans were everywhere. I discovered an island overflowing with muses. Their music was sweet and content. No vibrations of death. My mojo was on, and I could pull my pistols *and* whistle Dixie at the same time. Muddy Waters' ghost could've knighted me at that moment—somebody who you can always rely on for a good time. Cocaine-induced superpowers escalated the intensity. *I'm Caesar himself. No, I'm not, I've simply read the Romans to the point of exhaustion... The voice in the back of my head begs to differ. Maybe in some strange way, I really am Julius Caesar, crossing the Rubicon and vanquishing all challenges and enemies... Nietzsche advises us to be Caesar but to have the soul of Christ. What can I do but wonder? Tonight is my night.*

Strobe lights gleamed and beamed through the dark room, changing from green to blue, red, orange, and yellow on the walls. We were radically alive and wildly drunk. I finally located Jack. He sat, laughing with Vanessa on the couch. Across from them, two dreadheads from Alabama jeered and chain-smoked blunts. Over in the corner, a tall, skinny guy in an LSU football jersey hit on a charming blonde. She wore a pink top and bellbottoms. Their conversation was lifeless.

"So... Uh... You go to school here?" he asked.

"No," she said. "I'm graduated."

"Oh... Cool... Where at? What was your major?"

"Tulane... Nursing..."

"Oh, so what do you do?"

"I work at the hospital."

"Nice, how's that?"

"It's okay..."

Jesus Christ, take the hint, man. I concealed my chuckle, and nobody noticed through the laughs, hollers, and House music. I've witnessed this process a million times. I'll see some airhead hitting on a poor, pretty girl, interrogating her with boring questions about school or work, as if she isn't asked those *same* questions a million times at parties or bars.

Across the room from those two love birds, three people drank and talked.... I should say two... A girl and her friend faced each other and there stood a short, chubby, inebriated guy wearing a dad hat. He looked like a fucking narcotics agent. Or like a salivating dog waiting for a treat. He caressed his stubby little hand on the one girl's ass, and she repeatedly moved it away. Every impulse compelled me to go over there and crack a bottle over his head.

It didn't last because Clara called my name. "Get your ass over here. We're doing shots! Jack! Vanessa!"

Again? I thought. I nodded at Joe, who chiefed a cigarette a few feet away.

"Fuck it, I'm down," he said.

We reverted through the packed living room to the kitchen counter by Clara, Jack, Tony, and Vanessa.

"Thanks again for patching me up," I told Vanessa.

"Don't mention it. You feeling better?"

"I can run through a fuckin' wall!"

"Good." She smiled.

"What are we shooting?" Joe asked as Clara poured shots.

"Those motherfuckers on the street," Jack joked. "But wait, Morrison's dumb-ass forgot to load the gun!"

Once again, I couldn't defend myself.

"Tequila!" Clara yelled like a child.

"Fuck, it's game over," I said to him.

"No better way to end it."

"I love life!" Tony bellowed at the top of his lungs.

We echoed the phrase and drank to existence.

A Doomed Romance

Once the tequila settled in my stomach, I glanced across the counter. I heard a *SMACK* and saw the stubby guy rubbing his face as the woman he'd tormented roared at him like a lion. *Good for her.* I was then astonished by a girl I hadn't seen at the party. I was bewildered how I never noticed her because my jaws collapsed to the floor. She had long, wavy hair like one of the sisters from Heart. Golden blonde. She was tall, tan, and had earthy-brown eyes. An hourglass figure. She could fill a pair of jeans. I melted. From her angular face and red blouse, down to her Chuck Taylors, I fell head-over-heels.

Fuck. I'm going to Memphis tomorrow. But I couldn't conceal my emotions, and I was unbelievably turned on. "Clara," I called. "Clara!"

"Yeah?"

"Who's that girl who took shots with us? The tall one with the blonde hair?"

"Evangeline. She's here with her sister who's a friend of mine. Why? You like her?"

"Lord, have mercy, she's Aphrodite—I have to meet her."

"Okay, loverboy, I'll introduce you."

"Thanks. I'm simpin' hard, but I can't fuckin' control myself."

"Hey, Evangeline!" Clara drunkenly shouted.

"Yes?"

"Come over here, I have a good friend of mine I'd like you to meet!"

Evangeline strolled over to us.

"Fortune favors the bold," I whispered to myself, quoting Virgil.

"This is Pat Morrison. We graduated from LSU."

"Nice to meet you, Pat."

"The pleasure is mine, Evangeline."

"Please, call me Eva. I'm guessing Pat is short for Patrick?"

"Close but no cigar. Patricius."

"Now that's a name you don't hear every day."

"I mean, it's the Latinized version. You're right in a way. My folks thought it'd be a good idea to give me the name that Saint Patrick actually went by. He was Roman and all."

"How creative." She grinned.

"So, you have a last name, Eva?"

"Castille."

"Evangeline Castille... Now that's a pretty name. Are you French?"

She gave a flattered smile. "Thanks. And yes. Cajun. But my granny's a full-blooded Choctaw. You know, *Patricius Morrison* also has a ring to it."

Now I was the one blushing. "Pat and Eva," I said jovially.

"I'll let y'all talk," Clara said before vanishing.

"So, Eva, with a name like yours, you're from Louisiana, I presume?"

"Yes. I grew up in a small town outside of Lafayette."

"Which one?"

"Port Barre."

"For real?"

"Mhm, why?"

"My boys and I drove through there yesterday on the way back from California."

"Oh my God, you're kidding."

"Nope. Stopped at Billy's in Krotz Springs for boudin balls and some cracklins."

"I fucking love Billy's!"

"It's fire. I got the ones with melted pepperjack inside."

Her eyes sparkled. "Those are my favorite! I can't believe you're familiar with Porte Barre and Billy's. Where'd you grow up? Are you and your friends from California?"

"We're from Chicago—except my roommate, Jack. He's from Mississippi and is still living at the apartment in Baton Rouge before the lease ends. I lived here in Louisiana for a few years while attending LSU. We drove to L.A. and decided to come here before heading back up North."

"Fuck, that's a drive."

"Nothin' we can't handle," I boasted. "You wanna sit somewhere quiet and talk?"

"Let's do it. Where to?"

"The balcony's pretty nice. I was sitting out there for a while earlier."

"One second, I need to pour myself another drink."

"Me too," I said, despite having a full one in my hand. I gripped the nearest whiskey bottle and poured a little more.

"Let's go," she said.

"I'll clear the way."

We forced our way through the mass of sweaty bodies. I was terrified yet ecstatic. *How have I gotten a girl like this to talk to me?* I'm a fairly confident man, but this woman was different. Thank God we passed through Cajun country. I opened the door for her, and the midnight air cooled even more. Nobody was out there but us.

"Thanks," she said.

"Mama raised a gentleman," I warmly replied.

"You don't sound like you're from the North."

"I get that a lot. Since I was a kid, I've wanted to live in the South. I began to change the way I spoke when I was 12 after a trip to Memphis and San Antonio."

"Interesting you wanna move back here," she said, taking a seat. "But let me get it straight... You're from the Midwest, look like a California boy, but sound like you're from down here. A real American boy, huh?"

"Star-spangled! But what do you mean? About wanting to move back here?"

"It's not common for somebody from up North to want to live in Louisiana, I guess."

"Sure, this place has its problems, but, in my opinion, it's the most underrated state in the union."

"Well, I love it here, and I don't think I could live anywhere else. So, what are you doing now that you're done with school?"

"Livin' with the folks, paying off my loans."

"I feel that."

"Where did you go? You look young."

"I just turned 19. I'm about to be a sophomore at ULL, but I'll always be a Tigers fan."

"Ah, the Ragin' Cajuns. I'm glad to hear you're pullin' for the good guys."

"I was at Mike's when we won the natty."

"I've drank there a million times, but I was here for the game. My boy Jack was actually at the Superdome though."

"Jealous."

"Apparently, the Superdome will soon be the Caesars Palace Superdome."

"I heard! Isn't Harrah's getting converted into a Caesars?"

"I think so. If the rumors are true, it'll be a damn fine investment for the city."

"It totally would! I really want to live here someday, but only for a few years. Have fun in my twenties before settling down."

"Well, Eva, I'm convinced we're the same person because I have similar plans. New Orleans is unlike any other place. It's a city constantly under siege. America's very own Pompeii or Jerusalem. A lively city of artists, gangsters, and dreamers guided only by starlight and a taste for broken bottles and colorfully dark history. After I chase a few goals, I, too, intend to settle here to ride out my twenties."

"Eloquently put! I've lived in Louisiana my whole life but haven't been here more than a few times. But every time I do, I fall more in love with it."

"I relate. There's something special about this town for damn sure. However, I digress. You're having fun tonight?"

"It's the most fun I've had since the pandemic started. I stayed on campus as long as I could until my parents made me go back to their place. This summer's been boring. My ex broke up with me a couple of months ago, and I've been putting myself back together ever since."

"A lot of people feel that way. It's worse here because the cases are high."

"It's hard to imagine things getting better any time soon."

"When the world goes to shit, we have to make our own fun. It's easier said than done, but it's possible."

"How've you managed?"

"Playing softball with my friends, house parties like this one, and tons of reading and writing."

"You read and write?"

"Yes. Nietzsche, Hunter S. Thompson, James Baldwin, Dante, Homer... A shit ton of others too."

"Oh, Lord, that's a lot."

"Yes, it is. Do you like to read at all?"

"Yes, actually. I've read almost everything Shakespeare's ever written."

"Okay, now that is impressive. I read *Julius Caesar*. *MacBeth* too. Do you have a favorite?"

"*Romeo and Juliet* is my favorite because of the love story, but, for rhetoric, I have to say *King Lear*."

"I need to refresh myself."

"I recommend you do, Pat. You said you write?"

"Mhm." I nodded. "I've tested the waters with some poetry, but I want to explore becoming a novelist. I wrote a few poems out in the desert last week."

"That's awesome. There aren't many guys out there who write. Would you mind reading me one?"

"I sure can." I recited a poem I wrote while stargazing in Monument Valley.

I loved you sincere
in lands distant and near.
It's frightening how time flies,
how a mighty flame dies.
In this life I've been through much;
I've seen enough,
heard enough,
and hated enough,
But haven't loved enough.
As I fixed my eyes
to the bluest of skies,
I wondered what I'd tell The Lord when he asks me, Why?
To you who I love, I say,
Another world awaits.
I hope to see you there
so don't be late.

"You wrote that? It's beautiful," she said after a brief silence. "You have a way with words, I'll give you that."

"Thanks. It comes from my soul."

"So romantic."

"I can't help it. Can I tell you something?"

"Yes?"

"Your ex fucked up bigtime."

"Why do you say that?"

"Because I think you're lovely. You read, you listen attentively, and, I can't explain it, but I'm a sucker for girls with brown eyes." *Lord, have mercy on my wicked soul. Intentions are too obvious.*

"No boy's ever spoken to me the way you do."

"The reason is in your sentence, Evangeline."

"Explain."

"You said no boy has ever spoken to you the way I do. It's because they were boys. They weren't men."

She moved her hand up my thigh.

I broke out in a sweat. I slid closer to her.

"And you are?"

"Only one way to find out." By then, her hand found its way to my chest, and we were face-to-face. "May I?"

"Shut up and do it already, Patricius."

I pulled her body close to mine and gave her a kiss. I either became clinically insane or a chorus of angels sang gospel hymns from above.

She whispered something to me in French—game over. A full erection the size of Lake Michigan formed in my shorts. Our lips locked. I tasted her lipstick, sweet as sugar cane. I caressed her lower back as she ran her tiny, fragile fingers through my hair. For several minutes, we made out, and I sensed her hands gliding down my abdomen, toward my pants.

I couldn't fight it anymore. *Are we about to fuck on this balcony? Fucking outdoors?* If you've done such a deed, congratulations, you're a different breed of cat. Between public parks at 3 AM in Argentina and road head on I-44 outside Claremore, Oklahoma, I'm no stranger to copulating in public. But this particular situation was too risky. Inside, a hundred bodies partied, and, at any moment, we'd be busted.

"You wanna dance inside?" I asked.

"Yes! I've been in need of a dance partner!"

"Lovely."

We went inside and danced together as if we'd done so before. Unfortunately, I'm not gifted with the rhythm my father perfected while listening to *West Side Soul* in the '60s and '70s. But it didn't matter because Eva and I locked together, and we found a natural rhythm, spinning each other in circles, kissing and holding each other close. I swept her off the ground and spun her around as she giggled. Her bright red lipstick smeared around my mouth and cheeks. I didn't care.

She attempted to teach me a country-ass dance I embarrassed myself trying to master. Better luck next time. I've danced with plenty of women, but the vibrations with her were different. Never before had it felt so right, free of anxiety. Tony, double-fisting drinks, nodded a salute, and I winked back. In the middle of our fun, somebody nudged my shoulder.

Raven! She had finally arrived. "Hey motherfucker, I missed you!" she roared, clasping her arms around me.

"Raven DuFresne! How I've missed you!" I lifted her off the ground.

Her surname is DuFresne, like Tim Robbins' character in *The Shawshank Redemption*.

"Who might this be?" she asked in her South Louisiana accent.

"I'm Evangeline."

"It's a pleasure meeting you, queen. When did y'all meet?"

"Tonight." She blushed.

"Pat is an amazing friend, and he can write a damn good poem!"

"I know, he read me one earlier. It was beautiful!"

"I'll let y'all two keep dancing. I had to say hello."

"It's nice meeting you, Raven. I'm sure we'll hang out before the night's over."

"Absolute bet!" She hugged both of us and commanded Shane and Dre to do shots with her. "Shane, baby, get Dre's ass over here. We're shooting tequila!"

"She seems like a lot of fun!" Evangeline exclaimed.

"Oh, you have no idea. I've known Raven for hardly a year. Parties and bars ain't the same without her."

"I believe it!"

I crashed into a wall where I could no longer subdue my biological impulses. I wanted to connect with her in the most natural and vulnerable way. "Let's kick this up a level and go somewhere we can be more alone," I suggested.

"Yes!" She whispered in my ear, "I want you inside me... But where could we go?"

"We should have a couple of options."

She grabbed ahold of my hand. The only place that came to mind was the bathroom I took the molly in. Or a guest room, if possible. I fumbled around with a couple of doors in the hallway. Door number one led to a closet. The bathroom was occupied by somebody throwing up. Third time proved a charm. I knocked and not a sound came from the other side. I twisted the doorknob. A dark, empty room. But to our pleasure, it had a queen-sized bed. She shut the door and locked it.

The lights remained off, but I heard her undressing. I followed suit. The opening of "Electric Feel" by MGMT vibrated the entire apartment. In a matter of seconds, our lips found each other. We stood in the blackness, naked as the day we were born. I again lifted Eva off her feet and kissed her and she clung to me as if dangling from a cliff. I'd never let go.

We clutched each other on the bed while I stroked her. We locked lips again. Foreplay is important, but it got to the point where the ante had to be upped. I slid on the lone contraceptive I always store in my wallet. At that moment, she invited me inside. Her nails dug into my back and left red trenches. She placed one of her hands in mine. With her other, she grabbed my silver chain. Her shrieks and moans told me I was doing not only well, but unexpectedly well. In both English and French!

We smoothly switched positions over and over again. For an ambiguous period, we shared a beautifully painful passion that was completely foreign to us. She was closer and closer with each thrust of my body. Me too. *This exchange of good ole fashion free love is the best I've ever had, and it scares the shit out of me. Why do I fall so easily? Why am I like this?* I considered it obvious she felt the same because her body shook in erotic spasms the way a woman's does during an earth-shattering orgasm. Her French turned me on with ferocity. Despite suffering from the curse of a high orgasm threshold, bolts of lightning fired away, and we crashed together in ecstasy.

"No guy's ever done that before..." She gasped.

"Done what?"

"Made me come."

"Nobody? Never?"

"Not until tonight." She grinned, placing her hand on my chest. "You're good. I'll be sore for a week."

"To be honest, most of us guys are in it for ourselves when we fuck. It's our dirty little not-so-secret because you ladies know damn well how shitty we can be. Sex isn't a one-way street. It's supposed to be spiritual... Intimacy in its purest, most vulnerable form. Bonding hormones are intensely released. There's a reason it's sometimes called 'mating.' It took me a couple of years, but I think I've figured it out. I've read a few books and had enough practice. You should be proud yourself. Probably nine out of ten times, I don't finish. I usually can't help it."

"You are a rare find, Patricius Morrison. I can't explain it, but I just feel safe with you."

"That's the best thing a woman can tell me. In the best possible world, we'd all feel comfortable together. One can dream."

Her heart pulsated against mine. She played with my hair. *I'd lay here next to her forever if possible.* Beneath our skin, two skeletons, two hearts pounded together. We found each other, if only for a short period of time. To our dismay, the moment didn't last. A knock banged at the door.

"Morrison, you in there?" It was Joe.

"Yeah, gimme a second."

How the fuck does he know we're in here? I nearly tripped over myself in the dark but found the light switch. "Damn. It appears my friends are lookin' for me."

"It's okay. My sister's probably worried about me too."

"What's her name, by the way?"

"Samantha. She's out there somewhere."

"We can get dressed and I'll help you find her."

"Sounds good."

Within seconds, our clothes were back on, and I opened the door for her. I wiped away the lipstick stains. Joe sheepishly leaned against the wall with a lascivious smile. He was curious as to my whereabouts. I introduced him to Evangeline and alerted him of our mission to locate Samantha.

"What does she look like?" he asked.

"Short, tan, blonde, wearing a yellow tank top and a cowboy hat," she replied.

"I saw her talking to Clara on my way over here. By the front door."

"There she is!" Eva exclaimed. "Samantha!"

"There you are, girl. I was about to grab some friends and look for you outside!" Samantha shouted through the noise, making her way to us. "What are y'all's names?"

Eva blushed. "This is Pat and his friend Joe. They drove to California from Chicago and decided to come here on their way back."

"Wow," Samantha chuckled. "Y'all are nuts."

"We live dangerously," I joked, half serious.

"Well, it's nice to meet y'all! I'm sorry though, we have to get going."

"What?" Eva replied, looking like a little kid whose ice cream cone lost its scoop.

"I have an exam for my summer class tomorrow at 8, remember?"

"Oh... Yeah..."

"We should exchange contact information," I requested, with my heart sinking deep into despair.

"Yes, here's my number. We'll get the rest later."

After exchanging contacts, I said goodbye. My heavy heart pounded, watching her and Samantha exit the apartment. Samantha interrogated her about her smeared eyeliner, and that's the last I heard before they shut the door. I never felt so empty since suffering the wrath of rejection from my first crush in Louisiana in 2018. I asked out a girl whose name I've long gone out of my way to forget. Christmas had been days away, and that very night I boarded a flight back to Chicago.

Upon returning home, my parents knew something was wrong because I put on my headphones to go for a walk in the cold. I hate the cold. Lesson learned. Never ask someone out before boarding a flight. If rejection is your destiny, you'll feel all the more empty on the plane surrounded by total strangers. That fateful night, I found myself far away from the warm sunshine of the South, sitting on the icy steps of St. Bridget's, watching my tears melt the snow. *Pick yourself up, you hound*, I thought. *Worst case scenario: We never speak again, or cross each other's minds 40 years later in a pleasant memory. You need a drink.*

"You wanna do another shot, Joe? I need one."

"Yeah but give me some details. Were you getting laid?"

I stared at him for a few long seconds. "You tell me."

"It looks like you did. Is something wrong?"

"I'm fine. Just caught feelings, you know how it is. I'm a sick bastard who falls in love too easily. I destroy myself. Let's drink. David! David!"

He was across the room, talking to Tony.

"What's up?" he said, turning around.

"Shot, you too, Tony. Bring Raven over here. She'll want one."

I loved the pure love. My brothers and sisters all merrily gathered around the counter. Joe, Tony, Shane, Dre, Raven, David, Jack, Vanessa, Clara, and Dan Dunkel huddled around the table with what I estimated to be every single shot glass in the apartment.

"Tonight, we what?" Jack bellowed. "Tonight, we what?"

"Tonight, we fuckin' die!" Everybody cheered.

Dunkel veered my way, post-shot. "Morrison, you've dodged me all night, my friend, how's it goin?"

"My apologies, Dunkel. I've been all over this damn place tonight. But I'm great. Nearing the end of a crazy road trip with my guys, Tony and Joe over there."

My two companions arm-wrestled at the counter, shouting obscenities at each other.

"I met 'em earlier. Sounds like y'all had a wild ride in."

"You have no idea, man. But it's great to be here."

Dunkel is a hard man to read. It's part of what makes him interesting. He's a mysterious bastard, and it's impossible to figure out whatever it is he's thinking. No matter what, he's interested in drinking. A beer-guzzling LSU fan who will funnel a dozen beers without showing a trace of intoxication. Yes, indeed, he's a calm, relaxed individual who I've had the pleasure of calling a friend.

"Not for long," he said.

"Are you referring to hurricane season?"

"Yeah. They're predicting it's gonna be a rough one."

"A pandemic, a pathetic excuse of an election, and now impending destruction from hurricanes? What else could go wrong?"

"Tell me about it, Morrison. My folks out in New Iberia might be in trouble this year."

"Those poor folks in the rural parishes, man. I pray things turn for the better, but I don't think they will."

"Neither do I. Hurricane seasons are gettin' worse."

"I thought about these things while riding in this morning. Politicians down here gotta get their heads out of the sand if they intend to hold onto a state to govern."

"The fact a guy from Chicago gets it but our born-and-bred politicians don't. Our way of life in Louisiana is at risk."

"Revolution!" I screamed.

"Yeah, a booze revolution," he laughed.

"Come on, let's drink some more."

BACK ON THE ROAD

We partied on for the rest of the night and killed the rest of Watts' cocaine. Tony wrapped a gorilla finger with the L.A. weed to take the edge off. Jack and Vanessa disappeared for a while. I'm sure he boasted about scoring high enough on his first bout with the LSAT to get into LSU Law for points. He is, after all, a handsome guy. The rest of us smoked outside as the party slowly fizzled out, and we ordered a couple of pizzas to replenish. Us guys had to eat something or else there'd be no way in Hell that we'd make it to Memphis the following day. We fought deep into the AM hours, and I checked the time... **3:47 AM.**

We had a fantastic time, and Clara let us crash at her apartment. David left, then Shane, Dre, and the rest of our Baton Rouge group. Jack and Vanessa were asleep on the couch in each other's arms by the time we finished. *Good for them*, I thought. Joe claimed a spot on a chair next to the balcony entrance, and Tony fell asleep, sitting at the marble kitchen counter with his head down. I snuck into the guest room for sanctuary and chugged a glass of water to prepare for what I knew would be a rough morning. As I drifted off, I was at peace despite the pains inside.

The old city I'd known and loved came back to life at Clara's. It was a fucking madhouse. People from every background partied on well into the AM. Our only concern was having one hell of a time. I pulled my gun out on some troublemakers while swinging off the molly. It's hard to top smoking grass from L.A., snorting coke from Vegas, and guzzling ungodly amounts of liquor on a New Orleans summer night. The next day in Memphis would be rough, given my experiences there. Nevertheless, I looked forward to it. Laying in the empty bed, I recited the Lord's Prayer for the first time in ages and retired into my dreams.

The sun beamed through the window when I awoke. I checked my phone... 10:30. I made my way out to the living room and found Tony. He sat, eating an old piece of pizza. Vanessa had vanished and Jack lay on the couch, watching a TikTok. His dark hair lay messy on his neck covered in hickeys. Joe remained asleep in the armchair.

"*Buenos días*," I muttered. My body was drained, but my head wasn't throbbing. Nor was I nauseous. A miracle.

"Sup," Tony groaned.

"I'm drained but alive. How about you?"

"My head hurt earlier, but this pizza helped. Clara also gave me some water."

"She's an angel, ain't she?"

"You weren't wrong when you said she was somebody who knows how to have a hell of a time, sheesh."

"I told y'all, welcome to New Orleans!"

"We'll definitely be coming back here when this pandemic bullshit is over."

"An adventure in the making. The story must continue. Let's wake up Joe."

"Wait," he said, "we're going to Memphis, right?"

"Yessir."

"Hey, fuckstick!" Tony yelled, shaking Joe awake.

"What time is it?" he murmured.

"It's just past 10 o'clock. Eat some pizza and drink some water. We gotta go."

"Fuck, my head hurts."

"Same," Jack said from the couch.

"Y'all look like shit," Clara boomed, emerging out of her room in the hallway, holding my backpack.

"Thanks," I yawned. "Considering we've lived out of a car and driven in a 4,000-mile circle, you're giving us a compliment."

I fixated on Joe, Tony, and Jack. Joe looked green around the gills, Tony's nose was littered with cocaine residue, and Jack looked like a light breeze would knock him over. We helped Clara clean up the empty bottles off the counter and brought them to the garbage chute. I snuck the bedsheets from the prior night into the laundry.

"We gotta get going," I informed Clara in a melancholy voice. Parting ways with her saddened me. She has a contagious energy, one I miss whenever we're apart.

"I'll see you around, Pat. I can't wait to visit you in Chicago," she said, holding me close.

"Likewise. I'll be back in town soon enough. Thanks for having us. I send my best wishes to you and William."

The other guys expressed their appreciation and bid their farewells as we left. We headed back into the Quarter we terrorized in a psychedelic disaster less than 24 hours earlier.

The streets were empty, save for a few cyclists and drifters. A homeless man with long, gray hair and a scraggly beard slept on a manhole cover. Sights like these elicit saddening thoughts. The dirty old folks sleeping on sidewalks everywhere between New York City and Portland were kids at one point. They likely enrolled in school, pursued livelihoods, and perhaps had children of their own somewhere. Injustice will never be done away with, but it's possible to create a world with less of it.

Joe interrupted my rambling, puking up chunks of pizza into a cockroach-infested garbage can on Bienville Street. In the midst of Joe's misery, Tony joked about the car getting stolen. I told him to fuck off because I'm plagued by enough anxiety. Like how those frat boys could've squealed to the cops about a drugged-out Irish lunatic waving a revolver in their faces. *A revolver sitting in the backpack I'm carrying.* I expected sirens and squad cars to roll in, persistent in ending our nationwide rampage of drugs, booze, and violence.

Thankfully, just the two Jeeps waited right where we'd left them. Untouched.

"This is it, huh," Jack sighed.

"Yeah. A damn good time though, brother," I replied. "I'll drive back down in two weeks to move all my shit out."

"Don't remind me." His eyes watered. Both of us had developed a powerful bond, not just with our apartment in Baton Rouge, but the city and state as a whole.

"Joe, Tony, it was an honor getting belligerently hammered with y'all last night."

They both nodded and shook his hand. Goodbyes aren't easy, and the four of us had fought through a tremendous amount of disaster. A powerful bond had been born.

Seconds later, Jack peeled off into the sunshine, and I seized the driver's seat. With stops for gas taken into consideration, Memphis is a six-hour drive from New Orleans. We'd have to tear through the entire state of Mississippi before getting there. On Memorial Day in 2019, I drove from Baton Rouge to Chicago, and the Magnolia State was the most laid-back part of the journey. Not a single cop from McComb to Southaven. Aside from a couple bouts against possessed, road-raged motorists outside of Jackson, driving through Mississippi was a breeze. I blazed up the interstate at 110 miles per hour. It was incumbent upon me to do the same on our trip because Beale Street patiently waited.

We crossed state lines in a meager forty minutes. The bayous and swamps surrendered to hills and pines along Interstate 55. By 1:30, our trek led us through the quiet town of Hazelhurst—home to a Sonic, a few billboards, and humble shotgun houses. But talented people come from all places. Blues icon Robert Johnson was born there in 1911, and his birthplace remains intact. The tale of Johnson is a Faustian one, and all three of us had long been mesmerized by the story. "Little Robert" had a poor reputation as a guitar player. Crowds heckled him to get off the stage, and he left the Delta with a dirty chip on his shoulder. For a year and a half, nobody knew where he went. One night, out of the blue, he reappeared at a juke joint as a guitar virtuoso. His sudden ascent from amateur to pro raised questions among locals.

According to legend, Johnson met the Devil at a crossroads. In the blackness of night, he tuned the guitar and handed it back to Johnson. With the transaction complete, Johnson sold his soul to the prince of darkness. But, a deal with the Devil comes at a devastating price, and poor Robert died mysteriously at 27. For the occasion's sake, I turned on "Me and the Devil Blues." The eerie, supernatural voice of Johnson haunts even the bravest of souls.

Mississippi's dark forests possess an ominous energy. My understanding of the area is limited. But ghosts are everywhere, marauding among the pines and crossroads. The whole trip, we fired Muddy Waters, Howlin' Wolf, and Elmore James at top volume, but these legends hit differently in the land of their birth. The blues inspire me. These artists, from poor sharecropping backgrounds, never intended to get ripped off by a life of servitude. Johnson died in obscurity, but none other than Bob Dylan, The Rolling Stones, and Led Zeppelin covered songs of his.

One hundred years after his heyday and I'm writing about him. Throughout our travels, few emotions beat the thrill of raising Hell on the highway alongside Muddy Waters and our good friend, Howlin' Wolf. The Deep South is defined best by the words of its writers and musicians. Everything else is either conjecture or hearsay.

In suburban Jackson, it dawned on me that the car was in dire need of gas, and the air-conditioning would hastily deplete the dwindling supply. Besides, Joe's condition hadn't improved, and the poor bastard was in desperate need of food and water. He mentioned having no desire to give the car a vomit-colored paint job. I pulled in at a Shell in Madison, and he sprinted into the store before the car stopped. Tony volunteered to fill her up, and I ventured inside for provisions. Beef jerky and water would do the trick. Joe limped out of the restroom while I waited in line. He looked like death.

"Hey, Torres, how you feeling?" I asked.

Joe's a really lean guy with high cheekbones but, in the depths of a hangover, is hardly more than a skeleton with bags around his eyes. "Better," he answered in a scratchy voice. "My headache's gone but I'm still kinda nauseous. Probably gonna eat this beef jerky and pass out until we hit Memphis."

"Good idea. Get some rest, and I bet you'll be feeling fine upon our arrival."

"I hope so. This hangover is beat as fuck."

"Obviously. Take this water, too. You need some."

"Thanks."

Tony anxiously ripped his vape upon our return. "Let's go," he said. "I'm tryna get some of that Tennessee barbeque."

"Same," I replied, grabbing the wheel. "I know of a dope place there we can feast at."

"Bet," Tony concurred, switching to the dab rig in the passenger seat. "Joe, you want to hit this?"

"Sure, pass it back here. It'll help me sleep."

"Just be careful," I cautioned. "I don't want to sound like a tweak, but this is Mississippi. It ain't Colorado or California. Seeing cops out here is unlikely but, if they sense any drugs, even weed, they'll exercise any and all efforts to put us in goddamn cages." I didn't want to get a DUI. We came way too close with the Border Patrol. Whatever would happen in Memphis beats swinging pickaxes at the county farm.

"Don't be sweatin' us," Tony snickered. "Besides, we used up all the blow, we're all out of acid, and we drank our booze. All we have in the car are these dabs and the flower."

"I trust y'all will be careful. I'm just saying, I'm not tryna have a repeat of our encounter back in the desert."

"True," he said.

"Yup, this'll do it," Joe interrupted with a hacking cough after hitting the rig. He sipped his water and, within minutes, was catching Zs.

Sprawling housing developments, billboards, and trees encompassed the interstate. For a brief 10 minutes, we soared through suburban Jackson, until finding ourselves in the boonies. With the other two wrapped in THC comas, I was forced to retreat into thought. I discovered my next achievement to accomplish, thanks to the trip. Since 2016, my ambitions aimed at graduating college and being the first in my family to do so. I had to unshackle myself from student loan debt to pave the way for my dream life on the road.

I'll drive from Chicago to the coastal splendor of Georgia and the Carolinas. I haven't traveled out there since age 14. From the coast, I can visit friends in Alabama, Mississippi, Louisiana, and Texas before the big westward push. Gun it to Slab City and sing the High Desert Blues for a couple of months and become the homeless king of Venice Beach or visit my Uncle Bill in Oceanside. Something about falling asleep in Los Angeles one night and maybe Helena, Montana, after sounds too sublime to pass up. The eternal high of speeding on the interstate, witnessing daily life in our vast country, and living free of obligation enthralls my spirit. A return to the Land of the Diné also is necessary.

All the while, I can write about my travels and prepare for grad school. Infinite amount of time to do as I please. And whoever wants to come with or visit me is free to do so. I imagine Tony and Joe would ride along for at least a portion of my time out there. A smile formed on my face as I contemplated the endless possibilities the future held, pushing 105 down the Mississippi highway. I accept that I am a man in progress. There is much more to learn. The road will teach me.

Self-discovery is elusive for most people. One can transition from birth to death without knowing who they are— a frightening truth. For us guys, all three of us stepped closer to knowing ourselves, who we were, and who we were becoming. Once I graduated college, the fact I was aging finally struck. I wasn't getting old but older. But was I becoming wiser?

It's not so simple. Between the heaps of books, travel, and drugs, I preferred to think so. But who knows what's really going on? Humans live so damn long, I wonder if the idea of a mid-life crisis is outdated. You find yourself at the ripe young age of twenty-something, bombarded with bullshit expectations from every direction under the sun. Which is ironic, because in this stage of life, the sky is rather dark. Whenever someone discourages you from chasing your purest desires, it's best to ignore it because their bitterness has halted their growth, and their dreams, awaiting them from the grave.

On the road, the world belonged to us. Somewhere a presidential election was going on. Somewhere a pandemic wreaked havoc. Somewhere dark smoke from savage riots bellowed to the sky. People dyed in the fabric of hustle and bustle repeated their daily routines, as if routine as we know it isn't suicide. Come Monday, I would again join their ranks, but not by choice. Freeing myself from debt was my duty. My bout against the rat race would be temporary.

"One last ride with the boys," I whispered to myself. "Be in Memphis before we know it."

BEALE STREET BLUES

Sitting in Downtown Memphis is an old barbecue joint called Rendezvous. My first time eating there was at age 12, when my family and I drove to San Antonio in March of 2010—my first time leaving the familiar confines of the Midwest. The restaurant is renowned as a top-tier spot for elite barbecue. The workers, particularly our waiter, appeared to be in a shitty mood. Our service was abysmal. So much for Southern hospitality, right? Well, the reason for such a lackluster experience reared its head the next morning.

After hopping in the family minivan, the radio announced the founder of the place had died the morning we ate there. Our waiter was an older man, so we presumed he'd known the owner well. Awful timing. My dad and I returned to Rendezvous in 2016, the same trip we got booted from a bar. Expectations were superseded. Whenever in town, I never miss an opportunity to eat there.

"You said you knew a good place for us to get food?" Tony inquired as we crossed the border into Memphis.

"Yeah, Rendezvous. The barbecue is insane."

"Yessir, yessir!" he exclaimed. "How many times have you been there?"

"Twice, but both times have been great. Some of the best barbecue I've ever had. Shit, it could be the best."

"Fat bet. It'll probably help Joe get back on his feet. It's our last night of this trip and, even though yesterday was wild, I'm down to go all out again. How are the restrictions here?"

"Not bad, to be honest. Beale Street is open, which is where lots of the bars and restaurants are. It's sort of like Memphis' French Quarter or Broadway in Nashville."

"Sounds like a move. I've been to Nashville a few times but never Memphis."

"It's an underrated town. I've told both of y'all about my times here though, we'll have fun."

"It makes me more excited for it all."

"Take my phone for a second. Go to my hotel app and find a place downtown where we can stay."

He scrolled for a minute. "Hotel Indigo, two adults."

"How much for the night?"

"One-forty."

"Damn, man. We had a better deal in Vegas, but I don't give a fuck anymore. We'll finish this ride in style."

"Neither do I. One of us will be drunk enough to pass out on the floor."

"You're not wrong! I'm not sleeping on the damn floor. Last one to find a place is fucked."

"Neither am I," he said. "I crashed on the floor back in Baton Rouge."

"You were full of energy yesterday, give me a break!"

"I mean, I was, but still. We'll make Torres crash on the floor."

Joe snored in the backseat, out cold since getting ripped in Madison. We even debated pulling over a couple of times to check his pulse.

"Our room's all set. We'll Venmo you the money."

"Bet."

"Joe!" Tony called for his attention.

He showed no sign of regaining consciousness.

"Joe!" Still no sign of life aside from light snores.

"Torres! Your weed's on fire!" I yelled.

"What? What's going on? What time is it?" He shrieked, leaping up in his seat.

"There you are, we're officially in Memphis. It's half past 5," Tony informed.

"Damn, I basically slept through the whole state of Mississippi."

"You feelin' better?" I asked.

"Yeah, the nausea is gone, and my head feels fine, but I'm starving."

"We have a dope barbeque joint to go to."

"It's gonna slap, I bet," Joe replied.

"You tryna' drink tonight?"

"Yeah. I think I can, actually. I just need some food in my stomach other than pizza and beef jerky. More water would help too."

"We'll check into the hotel, freshen up, get our shit together, and go to Rendezvous."

"Bet," my companions replied together.

"Pat, I have a good song rec."

"Let's hear it, Joe."

"'Parchman Farm' by Johnny Winter."

"Aye, aye."

Merging off the highway, Memphis' skyline imposed itself in full view—the iBank Tower, the Memphis Pyramid, and the bridge over the Mississippi River connecting Tennessee and Arkansas. People were out and about. Aside from a minuscule number of masked pedestrians, there was little trace of a pandemic. The Southern states were notoriously less restrictive. Despite Tennessee's rebound in cases, the normality was inviting. Cathartic, perhaps.

The Memphis Rock N Soul Museum greeted us as we reached the hotel. Aesthetically, Memphis is a cross between an old Southern blues town and a large Northern city. The combination is peculiar, but the city has grit. It's impossible to predict what you'll encounter there.

We achieved a timely arrival, and it was relieving to have made it before 7 o'clock. As much as I detest lines, we were stuck behind couples, businessmen, and Northern tourists who fled the restrictions of their home states. On the TV in the lobby, MSNBC scolded Donald Trump for his rowdy, maskless rallies. Only in the 21st Century United States would mask mandates be considered "tyranny." There's an infinite wealth of issues more pressing than masks. Freedom of association is dead. The right to privacy is dead. The frontier is dead and has been replaced by a business enterprise known as the United States of America.

We are hellbent as a society on throwing our resources and energy toward the dumbest of trivialities, only to avoid the real problems that are slowly killing us all. Suddenly, MSNBC shifted the focus to Biden's rallies, which were bland and uninspiring, but at least attendees were masked and socially distanced, poising the media to kiss neoliberal ass like they always do.

"Why the hell do they give these clowns so much attention?" I thought out loud. "*It's not as if there's two other* branches of government to report about or additional issues. I'm sick of this election and it's more than three months away."

"There's a damn good reason news ratings have been plummeting," Joe pointed out.

"My biggest fear about Biden is his gun control plan. Even though two years ago, Trump actually muttered the words, 'Take the guns first, worry about due process second.'[12] It reaffirms what we agreed on back in Vegas. None of these rats in Washington are on our side. Every single initiative taken by politicians is geared for their own benefit, no matter what they try to sell."

"What's in his gun control plan anyway?"

"Good question, Tony. I read an article from the *Washington Post* the other day about it, saying he hopes to extend the 1934 law banning machine guns to what he calls 'assault weapons.' Apparently, it would include all AR-15s and even some handguns and shotguns." I did my best to speak in a lower voice. *Do we have a democracy if we can't even speak our minds for fear of pissing someone off who can't handle their emotions?*

"Not very freedom of him," Joe replied. "He campaigns on connecting to the working class and average person but wants to disarm them. Real smart."

"If we're lucky, it'll be another empty campaign promise," Tony speculated. "Biden's better than Trump, but his gun policies are fucking awful. Very elitist. Sure, he doesn't need to protect himself. But what about the rest of us? Let people be free and stand up for the little guy. Shouldn't be a hard platform to maintain."

"I can take the next in line," the receptionist announced.

"I have a reservation for two adults," I told her.

"What's the name?"

"Morrison."

"Here you are. Do you have a credit card?"

"Yeah."

She glanced at it and handed it back.

"You're all set. Here are your keys, the room number is inside. Check-out is at 11 o'clock tomorrow morning.

---

[12] Sarlin, Benjy. "What Trump Said vs. What Trump Did." *NBC News*, 2018.

Unfortunately, our recreational services won't be available due to social distancing measures. Enjoy your stay!"

"Thank you, ma'am."

We hauled our bags up the elevator and into the room. It had a balcony overlooking the street—an auspicious advantage. A goodnight blunt to close the evening is always ideal. We freshened up and hastily departed from the room to explore Memphis. Rendezvous is only a couple blocks down B.B. King Boulevard from the hotel. There's nothing but parking garages until turning into the alley by the restaurant.

Upon stepping in, the joint was no different from how I remembered it. You went down a flight of stairs. It's a basement restaurant in an obscure location, like the original Billy Goat Tavern on Michigan Avenue. The tablecloths were checkered red-and-white. Antique rifles hung from the walls, in addition to a wide assortment of blues memorabilia and photographs of famous people who've enjoyed meals there—former presidents, athletes, and musicians. It's where Mick Jagger celebrated his 55th birthday. Therefore, it's safe to say Charlie Vergos' Rendezvous has unprecedented clout, and it's well-deserved.

"This place is fucking dope." Joe smirked.

"Yessir," I said. "A classic, old-school blues vibe."

"I can already tell this is gonna be amazing." The air thickened with the aroma of ribs and barbeque sauce.

A young employee approached us. "Table for three?"

"Yessir."

"Right this way."

Our table sat adjacent to a mural painted on the brick wall. It depicted workers carrying barrels, a man jamming with a banjo, and women dancing on the barge. Obviously, the river was the Mississippi. Meanwhile, we had morphed into savage beasts, drooling for a bite. My last meal was the pizza at Clara's. Joe and Tony snacked on nothing but beef jerky while driving in. Our need for nourishment hit dire levels. Within minutes, a kid our age brought us water and obsequiously wrote down our orders. He was clearly busy but a well-mannered individual. We each pounded into our waters and, in 20 minutes, our food arrived. It felt much longer.

"This meat is sliding right off the bone," Joe said, digging into his ribs, diverging from his tradition of consuming the side first. "That's when you know you have some fire barbeque."

"Damn right," I replied while assaulting my pulled-pork sandwich drenched with Memphis sauce. A side of peppers was the cherry on top.

"The South has the best food in the country, hands down," Tony said, diving into his beef brisket.

Joe and I nodded.

"Without Chicago, Illinois would probably have good burgers and steaks but that'd be it."

"Hell, Joe, one of the best things about Chicago is the food," I replied after chugging some water.

"There's something for everybody there. The local stuff...pizza, hotdogs, and beef sandwiches... The barbecue back up in the Windy City is gas, too, but not quite like here. The Mexican food is even supposed to be some of the best in the country, I've read before."

"There's a lot of us up there!" Joe boasted.

"Tacos Por Favor, though. I'll miss it."

"Same here, Tony. I'll miss this for damn sure, too."

I ripped further into my sandwich as the sauce dripped from my chin.

"We should take a road trip all the way through the South. The past couple of days are the only time I've been, and I really like it down here."

Even before our trip, Joe dreamed of driving across the South.

"Hell yeah, we have ourselves a future endeavor."

"We'll get a tradition going, boys!" Tony exclaimed.

"A tradition I can get behind," Joe said.

"We could start on the coast in Charleston or Savannah and then hit ATL, the Gulf, New Orleans, and then hang around some Texas cities," Tony suggested.

"Legendary. We should try to hit the road as much as possible. There's so much out there we still have to see."

"Facts, consider all the places in the world, countries we haven't even been to."

"I saw your stories and posts from Argentina last summer, was it really as awesome as it looked?"

"Yes. And then some. One day we'll go. Flynn desperately wants to return."

"How long did he study there?"

"Six months."

"Lucky motherfucker," Joe scoffed.

"You'd love it, Joe. Especially you, Tony. Most of Argentina's population is Italian. In fact, Argentines are sometimes described as Spanish-speaking Italians."

"Ahhh, my people. Descendants of Rome."

"Some people say certain areas look a lot like Sicily."

"Half my family's from Sicily, let's do it!"

Our conversations continued, and we picked our plates clean. We tipped the waiter and quickly hit the streets, content and ready to drink on Beale. En route, we strolled along Main Street and found another mural. This one spanned a sizable portion of the block and portrayed Black sanitation workers on strike, armed with signs reading, **I am a Man**. A quick search revealed the march happened in 1968. I recall seeing pictures of the demonstration in one of my history books in grade school. The civil rights movement is easy to paint as a brief moment in history, a spark in time that came and went long ago.

But a hefty sum of our parents lived to see it unfold. My father was almost 10 years old by the time it drew to a close. He remembers the era vividly. The day Dr. King was assassinated, his entire neighborhood went up in flames. He, my aunt, and my uncle hid under their dining room table to avoid getting pelted by bricks crashing through the windows. Photos of the area look like ones taken of Hiroshima or Nagasaki, reduced to rubble and what essentially was military occupation because the streets teemed with swarms of National Guardsmen. Chicago's West Side has yet to recover.

The mural reminded me of my own experiences marching. When George Floyd was murdered, I figured I could no longer remain ass-to-couch while my fellow Americans were losing their lives at the hands of flunkies who think a badge and gun gives them the right to act as a Gestapo. The first civil rights demonstration I ever participated in occurred in June 2020. With sign in hand, I rode the Blue Line to Division Street, hopped on a bus, and took it to Roberto Clemente High School, where I connected with my good friend Max Ward and his older brother, Terry.

Streets weren't fit to be on, and a sublime atmosphere absorbed us. I'll never forget it. 30,000 people marched in Humboldt Park down Division Street. Never, was there a hint of trouble, nor was a single arrest made—a victory for We The People, and a loss for the fearful fascists who fight tooth and claw to mitigate voting rights and pass legislation against protesting. Justice gave us her blessing and, within us, was a universal sense that history was on our side.

The old guard had fallen in retreat, just like in the '60s... It could've been the largest storm of protest since 1968. But for how long? I already feel the fires simmering down. The walls are caving in, and I fear our victories that summer will be insufficient in the long run, leading to a crippling reactionary wave. Time will tell. I succumbed to a tangent elicited by a mural and, before long, Beale Street's chaos invited us in.

The bars atop the cobblestone streets sang their bustling song as the neon lights outside B.B. King's Blues Club, Silky O'Sullivan's, Blues City Cafe, and Kings Palace Café/Tap Room flickered against the darkening sky. We were a pack of carnivores, baring our teeth and foaming at the mouths, ready to attack the evening. Joe experienced culture shock, again. Memphis is nearly two-thirds Black. To put things into perspective, our Chicago Ward is the Whitest in the entire city. I've even heard tell of parents who moved there to "get away from" Black and Brown people. Of course, the words they used were heinous racial slurs. Hence, a majority-Black city situated in the Deep South will leave a distinct impression on anyone raised under the heavy hand of segregation.

"What are the hours like at the places here?" Joe asked.

Tony grabbed his phone. "It looks like most of the bars close at 10, but Tin Roof and Rum Boogie Cafe are open 'til 1. I don't know though. Those two could be pre-pandemic hours."

"Weird. Maybe some places can pull a few strings and get around the reduced hours," I speculated with a smirk because Rum Boogie Cafe is the place I was kicked out of back in high school.

"We can start here and work our way down the street. Let's go to B.B. King's Blues Club."

"Let's do it. It's 6:30 now. We'll take some shots there, listen to live music, and run Rum Boogie Cafe," said Tony.

"It's beat," I growled. "Does COVID have a higher infection rate after 10 PM?"

We veered towards the club entrance.

"*A Mexican, an Italian, and an Irishman walk into a bar,*" Joe jeered as we went inside.

A fine, familiar scent of barbecue and liquor wafted as we walked in. Black-and-blue checkered floors, a band onstage, an old piano, black-and-white photographs of blues icons, two levels, and multiple bar areas revealed to me a classic juke joint. Full capacity remained a pre-pandemic flashback, but a solid crowd of people ate, drank, and nursed beers on barstools.

We copped a table near the stage. Immediately, I recognized the song the band was playing—"Smokestack Lightning"—a song about heartache by Howlin' Wolf. *Damn, these lyrics!* I thought. Evangeline crossed my mind. That lovely Southern belle, Lord, how I missed her after a minuscule 18 hours. Emptiness replaced the butterflies. Thanks to our busy arrival, I had little time to check my notification-overflowed phone.

I scrolled through Snaps from Tara, Tommy O'Shea, Fergus Flynn, and finally one from Evangeline. She had gone on a walk in New Orleans' City Park. It was captioned, "Sorry about last night," to which I replied, "Sorry about what? We had fun while it lasted."

She felt guilty about leaving so early.

I was overwhelmed by unending fits of grief, mourning the fact I'd never found real romance. The heartbreak expressed in poetry typically stems from breakups, but what about those who have never felt the affection of a significant other? Who's never held the hand of somebody who loves them? Where are our songs? Where is our poetry? For years, I've mired in the dirt, waiting, praying for a beautiful person to belong to, and who will simultaneously be mine.

Thoughts bothered me. *My human addiction, your whereabouts are a mystery, but when our paths cross, I vow to give you whatever remains of my flesh and blood. I loved you long before we met and will until the end of time.* I remember hearing those pop songs from the 2010s about arms being castles, beautiful sunsets, and the wealth of a lover's eyes; I hated those songs but never wanted anything more than to be the man being sung about. A lover to hold, and for her to hold me, is all I've ever needed. *Fuck this.*

I couldn't afford to let the lovesick blues get to my head on the final night. I just wanted to get drunk, laugh, philosophize, and enjoy a wild night with my friends.

A waiter showed up. "What will y'all be having?"

"Three shots of Fireball," Tony requested, pulling out some cash from his wallet.

"Yessir," said the waiter. "May I see some ID?"

We each showed our identification.

The waiter nodded. "$12," he said.

Tony handed him the money. "Keep the change."

"To the last night!" Joe said as we cheered our shots.

"I'll cover our next round," I offered. "What are y'all trying to shoot next?"

"Let's have some Captain."

"Good choice, Tony," Joe replied.

I shared the sentiment, graduating from beers to harder alternatives, I became loyal to brown liquor.

"Memphis was a dope choice, Morrison," Tony said.

"I mean, it was definitely our best option. We sure as hell weren't going to St. Louis. Memphis has more flavor, and those are the only major cities on the way between New Orleans and Chicago. Nashville's a bit out of the way."

The old bluesman maintained pace without a hitch. Again, I recognized the song with ease. "Rock Me" by Muddy Waters. I sang along off-key.

"I feel right at home in this town. The blues, the grit, the neon signs; it's like I'm 50 years back in time."

"We'll definitely come back here when everything's fully opened up. We have to," said Tony. "It's nice to know there's still wild places out there. Old-school towns that can throw down."

"If you had mentioned to me 10 years ago, I'd be here with you guys after doing everything we've done on this trip, I would've confidently called bullshit."

"So would I, Joe! We're only warmin' up, boys. We'll pay off our loans and the world will be at our fingertips. We can be whoever we want to be, do whatever we want to do."

"Our future and our meaning depend on our actions. We can choose to live free if we really want to. I value being an individual. Colleges don't help much anymore, and I almost think school is a mistake, but I'm too invested. Can't turn back now... I see people's profiles on LinkedIn and I want to throw up. All the plastic fucking smiles we're forced to look at and present, nothing but scared kids joining the bourgeoisie. We wear our withering souls on our faces. Why are we all funneled into the system like this? Why all the rush? I think we can take a breath, step outside ourselves, and think hard about what it is we intend to do with our lives. Lots of people don't want to have that conversation. I don't think life should be taken too seriously. But what we do with our lives should be. If that makes any sense."

"I'm catching your drift, Joe. Colleges once were centers of intellect. They had depth. A student was an individual of distinction. Today, the university is a dead horse, a bland factory, producing a new generation of conformists who end up nothing more than products on an assembly line. And human beings have no purpose on an assembly line."

"Amen, Morrison. Too many people think they can't control their destinies and it's fucking depressing. Deadass, do you have any idea the number of times people have basically told me they can't chase their dreams because of pressure from their surroundings? It's insane! If you aren't doing what you love to do for the rest of your life, you're not happy, and you definitely will have a Hell of a hard time finding meaning."

"You're spot on, man. We're in our early twenties, we got the rest of our lives to work and make a living. These are the years to be selfish and take risks, while we aren't married and with kids," I said. "There's no good reason to sacrifice our most vital years chasing a fuckin' dollar sign."

"This is why I love you pricks," Tony said. "We're on the same page. I sometimes think about those things and how I'm going to handle it all when I graduate. What's next? I don't want to be stuck doing something I hate until I'm 65. I want to work and have a family and all that good stuff, but I better make sure my livelihood is something I genuinely enjoy. My grandpa came over here from Sicily with nothing. He worked in the stockyards on the South Side in the '50s. He died when I was 8, while living with us. He came here with nothin' and died with nothin'... I hate the idea of toiling for the man and never getting a leg up. It's hard to think about the millions of people stuck in the cycle... Good, hard-working people stuck in the game."

"You're singing the blues of our whole generation, brother," I said to him. "And then some."

The waiter returned, and I bought us another round.

"And many who've come before us," Joe said, continuing the conversation.

"I've never told anybody what I'm about to tell y'all, because of the stigma attached, but here goes... I confess that, although I don't like the concept of ideology, the one closest to my train of thought is anarchism. We're cursed by a dishonest, money-driven society constructed by thieves upon illusions. Scripture says we can't serve two masters. Both Capitalism and the State damage this truth. The annals of history prove that hierarchies crumble. Their power is secured by swords and tears, from Rameses and Nero to Hitler and Stalin."

"I don't disagree with you, man," Joe said sullenly.

"What do you think, Tony?"

"I think you're spot on. I still believe in some type of government, but you make a good-ass argument. I'm convinced you can make any ideology sound appealing!"

"It's the art of rhetoric, my friend. Cicero. Marcus Tullius Cicero. Check out some of his stuff when you get the chance. Particularly his oratory against Catiline. His conversations with Scipio Africanus are gold too."

"I'll be dead before I get through half of the books you recommend, Morrison!"

"Even so, you'll be glad to have read half of 'em!"

There comes a point when you read enough books to drive you to the brink of mental collapse. I have awoken to an endless gust of terrifying and absurd realities. They've pressed me beyond the point of no return. A world of philosophers and artists would be a better one, but this is a pipe dream. Few people dare to follow the rabbit hole of philosophical thought. I chose the path and don't know how to handle it. I don't see what other people see, and what I see is a bottomless rut of insanity and we're all sinking down. Yes, I have attained knowledge that most other people don't possess, thanks to my extracurricular studies.

There is a fantastic level of freedom in seeing the bigger picture. Achieving a rare level of consciousness is a double-edged sword, and I am only funneling downward into a viper pit, bound for something monstrous and inexplicable. Come to think of it, I don't recall a book I've recently read that wasn't written by a dead author, which in some way makes me a literary necrophiliac. It gets awfully lonely here in the world of the living. Lonely enough to where one must hide what they've learned to avoid freaking out the average person.

I detest concealing these anarchist tendencies. Anarchy is the only ideology humble enough to admit there's no utopia, no grand society worth killing for. When was the last time an anarchist orchestrated a genocide? Interfered with the right to vote? None that I know of. It takes an organized hierarchy to commit such horrendous acts. Yet I remain treading on glass for sensitive people who might be disturbed by my beliefs.

We can't even imagine what a truly free society would look like. Hence, we loathe unshackling ourselves, the same way the Children of Israel didn't want to leave bondage in Egypt. As Nietzsche writes, "All great things first have to bestride the earth in monstrous and frightening mask in the hearts of humanity."[13]

Behind its mask, freedom is a muse that frees us from deception. All human beings are works of art. The problem is most of us have yet to recognize it. I don't know where this hard road of radical individualism leads but, if I die penniless, at least I can say I lived an authentic life without compromise. I will die free.

As my mind wandered, Joe and Tony laughed about something. I was zoned out and staring at the empty shot glasses. Glasses clinked and laughter filled the room. I wanted to join in but was unable to. *After tonight, the next time I'll see the*

---

[13] Nietzsche, Friedrich, and Kaufmann, Walter. *Beyond Good and Evil: Prelude to a Philosophy of the Future.* Vintage Books.

inside of a bar will be in the neighborhood up in Chicago— something I do not anticipate warmly. The atmosphere up there is soul-crushing, disproportionately populated by knuckleheads, swingers, racists, wine moms, divorcees, and cops whose thirst for life has dried up with their gametes.

These troubled souls grew up in the neighborhood, raised children there, and will die without ever tasting what it's like to dwell outside their comfort zone. Never since the day that whiskey-guzzling, acid-eating lunatic named Heneghan stormed into Paddy O'Fallon's Pub during a fundraiser for cops screeching, "Fuck the pigs," have I stepped foot in any of those havens of alcoholism, broken dreams, and plastic patriotism.

Word of advice—if you wind up at any bar along Northwestern Boulevard and a fat, mediocre country singer instructs the audience to remove their hats for the national anthem, don't hesitate. Just do it, unless you want an emotionally unstable mob of morbidly obese phony patriots threatening to sentence you to the guillotine.

One night in the middle of June, I took a stroll to clear my head. Outside the bars, I heard a drunk, middle-aged woman wailing at some poor fool, "You liberal piece of shit!" A millisecond later, two braindead muscle-heads were screaming at the same guy about how much of a pussy he was for questioning the "people who put their lives on the line for us every day."

How did we get to this point? Have we devolved as a species into tribalistic primates who sling shit at those ideologically opposed to us to obtain a sense of validation?

"Morrison," Tony said, jolting me back to the moment.

"What's up?"

"You've been quiet for a while, you okay?"

"I'm fine. Just dreading the idea of heading back up north, feeling pretty hopeless. This entire trip has been an insane high, and I don't want to come down... But I know I have to."

"I get it, man. I don't like falling into the routine either. But we gotta swallow nails if we ever wanna get ahead."

"Can't argue with that."

"I'll be right back, I gotta use the washroom."

"Somebody's got the liquor shits," Joe jeered.

"It's the pain of the game," Tony giggled as he faded away into the bar.

"Like both of you, I'm not trying to fall back into the routine of school and the weekends, but I anticipate graduating in December," Joe said.

"Graduating is an amazing feeling. I'm having a hard time summoning the words... You've accomplished the tedious job of graduating college. A crushing weight is pulled from your shoulders, only to be replaced by another, and we've discussed the horrors of bourgeois society this entire trip. But the beauty of graduating college is that you have some type of credential. Did you know only 6% of the global population has a college degree?"

"No, I actually didn't. Where'd you hear that?"

"LSU's president gave a speech and said so, and I don't have any legitimate reason to doubt it."

"Tony and I will join you as a six-percenter soon!"

"Ride the high wave, brother. I don't want to sound pessimistic, but I hope we don't change."

"Explain."

"I guess what I'm trying to say is we can't lose our edge, our ambitions. Reach for the sky and don't settle. Be a grown man but stay a kid in the best of ways."

"I won't cave in... If there's something about our generation I admire, it's our drive to live differently from our parents. I think we're coming to realize the fake authority our world's been built around. We don't want our lives defined by bullshit sedentary work surrounded by blue light, only to get stupid-hammered every weekend to numb how empty the cycle is. The memes of text messages between teenage employees and their overbearing bosses are great. We give less of a fuck. Maybe it's because of how young we are. Maybe it's something more. I don't have the answers."

"Nor do I, my friend. We have been failed by earlier generations. They haven't left us with a better world. And now we're at bat for our children and for our children's children. From what I see, the three of us are doing our best. Whatever our best may bring."

"Cheers, brother! I say, we grab another round of shots before heading to Rum Boogie Cafe."

"You got yourself a plan. It's almost 8. We have a couple hours."

"Bet," he said with a silly smirk.

"What's so funny?"

"I'm thinking about the Fourth of July."

"Lord, have mercy, what about it?"

"All of it. The softball game, the beers, the party at Truck's... A damn good time."

"I woke up and had acid for breakfast. Smoked and housed beers for the next five hours before the game. When those kids started throwing M-80s into the outfield, it felt like Vietnam! Then all those deer ran through, and a bunch of cops showed up. I was like, 'Shit, Pat, you gotta be hallucinating!'"

"You played good as fuck too," he cackled.

"Yeah, pitched the whole damn game, batted six-for-seven, and we won. You kicked some ass yourself."

"Sure did, it was fun. I had two triples. We had nobody over six feet tall on our team either."

"With democracy at work, Flynn and I were voted captains and, when he picked all the bigger guys first, I was like, *no way*. You jive-ass motherfucker, you think you're gonna win this!"

"They had the size, but we had all the athletes."

"I caught on," I chuckled. "There's a reason you were my first pick."

"Remember when Tony's parents took us to see fireworks at Lake Michigan?"

"Damn right, I remember. Back then, all we needed to have fun were a lake and some good ole fashion fireworks. I remember staring at the skyline, the John Hancock Building in particular, and feeling so proud to be from Chicago."

"Things were magical when we were kids. Neighbors didn't shun each other because of elections. Social media wasn't around, not like today. We didn't have to go out in search of something beautiful because we were pure, and life itself was big and endless."

"Poetry, Joe. Pure poetry, you're speaking."

"Are you still proud to be from Chicago?" he asked.

"Yes, I am. First of all, I wouldn't have met you, Tony, or any of our people. I can't imagine life without our crew. For that reason alone, I'm thankful to have been born and raised there. It's one of the greatest cities on earth. I love Chicago with all my heart. It'll always be a home, but I have to leave it. Living in a metropolis of 10 million people with zero natural beauty is suffocating for me. I need to breathe. I need sunlight. It's why I moved to Louisiana and hope to return eventually."

"You really were at home there, huh?"

"Totally. It's the first place I've felt like I fit in. For the first time in my life, I found a group of friends who immediately accepted me for who I was, no questions asked. I'd take bullets for our people back up north, but I don't have the best history with all of 'em. My Louisiana people rode with me from the second we met."

"Not gonna lie, you had to put up with some shit back in the day."

"Didn't we all?"

"Yeah, but it was different for you, man."

"I guess. It wasn't fun having guys twice my size pin me to the ground and dump beer on my face, try to put cigarettes out on me, or set my hair on fire. I didn't appreciate the racist bastards who'd speak to me in Ebonics because I sat with the black kids at lunch. Or the cancer jokes. I've been called some pretty nasty shit, but it's water under the bridge. Growing up ain't bad in its entirety."

"Here we go, boys!" Tony shrieked, returning with three Vegas bombs.

"Somebody better be prayin' for us!" I boomed.

"Last night on earth!" Tony cheered as we slammed our shots.

"Alright, let's blow this popsicle stand." I scowled.

This road is damn hard, and childhood flashbacks slammed me like a semi barreling down a busy street at a hundred miles per hour. I was 8, maybe 9 when a demented mob of preteens stormed after me for reasons I don't remember. Kids saw me as a target and, to this day, I don't understand why. It was summer... The Northwest Side Festival... Rocks flew past my head and several struck my back until I found refuge in a large oak tree. One brave soul, a short blond kid, pursued me up the tree until I kicked him off into the dirt. He wailed, claiming I broke his arm. He played a stupid game and won a stupid prize. Good riddance. I climbed high and fast until I couldn't climb any further. Boy, did I climb! For about 15 minutes, the devils below cheered and slung rocks, but I climbed too high for any to make an impact.

I came down once the bastards left and sprinted home like I'd never run before. I didn't tell my parents and never spoke of the incident to anybody until high school was almost over. I suppose that poses yet another example of how I've become the beautiful monster I am today—a booze and drug-consuming pseudo-intellectual who tirelessly romps it up in the cities of our star-spangled land, desperately seeking to put the past behind him. Bullies are like hyenas. They either choose the weakest target or band together against the lion, their strongest competitor. A slight buzz is all it takes to cast me deeper and deeper into wells of curiosity.

Meanwhile, Beale Street boomed. Live music everywhere on that July Saturday night. Neon signs flashed and the vibrations rang of chaos. An all-out brawl unfolded in the street outside of Miss Polly's Soul City Cafe. A heap of at least 10 people who threw punches, kicked, and spazzed out. One hopelessly intoxicated human tornado shrieked, "I'll cut you like a goddamn fish" at the top of his lungs. He brandished a large buck knife. The blade must've been 8 inches long.

Suddenly, the madness was interrupted by a barrage of cops tackling everyone in sight. *Time to find refuge at Rum Boogie Cafe.* Memphis appeared to be almost as rowdy as New Orleans. Its murder rate is insanely high. Chicago's is rather modest in comparison. You never know when you'll fall victim to an act of senseless violence. Therefore, it's imperative to be armed at all times. A night out can be instantaneously ruined by a malevolent cop or some inebriated wannabe G.I. Joe who threatens your life for looking at him the wrong way.

Despite the risks, danger exhilarates me. I deeply pity those who have never danced on the edge. Throwing yourself into the fray makes you more alive and in touch with your instincts. Risk, danger, chaos... They're merely a part of life. Add life to years, as opposed to years to life. My bout against death taught me the importance of making the best of the life I'm lucky enough to have. Henry David Thoreau says, "The mass of men lead lives of quiet desperation."[14] I intend to live dangerously, because, if I don't, I may not live at all.

Throughout human history, we've had famines, wars, diseases, predators, and starvation to contend with. That kept us on our toes. The English philosopher Thomas Hobbes once said, "Life in the state of nature is nasty, brutish, and short."[15] I don't think we should rely on much more than this unforgiving state of nature. I brood deeply about the affairs of human beings because I wish the best for our species. But without hardship, without tests of our survival, I fear we will no longer be human. Our pain is a part of what makes us who we are. Exposing ourselves to the desert heat, the Rockies, and the concrete jungles of the South humbled us.

This world will kill us all eventually, but we are gifted with the chance to raise Hell while we're here. We're conditioned to pursue happiness at all costs, but such an endeavor is foolish, naive bullshit. The Promethean struggle lies in the fight to live a life of purpose. Happiness will follow.

The night flung us into all sorts of places, mentally and physically. Alcohol flowed through our veins, lowering all inhibitions, and it was outstanding. Our time was running out. We had to make the best of it, and I felt certain we'd pull through in fine style. "I got our first round!" I announced.

"Bet," Joe said as we approached the bar.

Hanging above our heads was the colorful sign reading **Rum Boogie Cafe, Since 1985.** I handed the bouncer my ID—a fat, bald, bearded individual with a tattoo sleeve. "You think I was born yesterday?" He scowled at me.

"What are you talkin' about?"

"This is clearly a fake ID, and you don't look 5'10 anyway."

"That's my ID, I promise you, it's real. I get it. I look young but trust me. It's all real, I sat at the DMV for two hours getting it." I'm used to such treatment.

---

[14] Thoreau, Henry David. *Walden* and *Civil Disobedience.*
[15] Hobbes, Thomas. *Leviathan.*

"Listen, kid, you can either fuck off or I'll make you! You don't want this to go the hard way!" His face flushed red.

"We're all 22," Joe said with his ID in hand.

"You're not gonna make me do shit," I told him. "Now do your fuckin' job and let us in."

"Quit jerkin' us around, pig!" Tony roared.

The bouncer shoved him, forcing me to see red.

I decked the prick, and he pushed back at us when the owner, manager, or somebody official jolted out the door.

"The hell is goin' on out here, Otis?" the man asked in a deep Southern accent. He was thin, wore an Ole Miss hat, and looked like Eric Church.

"These little shits are trying to get in with their fakes!"

"Did you even scan their IDs?"

"Well, no, but check their IDs! They're outta state and obviously fake!" he fired back in a panic.

"Scan their IDs," the man ordered.

Sure enough, they each scanned.

"Clearly their IDs aren't fake. Gentlemen, I apologize for my employee's behavior. He'll be dealt with."

"Thank you, sir," we each replied.

I turned around to see the bouncer rubbing his face where I'd hit him.

"First drinks for y'all are on the house. Once again, I apologize," said the man.

"We greatly appreciate it," I said, taking my mask off. "Could we please have a round of Old No. 7?"

"Comin' right up!" he obliged as we secured a seat near the stage, where a band played some tunes we didn't recognize.

For fuck's sake! First, I'm kicked out of high school, and then this happens. Admittedly, Rum Boogie Cafe is a cool joint. Guitars hang from the second story, surrounded by brick walls with writing on them. Each of the bar's windows has neon signs, one reading, **Memphis Style BBQ and Ribs**. The setting really takes you back a few decades.

The man who'd scolded the manchild at the door returned with our shots.

We knocked them back after expressing our gratitude, in love with the warm trickle of whiskey running down our throats.

"The fuck was up with the bouncer?" asked Tony, his voice still raspy from the shot.

"You know how some of those fuckin' meatheads are," Joe scoffed. "They think they're the shit because they're given a sliver of authority so they think they can treat young guys like us however they want."

"Pseudo-tough guys, that's all they are," Tony said.

"Preach, y'all. Always some type of trouble."

"It's you, Morrison, you're the bad luck."

"Well, Tony, I suppose they never specified which direction the Luck of the Irish is supposed to go. A fuckin' Irish history book would quickly answer that question."

"I miss the days when we didn't have to worry about bouncers and all that shit, even the booze."

"We didn't have to worry about douchey muscle-heads while climbing the monkey bars or hooping at Brooks."

"No lies detected, Torres," I replied.

"I can't put my finger on it," Tony began, "but we lose something when we age out of childhood. As kids, we have no conception of anxiety, depression, obligations... None of it. We lived and looked at each other as people, nothing more."

"How it should be," I said mournfully. "Whether it's a boss of ours, a girl we like, even the damn president...they're *people* who have issues, insecurities, and imperfections, no different from us."

"We tend to let our thoughts control us, but they shouldn't. Our fears don't exist outside of our minds. We can be free if we truly want to be, it's just up to how far we're willing to push ourselves."

"I don't think anybody wants to be free," I said. "Freedom scares us. What do you think, Tony?"

"Maybe we're afraid of freedom because we're afraid of ourselves. We fear what we'd do with true freedom. I don't know if we'll ever find it."

"Even if we never are free, it's worth pursuing. Live free or die... It's a phrase I'll always stand by. Hold up, let's shoot somethin'—y'all up for more whiskey?"

"Sure."

"You, Joe?"

"Yeah... Surprise us!"

"You got it, homie."

On my way to the bar, a group of girls hovered around the barstools. Great. My genitals dictated I would not be served any alcoholic nectar for several minutes. "Ladies first" is an expression I strongly stand behind but, around a bar, give me a break. Are these bartenders genuinely gentlemen or are they not? Perhaps they're sinister, serving sugary mixed drinks to endless tsunamis of pretty girls in bellbottoms only to hit on them. *My men need booze, damn you!* The bartender looked 30, was balding, and laughing with the group of women. *This bastard's intent on keeping me in wait.*

Elderly couples happily drank at their tables, and tourists... My God, the tourists... In the nexus of a global pandemic, the sheer number of tourists in Memphis nauseated me. I wasn't kidding about Northerners flocking to Southern states to flee pandemic restrictions. These old people in their damn campers, thundering down the highways... It was a domestic blitzkrieg of Baby Boomers named Jim and Karen. Jim's complaining about the heat, and Karen is scolding him to pipe down. My stomach turned and twisted, pondering this hypothetical situation. Thank Christ the girls abandoned the area. My turn had come. *I see you, bartender. I'm flagging you down.*

"What can I get you?" he asked.

"Three shots of Wild Turkey."

"15 bucks. Cash or card?"

"Card. Closed."

He fumbled around and poured the Wild Turkey into three glasses. "Here you go."

"Thank you, sir," I said, leaving the man a modest tip.

At the table, the other two smiled in my direction, like parents when the doctor brings them their bouncing newborn.

"What we got?" Tony asked.

"Three shots of Wild Turkey from yours truly."

"Never had it."

"It's smooth. Hunter S. Thompson notoriously drank this stuff."

"You really love that bastard," he jeered.

"I've read almost half of his books. The man told it how it is. Some people are so madly in love with truth and freedom that they're willing to live and die for both. They listen to the voices in their heads telling them that there is something seriously wrong with the system, the lives we're pressed to live, boom or bust. Thompson was one of those people. I'm beginning to think I am, too."

"What do you mean?" Joe asked.

"I want to write and make my living on it. I'm ready to put all my chips in. If I lose, I'll try again. But if I make it, I'll be the happiest man on earth. There's too much to see in this world... Too many books to read... Too many beaches, mountains, and forests to wander around... There's an infinite amount of adventure to endure and an infinite amount to be written about. I'm overwhelmed by how fearful and in love I am with what can't be measured."

"You know I support you, Pat. I always will," Joe replied.

"Me too," Tony said. "I appreciate how deep you get into these things, man. These conversations we've had make me think about what I want. We talked about it while tripping balls at Monument Valley, but as long as I'm free from debt and can travel, I'll be fine."

"We've done too many drugs," Joe interjected.

"What?" I asked.

"We've done too many drugs. That's why we dive so deep all the time."

"To be honest, man, the drugs definitely have something to do with it, but they're not the end-all-be-all. They complement our literary influences and the cocktail is overflowing with questions, doubt, and absurdity."

Why do I take these drugs? I ask myself all the time how I've become this hedonist. Yesterday's uniform-wearing, conservative schoolboy is now a long-haired, drug-crazed anarchist whose most potent kryptonite is a beautiful woman. I sat there wearing a white button-up shirt, my hair messy, and my breath reeking of rum and whiskey. I've splashed in a booze bath for years and feel fine. Some uppers would've been nice, but we dug into the bottom of the barrel last night. How did I arrive here?

First of all, I do drugs because they're fun. Children play and adults have to as well, right? Some people load up on drugs to numb themselves, and those poor fools are the worst kind. If you can't feel anything, you're a ticking time bomb. Hence, I don't take drugs to numb myself but for the intensity... Explore the unknown, have fun, and experience thoughts and worlds unknown to the sober. They don't teach you this in D.A.R.E..

Joe and Tony can vouch for me when I say we all graduated D.A.R.E., that naive propaganda program where a square cop is forced to abandon free food at the airport for a classroom to educate children about drugs he's never done. I vividly recall the spectacle of 30 ten-year-old Caucasian kids in the classroom listening to some porker explain how weed is smoked from a "tube."

Parents of America, heed my warning! Your children are being indoctrinated with lies! Your children *will* grow up, and if they dare to engage in the scam of an American college education, drugs *will* be on the menu. Your little darlings can't be hidden from the dirty grit of American hedonism forever! Children become adults and do drugs. Most end up fine.

"Drink responsibly," reads every single package or bottle of alcohol, and I'm wondering why nobody bats an eye. To imply there's such a concept as "responsible" alcohol use and no such unicorn as "responsible" drug use is utter nonsense. Thousands of people die annually from alcohol-related complications but, in rural Alabama, a man is doing hard time behind bars for multiple marijuana charges? I smell an agenda at work.

I may guzzle whiskey and use an assortment of drugs, but at least, when I raise a child someday, it'll be firsthand experiences guiding my parental advice, instead of leaving the poor kid in a room with an armed stranger lecturing from his own ass. Drug education in the Land of the Free is among the most ignorantly poor systems of schooling ever conceived, and I'm an example. Drugs are like life in one specific context; you never know where they'll take you. A high is a wave you must ride.

"Let's hit Tin Roof, it's 9 o'clock," Joe suggested.

"Last hour probably," I mournfully murmured.

"We'll drink and smoke a blunt at the hotel," Tony said, attempting to cheer the mood.

"Sounds lovely."

We followed the golden liquor trail to Tin Roof to finish our Beale Street adventure. Drinking hard and talking hard, as always. The bar in Tin Roof was empty, and with an unknown number of shots in our systems, we concluded we'd had enough hard stuff. A few cold beers were in order. Joe and I ordered a pair of Millers, and Tony grabbed a Coors. Sporting events were virtually absent from television screens that summer and most places supplemented this absence with the news, disappointingly enough.

An anchor on TV spoke with the familiar monotone voice about the 700+ people who'd succumbed to the virus that day alone. I cringe at the sight of wealthy, entitled, phony anchors reporting unapologetically biased "news." They do nothing more than regurgitate what powerful people, *their friends*, spew. One more time hearing the monotone voice reference "social distancing" and I would've suffered an aneurysm. My tombstone was in sight. "Here lies Patricius Morrison, faithfully departed on July 18, 2020. Among the youngest to ever die of an aneurysm." I hate speculating on my death, but you can understand the idea.

"We're all losing our damn minds," I groaned, listening to the TV. "Another 700 people died from COVID."

"This has been a long time coming. Think about it, man. Shit's been hitting the fan for a while," Tony said after burping obnoxiously.

"You're preaching. We've lived through 9/11, seen the first Black president, a second civil rights movement, the rise of right-wing Populism, a global pandemic, and two of the worst economic disasters since the Great Depression, and we're not even 23."

"Don't forget, the War in Afghanistan is set to be our country's longest war," Joe pointed out. "There's nothing I find more fascist than policing the world."

"They don't call them the 'forever wars' for nothing. I bet half the country can't even find Afghanistan on a map," Tony drunkenly roared.

"Do either of you remember that goatfuck at Charlottesville?" Joe asked.

I knew exactly what he was referring to. So did Tony. The goatfuck of Charlottesville remains a dark moment, a scar on our nation. A white supremacist rally there in the summer of 2017, better known as the "Unite the Right" rally, caused a shitstorm of problems. Neo-nazi shrimpdicks parading swastikas and Confederate uniforms claimed the city for their own, brandishing tiki torches, chanting a series of slurs and dreadful slogans, clearly unaware of which country they were in. Tiki torches! Three people died in the fuckfest... Two state troopers and a counter-protester who was run over by a nazi maniac barreling through the crowd at high speeds.

"Damn right, I remember," said Tony.

"It'll go down as one of the darkest days of the 2010s, guaranteed," I said.

"The nazi son-of-a-bitch killed that girl, too... I forget her name..." Joe said sullenly. Everyone forgets in the end.

"Back home, people act like it's the Left starting all the problems. But it's everybody. The bullshit's all around us."

"The Top vs. Bottom metric is much more important than the Right vs. Left one. Going too far right or too far left almost always makes a person more authoritarian, which perpetuates totalitarianism. It's a threat to freedom."

"Kinda like I said in Vegas. The people who control everything... They're a club and people like us don't fit the mold. Plain and simple."

"That accidental ejaculation with a bowl-cut killed those poor folks at the church in Charleston in 2015, Charlottesville in 2017, and the Synagogue attack in Pittsburgh... That was in what? 2018? Those racist pricks can kiss my Mexican ass."

"All this shit happens, and a fat number of us wonder why there's so many civil rights protests. People are dying! These idiots in Washington will go after the guns instead of pausing and carefully analyzing the situation."

"I gotta take a piss," Tony announced, getting up to leave the table.

"These are some hard times," Joe said, fidgeting.

"They are, but hard times create stronger people," I replied.

"I guess if generational success is measured by leaving your kids and grandkids with a better world, we really have been failed. Not a single honest person anywhere can disagree with that statement. Do you have faith in our generation, or do you think we'll end up like the ones who came before us? Who briefly, for only a few moments in time, secured a genuine counterculture, just for it to be pissed away?"

"I have faith, alright. We are a peculiar generation. We grew up watching *Courage the Cowardly Dog*, after all. But we need unity, and that's hard to come by. Between the pricks at the top who're pulling the strings dividing us and our own domestication, I don't know. Thankfully, there are plenty of issues our generation largely agrees on. But the clock is ticking. The population is aging. Our energy won't last. The time has come. It's counterculture now or never. We need to read more and base our views on solid ground. Malcolm X described books as his alma mater and, to be honest, every American should read C. Wright Mills."

"A new revolution is badly needed. You've mentioned that guy, C. Wright Mills quite a bit. Tell me about him."

"He was a gun-toting, motorcycle-riding, whiskey-drinking Leftist intellectual who wrote primarily in the '50s. Counterculture activists devoured his work. I was combing Jim Morrison's reading list a few months ago and found Mills' book. It's called *The Power Elite*. In the book, he more or less provides a map of the power structure in our country. Essentially, three elite classes form the 'power elite.' They're divided into military, political, and business elites. This is a very tricky road because generals run for office and so do businessmen. Hell, one of them is sitting in the Oval Office right now. The elites do compete with each other, but Mills contends that their division is much less stark than the division among the general population. They fight amongst themselves but are unified enough to enforce their agendas. Meanwhile, we the people persist in biting each other's heads off because of our prejudices and political allegiances. His views on the middle class are fascinating, also. To Mills, the middle class is a prison of mediocrity. No passion, no thrill... Just unending servitude to the man while begging and pleading for more money to get that new lawnmower or more golf clubs. This view has rubbed off on me too. Like for fuck's sake, man! You, me, and Tony have microplastics in our blood. The party last night? Every single person there does too. The people in charge don't care about how sick, sterile, and tired we get, as long as we're kept weak and passive. We are crashing headfirst into Huxley's 'dictatorship without tears.' We have allowed life to become an endless series of tedious chores."

"I don't know much about this guy, but I need a couple copies of his, ASAP. I believe in reading good books... And if more people did, we'd be in a better place. I guess the elites benefit from keeping us in the dark, though. Nothing like an episode of 'reality' TV or a news binge to keep us blind and dumb. Shitty food loaded with toxins and carcinogens to keep us sick and fatten us for slaughter."

"Preach. man! To be honest, these conversations are worth having. When you discuss important issues, you brood over them and, if you're passionate enough, you participate in what's going on. People should be involved, I believe it to my core. Complicity is a damn sin. It's so fuckin' easy today to fall into a bland, comfortable routine, tuning out the injustices of the world, and to die without at least attempting to make a mark and fight for what's right. I may be gravitating towards an anarchist mindset, but I don't condone violence. I wish we'd all band together and tell the penny-pinchers in Washington we ain't afraid of them, that, at the end of the day, we the people are in charge. And that they cannot take whatever they want. In the absence of accountability, democracy becomes a dictatorship."

"Damn, dude, that was perfect. I would say you should run for office, but I'm aware of your thoughts on that stuff. Besides, running for office isn't the only way to make an impact."

"Hell no, Joe. Voters, demonstrators, writers, and even musicians have led social and political movements. Jimi Hendrix, Jefferson Airplane, The Doors, particularly Jim Morrison... The list goes on. All successful revolutions find strength through artists."

"Facts. I think music fueled the success back then. Especially your cousin, too."

Because of my surname, he occasionally refers to the Lizard King as my "cousin."

"You're onto something, man!"

"Howdy," said Tony, returning to the table.

"What time is it?"

"9:15, we should kill these beers to make last call."

"I'm down. Last person to finish their beer buys the last round! You down, Joe?"

"I'm up for the challenge!"

I proceeded to chug the rest of my beer, cracking open the next one and sipping aggressively. "I'm drunk," I groggily stated.

"Damn, me too, man," Joe replied.

"Me three," Tony followed. "No better way to finish our odyssey than with a relaxing buzz."

When 9:30 rolled around, Joe lost the bet. Given his state of illness all morning, I was impressed he drank at all. He grudgingly copped our final round of beers. We knocked back our brews and left Tin Roof, searching without success for another spot to drink. Tony roasted Joe for his inability to keep up, and Joe clapped back by defending how much he drank in New Orleans.

The voices and music of Beale Street faded behind us as we turned onto B.B. King Boulevard. A dog barked somewhere in the distance, reinforced by other noises common to a big city. Last night on the road, last night of *freedom*... Freedom... It's constantly on my mind, although never easy to figure out. Hence, I've developed my own definition. Freedom is being exactly who we are without compromise. Without it, we're pacified rule-followers moving mechanically, diminishing the internal and all its unique capabilities, as sacrificial lambs. Like a crack of lightning, death sweeps in and the lights go out.

Tony's comment about us mortals fearing freedom because we fear ourselves made sense. Freedom terrifies us because it forces us to acknowledge who we truly are. No matter where we come from—the city, suburbs, or sticks— roles are imposed on us, roles we are expected to fulfill. Any diversion invites alienation. But are we not already alienated by selling out and living false lives? Willpower is required to defy these piss-poor odds. In *Will to Power*, Nietzsche said,

"This world is the will to power—and nothing besides! And you yourselves are also this will to power—and nothing besides!" His theory of the will fits hand-in-glove with his idea of the *Übermensch*, the superhuman of the future who transcends all imposed limitations. The superhuman rises above the mediocre masses, playing by their own rules. We *are* Nietzsche's superhuman, if we choose to be.

I'm convinced that Nietzsche's work can remedy lots of our problems because he doesn't want his readers to think like him. He only wants them to think. Period. I won't go into a corny tangent about how *anything* is possible, but, in truth, we're capable of much more than what we're told. The human being is an exceptional species, gifted with unprecedented intellect. This intelligence leads to enlightenment, destruction, or both. Therefore, expanding our minds is akin to playing with fire. In the desert, I discovered a dormant power within me—a veil had been removed and I understood my purpose in this world.

I'm suddenly reminded of *A Bronx Tale's* quintessential quote: "The saddest thing in life is wasted talent." Thanks to the trip, I'm convinced I won't collapse into the ranks of wasted talent. I've allowed the world to teach me.

Tony rolled a fine blunt in the hotel room. Joe lay sprawled on the bed, facing the ceiling. I sat next to Tony, learning from him to the utmost of my abilities. Joe turned on some tunes when we stumbled through the door. "Yosemite" by Travis Scott. Between the three of us, we each did fine, and a memorable sendoff was in the works.

"She's done!" Tony shouted from the table. The blunt hung from his mouth.

"Big bet. Let's head to the balcony. Joe, you in?"

"Of course, I am. Give me a moment." He sluggishly rose from the bed and followed us outside.

"Let's fire her up!" Tony whooped, sparking the blunt.

"We're finishing this journey the best possible way. I wouldn't change a damn thing about this trip."

"Neither would I, Joe," said Tony.

"Even getting jumped?" I laughed.

"Yes, even that. I'm not kidding, Morrison. When you hit the road, I'll be seeing you out there."

"Count me in, bruh," Joe muttered through a cloud of smoke.

"Lovin' the sound of it. Nothin' but the car, a couple pairs of clothes, my friends Camus, Thompson, Baldwin, Hemingway, and myself. We'll put together a rowdy group of travelers, just like the old writers did. No town, no city, no mountain, or sea will be safe!"

"Sounds like a dream. A dream that can become a reality!" Joe cheered.

"New Hampshire has the best motto of all the states."

"What is it?" Tony asked me.

"It says, 'Live free or die.' For the past week and a half, we've been living free as birds. While standing on the rocky cliff at the Valley of the Gods last week, I felt as if I'd sprouted wings."

"That is sick; it should be our national motto. But 'E pluribus unum' is great. 'Out of many, one.'"

"Either will suffice. I had a similar feeling when we were out there. For once, the world seemed to make sense, and I was okay with everything. I already want to go back to the desert, and we were there only three days ago."

"Same here, Joe. I doubt any of us will be climbing mountains anytime soon... Literal ones, I mean. I'm two grand deep into my mountain of student loans. Two grand down, 23,000 thousand to go. Man, I'm high as hell."

"I'm amazed we never ran out of weed," Tony chuckled.

"We've had a steady supply. Joe and I packed the car full the night before. We left Chicago well prepared, and the dispensaries along the way were a Godsend."

"I think it's safe to say we smoked some of the best stuff of our lives on this trip and then some," Joe said, passing the blunt to Tony.

"Long live freedom! Long live the outlaws!" I screeched at the top of my lungs.

"I'll smoke to that, my brother," Tony replied. "This weed is slapping. I'm drunk as fuck, but this is mellowing it out."

"True, I could see all sorts of purple and gold in the green when you were breaking up the nugs," Joe laughed.

"Purple and gold, my favorite combination of colors!"

"Sorry, Morrison, but— Go, Hawkeyes!" Tony jeered.

Joe nodded with a smirk.

"Call me when y'all get a natty, y'all's crusty-ass football program hasn't won shit in at least 50 years."

"God dammit, Morrison, not everybody can go to an SEC school!" Joe shrieked. "But I have a question. What was it like watching Joe Burrow play?"

"There's nothing I can tell you that would suffice other than that he was a demon on the football field. 100,000 LSU fans going berserk while he slings a pigskin down the field. I wish I knew just how far we'd go while watching him play but, at day's end, I'm happy I got front-row seats to his rise as a football player. During his Heisman acceptance speech, he thanked the people of Louisiana for allowing him to become a native. Jack and I were watching the ceremony at the apartment, and since we're both out-of-staters, Burrow's comment resonated with us. The whole team was an army of steel, crushing all resistance in their path, legionnaires crossing the Alps... Complete and utter domination to achieve the ultimate crown. I'll miss Baton Rouge Saturdays and cheering from the student section 'til the day I croak."

"I bet the natty was unreal. I've watched your stories. The championship being in New Orleans worked perfectly for LSU."

"I thought the same thing, Joe. Drunk kids getting curb-stomped by bouncers, leading a 'Geaux, Tigers' chant through the French Quarter, losing my group of friends but finding more at random bars or any street corner, a pint of ole No. 7, and a one-sided LSU victory to win it all... What's not to love? It feels like years ago, but it's only been months."

"Maybe I'll go to grad school there."

"You'd have to cut the 'Go, Hawkeyes!' shit, Tony."

"Sure, but if what you've told me about Louisiana is true, I'll live with it. My limited amount of time there on this trip tells me you don't have a sliver of bullshit in you."

"Hell no, I don't. But I have a question for y'all... This adventure has been unlike anything I've ever done. Never have I loathed or believed in myself more all at the same time. What have y'all taken from the past week-and-a-half?"

Silence for several moments. Such a question isn't simple to answer.

Suddenly, Joe broke the quiet. "Not as much as I thought... I have a million questions, and my vision of what comes next is blurry. But I've learned a shit ton, don't get me wrong. We've seen the whole country! Our conversations helped put things into perspective, too. I guess the gist of it all is I better make a life worth living before it's too late. I might even move to the South someday. Thanks for that, Pat. I'm not kidding. It's beautiful here. All the trees down here, they droop. It makes me think of the blues... The nature, the music, the ugly past. They all come together as if the trees are crying tears of Spanish moss. It just makes so much sense to me. I guess the South is a paradox. A beautiful but grotesque story of triumph. I'm just afraid... Afraid that our youths are coming to an end. Time rushes by so damn fast now. Clocks are ticking. What about you, Tony?"

"Ah, tough question. The reality that I'll be graduating in December hit me hard on the beach in Los Angeles—"

"Before or after you became Paul Revere?" I interrupted.

"You bastard! Well, smartass, before... I think... But thinking about graduation made me wonder what to make of my life. It hit me in a weird way that I'm still a kid. All three of us are. With all the pressure to do this and that, it's easy to feel like we're already getting old. I also relate to what you said, Joe. We're far from old, but we're not getting any younger. If this vacation's taught me something, it's that I shouldn't take other people's expectations too seriously. Not even family. Most people spend their lives in no man's land. Their vision doesn't go far beyond their immediate lives. They live at the mercy of the powerful. Then you have people like us who tend to observe, who see all the bullshit for what it is. Finally, there's that small fraction at the top who really make waves. You wanna be in that position. The road ahead is confusing, but I'll make something of this uncertainty. Like both of you, I don't want to be just another brick in the wall. I never thought like this until this summer. I'm not sure. Maybe the elevation got to me. You sound confident though, Morrison."

"I am. It's no secret to y'all that my heart beats to a strange drum. If I can make it through life writing and traveling, I'll be the happiest man in the world, yessir. I want to be a novelist. Journalism caught my interest too, thanks to Hunter S. Thompson and Joan Didion. The skies are dark, but the clouds are giving way."

"I wish, man," Tony sighed.

"You'll find your way. And so will you, Joe. I've got a feeling we're gonna be alright."

For another hour or two, conversations flowed freely. Our freedom on the hard road lifted us to high heights. A dangerous freedom. We played by our own rules. In the face of tenacious risks, we'd return home in one piece, a preferable alternative to winding up dead or behind bars. Between our philosophical banter, the drugs, and the places we'd seen, we wouldn't be the same ever again. Our brotherhood strengthened with each mile traveled, and a lifetime of growth lay ahead.

Jim Morrison believed self-discovery to be at the center of what it means—not only to be young, but human, a timeless, mountainous rock upon which we shape our character. Nietzsche speaks through the message. Becoming who we are falls in with the heap of habits too often lost in childhood. It cures our ailments through how we express ourselves in a world shaping up to be completely empty and without love. A world where people aren't people but numbers, statistics, and worker bees.

I missed my siblings and my parents, but something about roaming this land made it tolerable. Years henceforth, when asked about the life experiences that shaped us into who we've become, all three of us will give the same answer: We went West and South to see what the fuck could happen.

The road can take you anywhere. We'd witnessed how different people live and survive through turbulent days. The weirdness of the 2010s peaked with the pandemic. 2020 marked the onset of a dormant cancer that will eat the Western World alive. This coming decade won't be any less nauseating than its predecessor. The Post-war Order is crumbling before our eyes. When will it end, this American chaos?

I doubt the madness will stop until this centuries-old experiment of republican democracy ceases and is replaced with something healthier. D.H. Lawrence's words hit home. I reference his honest opinion of the rugged American individual—"the essential American soul is hard, isolate, stoic, and a killer. It has never yet melted," he wrote within *Studies in Classic American Literature*.

Violence is embedded in our DNA. There is an inherent aggression in the American spirit. It is both our national doom and our pride. We allow the worst human beings, the lowest specimens of our species, to hold positions of power. They worsen this dilemma without guilt or apology. They care naught for the downtrodden.

Speaking of powerful people, the boss sat in wait at the job site, grinning deviously, anticipating his dominion over me on Monday. Fuck! I slaved away for a 400-pound millionaire whose emotional maturity equaled a 16-year-old's from Winnetka, Illinois, who wasn't gifted a Range Rover for their birthday. I worked in construction for an old angry Polish man and the job reduced me to a crippling status of cheap labor, making pennies compared to his dollars. $400 a week, post taxes. When the older guys requested hazard pay because of the pandemic, Bossman pointed at us young workers. "They're your hazard pay," he said.

I was the lone college graduate there but made the least, and I worked the grind for almost five years. Five years, and I was earning less money than ever before! My hours were cut, and some fool named Victor had taken my place on Fridays. He was not strong enough to carry a tool belt. The boss scolded me for my "unprofessional" attitude, but does attitude not reflect leadership? He must be going out of his way to turn young guys into communists.

I've read Marx and, quite frankly, am unimpressed by his solutions, but I empathize with his attacks against bosses. The job possessed two moderately redeeming factors: I was essentially paid to stay in shape and allowed time off as I pleased. A week off work was a week the bossman wasn't obligated to pay me.

Why did I persist, rolling this boulder of shit up the hill only for it to tumble back down?

I lacked choice. I'd applied for five jobs since the spring, and nobody gave me a chance. If some dingbat is paid to write articles about how Donald Trump prefers his steak or what Joe Biden's favorite ice cream flavor is, I can doubtlessly earn a living writing passionate, educated thoughts on *real* issues. These employers, cradled in ivory towers, speak the same dull language. "Thank you for your interest in our company. We regretfully inform you we've decided to move on to candidates with more experience."

I'm due for another rejection next week, I thought. The employers rejecting my applications would probably hire some dull kid whose laces are strait but lacks talent, heart, grit, and vision. The shitshow had gotten to the point where I began to consider myself unemployable.

My destiny will either involve securing a spot as an American writer, or a beer-guzzling slob who crashes with Mom and Dad until they croak. I didn't know what option was more tragic. I refuse to believe that the human experience is limited to the 40-hour work week. We are never ourselves between Monday and Friday, nor are we ourselves on the weekends when we drown in booze to remedy the emptiness that comes from decades of monotonous work.

It's dangerously unhealthy for one to constantly be on their best behavior. Whatever is waiting for me, I'll brave the storm. One day, I'll be free. My blood will run cold before I surrender. The crippling pain of inhabiting a gutter of servitude is only alleviated by conscientiously objecting to the system's demands. It's called dignity. I wish only for my spirit to smile when it hovers over my casket after the lights go out.

All these years I had something to work towards. Since 2016, surviving college was my saving grace. No longer was this the case. Ahead of me, stood a series of appeasements just to earn some bread, a brutal limbo state. But I mustn't torture myself any longer.

The present is the future in the making, and the future answers innumerable questions.

We've all sung the blues. It's part of being human, but with the blues comes Rock 'n' Roll. This mustn't be forgotten.

OFF INTO THE SUNSET

Groggy and hungover... Again... Memphis was worth it. An unopened Snap from Evangeline greeted me. We spoke all night. I should've never asked for her contact information. My love for her in New Orleans on Friday night was real and, if I weren't trapped in Chicago, I don't doubt we would've made the finest couple on the bayou. How much heartache must one man suffer? I had to wake the guys. A return to the highway would help mend the pain.

"Wake up, piss-breath." I nudged Tony.

"Ah, what time is it?"

"Almost 11. We have to check out."

"Where's Joe?"

"He passed out on the balcony."

"I'm gonna pack up my shit."

"Cool, I'll go wake his ass up."

I clumsily opened the door. "Shitstain, get your ass up, we gotta go."

"Got it," he groaned.

We moved hastily and, within 10 minutes, were back in the car. A radio station was discussing leads regarding a vaccine. Moderna had begun phase two trials in May and, with luck, a vaccine would be available by Christmas.

"Either of you plan on getting that shit?" Joe asked.

"Probably. Especially if getting vaccinated helps end this bullshit."

"What about you, Morrison?"

"I'm not a virologist, so I don't see a problem with it. Like Tony said, if these vaccines will help end this nightmare, I'm all for it. You sound skeptical, Joe."

"I am. Sure, scientists have worked with coronaviruses for decades. Doesn't a vaccine released less than a year after the pandemic started to sound a bit suspect to you?"

"A bit," I said. "But what do I know? If hundreds of millions of people take the vaccines and somehow there's something sinister about 'em, well, it would be one of the biggest crimes against humanity ever achieved. The lawsuits would be fucking nuclear."

"I'm on board with Morrison, but I understand where you're coming from."

"I get it too, man," I said. "There's so much misinformation and this pandemic's been so fuckin' politicized, I understand if people are hesitant to get it."

"My grandma says the vaccine is the mark of the beast."

"Rather ironic, don't you think, Joe?"

"Yeah, considering she's in her eighties, she's more vulnerable to Covid. I haven't seen her since February."

"I haven't seen my grandma since Christmas," I sighed. "I miss her. It's part of why I'll get vaccinated once they're available."

"Even then, don't you think the politicians will try to enforce restrictions?" Tony asked.

"They'll definitely try to milk this shit as much as possible. I mean, does anybody really believe that the politicians enforced these bullshit lockdowns for the public good? There are millions of zombies out there who still cling to such an illusion. The ruling class's repressive response to this pandemic serves as yet another horrific example of man trying to control nature. Attempting to manage what can't be managed, and each of us is paying the price."

"We're in for a Hell of a ride," Joe said. "I hate to change the subject, but I'm hungry. Either of you wanna grab something before hitting the interstate?"

"It's the South. There'll be a Waffle House we can hit somewhere."

"Bet," my two companions said simultaneously.

It was a rainy, sticky, morning as lightning bolts cracked across a tide of dark clouds rolling southbound over the Mississippi River. Determined and eager, we devoured our food to make some heavy miles. As we hopped in the car "Mama Tried" by Merle Haggard emanated from KWYN. My mama tried, alright. Although I didn't spend my 21st birthday in prison, I've accepted that anything troublesome that I'd dive into headfirst is on me.

An hour later, Memphis was long gone as the car zoomed deeper into Arkansas. To our delight, the weather cleared by the time we hit Blytheville. This region is flat, defined by cotton fields, rice fields, and pretty, purple flowers I'm unable to identify. The Mississippi Delta jutting from New Orleans up to St. Louis is a forgotten land of little white churches and country homes. These towns are desolate—baptized in fire and buried in anguish.

We stopped for gas in Jericho, and not a single, solitary shop on the main street was open for business. Pandemic lockdowns likely didn't inflict the damage. These towns are too poor to fall any further. People there have nowhere to turn. Coincidentally, the heartland struggles immensely with opioid abuse. How tragic that such a beautiful land is hopelessly cursed by heroin and meth. Rural America once ruled supreme because of our nation's agrarian heritage. At present, less than 1 in 5 Americans reside in rural communities, and the decline of this population dried up the well. The rural residents of the land between the coasts don't understand those of us who call the city home, and nor do we understand them.

Andrew Yang is sharp in this department. On a quiet night in Baton Rouge, Jack and I watched the Democratic debate. To a room of applause, Yang declared, "These communities are seeing their way of life get blasted into smithereens." Too bad, he suspended his presidential campaign a week later. Good people don't win elections. I pray the culture wars subside, but I don't think they will, not in the foreseeable future. Much of the country shamelessly insults people living in these rural, conservative counties who fight tooth and nail to remain above the poverty line. As we've fed our inner cities to the wolves, so have we done to our fledgling towns.

Cairo, Illinois, is the first town on I-57 upon entering the Prairie State. Sunshine glimmered through a series of trees and bluffs. I was thrilled to be alive. Despite the impending task of having to drag myself to work, I recognized our return as a gift. Every day is a blessing. Such an optimistic belief sounds cliche, but my circumstances provide me with no choice. I was born in a state of war. My struggle against childhood cancer is responsible for my lust for life. I was diagnosed with stage four neuroblastoma within hours of my birth, my parents were informed of my impending demise. A priest read me my last rites.

My father was enraged. He'd coached football since the '70s, and motivated them with an impassioned speech, saying he's never taken the field anticipating defeat. I survived those ugly nights of surgery. On Halloween, the doctors assured my parents that I could head home for a few nights. Once home, they refused to take their eyes off me. My mother told me recently that I looked like a corpse during that time. She cradled my little body in her arms, only to realize I was unresponsive and sleeping with my eyes open.

I was rushed to the hospital... I had fallen victim to sepsis due to an infected rash. The doctors placed me in intensive care and, adding to my horrid condition, my mother fought off a brain tumor around the same time. Fortunately, it wasn't cancerous, but my father, understandably, was a wreck. Three short years before, he was a single man, golfing and drinking with his buddies without a care in the world. In a nick of time, he found himself tortured by the pains of an infant son dying of cancer and his wife undergoing brain tumor removal. My mother suffered then and, as I lay dying, I like to think we held our hearts in each other's hands.

My narrative isn't limited to rebellion, adventure, individuality, or freedom. It is a story of cancer, and what it took from me...and how a mix of highs and lows shaped me into who I've become. Chemotherapy's devastating toll on my body left me sterile. It stunted my growth. Chances are, I will die two decades earlier than all of my friends. My hormones are royally fucked up. The doctors considered me even walking a stretch; it took long enough to learn.

I crashed into this world a month premature, forced to abandon the comfort of my mother's womb because, had I stayed any longer, a stillborn birth would spell my fate. I escaped the womb as if aware of this terrible fact and forced my way into life for a fighting chance.

This was my first superpower.

I was 19 when I discovered I couldn't have kids. I remember sitting in the waiting room at the fertility clinic as if it were yesterday. There I was, surrounded by nervous millennial couples desperate to fulfill their dreams of raising a family, some of them glaring in my direction, probably asking, "What's this young kid, this *boy*, doing here?"

I sank into the cushion of my seat, avoiding eye contact at all costs. A week later, my doctor broke the news to me. No little Pat Morrisons will ever roam the earth. I buried my own children before they were ever born. And that was the worst part of it all, the crippling fear of never giving anything to the world. I'll never father a child, doctor's words.

Adding gasoline to the fire, those words were received after I'd returned from my great aunt's funeral, already in a shitty mood. Phone calls change lives in ways none of us can imagine... I hung up and sobbed uncontrollably, sounding more animal than human. I matured in that moment. I saw through hot streams of tears, the setting sun of my youth. At that point in life, all I desired was starting a family of my own. Through all the pain growing up, having a family would make up for it. Yet fate rendered me powerless, and I watched my dreams fall into a heap of ashes. From every corner, the walls caved in, objectively the worst, most unbearable pain of my life.

However, I remain persistent in making the best of these struggles. I humbly admit, that although it may never come true, I still dream the same dream. Days after lockdowns went into effect across the country, an epiphany fired in my direction. I can't perform the basic biological duty of impregnating a woman, but I have a chance to give something to the world: my words. And words burn forever.

When I write, I turn pain into art. My work will be seared forever into the sands of time. Through surviving cancer and all the sorrows and joys since, I've realized that life itself is both God's gift and His curse upon me. I must choose which direction I want the balance to sway. If my survival proves anything about this mad and nefarious world, it's that miracles do happen.

By 4 o'clock, we reached Champaign, Illinois. Home of the Fighting Illini. Aside from their abysmal football team, the University of Illinois is a fine place to spend a weekend. My sister attended there. It's Illinois State on steroids. Between game days, parents' weekend, and bathroom cocaine, there's something for everyone. But, as every stop did, Champaign came and went. Rolling cornfields and downstate prairies brightly lit by the sun spanned for miles in every direction.

In Effingham, a massive cross shoots to the sky within a stone's throw of the interstate. We passed it a couple hours prior. The sight soothed me; the Sunday scaries disappeared. Somehow, someway, we'd be okay. Tony and Joe silently stared out the windows, contrary to our entire voyage. None of us had spoken in an hour. The only noise came from *The Jimi Hendrix Experience*. We rode the tail of a beautifully turbulent wave as the opening of "Voodoo Chile" gave the perfect homecoming serenade. For 11 wild days, we roamed this star-spangled land, hungrily consuming drugs and testing our grit nearly to the point of destruction. 11 days of Rock 'n' Roll and heart 'n' soul. Truth be told, Rock n' Roll is more than a genre of music. It's a way of life.

Joe's boss granted him three weeks off from Costco—a pandemic precaution. At least seven states we traveled through were blacklisted by the Illinois *and* the City of Chicago. A two-week quarantine was mandatory for the weary traveler, but not me. The boss didn't give a shit about Governor Pritzker's or Mayor Lightfoot's mandates. Employees are money.

Back to reality in 18 hours, I thought, but it didn't bother me. We'd return to our posts with stories to tell. Stories nobody could match. Perhaps the upcoming week would be long and soul-crushing. Perhaps not. Escaping authority only to wind up in servitude again is ironic, but the future was bright. I seized the opportunity to declare nuclear war on my student loans and, when they were gone, the road would stay put, anticipating my return.

Eyes to the sky, I saw the stars. They're within reach.

Thanks for reading! Find more transgressive fiction (poems, novels, anthologies) at: Outcast-Press.com

Twitter & Instagram: @OutcastPress, @OutcastPress1

Facebook.com/OutcastPress1

~ ~ ~

Email proof of your ~~Amazon/Goodreads~~ review to OutcastPress@gmail.com & we'll mail you a free bookmark & stickers!

Our city is an ocean. Every night one of our neighbors drowns in a crack on the sidewalk. Every night we call it hope to climb our way to the moon—just to panic when we can't find an airplane or meteor to catch a ride home on. We spend days treading water with someone we love, hoping that a wave doesn't rise and block our view of the sun. These 30+ illustrated poems exemplify that floating feeling of being between sobriety, society, and stillness.

More From
Outcast Press

Percocet Summer encompasses the rush of the solstice, odd obsessions, and other crushables (people and pills and moods). From Florida sweat to Georgia peach sweetness, NYC high-rollers to skidding-by wannabes, these 35+ illustrated poems cover all the shady crevices of a summer well-wasted. The throes of psychedelia and romance. Gas station syringes and cotton candy softness. This collection blurs dirty realism and noir like a Lana Del Rey love song.

More From
Outcast Press

~ ~ ~ ~ ~

International travels and ayahuasca, oh my! A novel about friendship dragged through the Amazon jungle and spit out through the stars with the aid of decades, DMT, and well-meaning debauchery.

Now available on Amazon, Kindle, SmashWords, Barnes & Nobel, & more!

About The Author

Twitter: @AnOutlawWriter **Instagram**: /StillBrendanHeneghan

Brendan Heneghan was born and raised in Chicago, Illinois, but the road is his home. Name a town between Charleston and Los Angeles. Chances are, he's been there. No stranger to the swamps, cornfields, and sprawling desert expanses of North America, he uses this experience to document an America he deems increasingly dystopian.

Heneghan graduated from LSU with a political science degree in 2020. Inspired by the upheavals of the 1960s, he fuses the political theory he's absorbed with his existentialist literary muses. *The Hard Road* is his debut novel with a sequel in the works, as well as a plethora of essays and poems you may find at BrendanHeneghan62.Medium.com

Made in the USA
Monee, IL
12 January 2024

51653700R20143